A  BOOK

Highlighting the lives and experiences of marginalized communities, the select titles of this imprint draw from sociology, anthropology, law, and history, as well as from the traditions of journalism and advocacy, to reassess mainstream history and promote unconventional thinking about contemporary social and political issues. Their authors share the passion, commitment, and creativity of Executive Editor Naomi Schneider.

WE ARE THE UNION

How Worker-to-Worker Organizing Is
Revitalizing Labor and Winning Big

ERIC BLANC

UNIVERSITY OF CALIFORNIA PRESS

University of California Press
Oakland, California

© 2025 by Eric Blanc

All rights reserved.

Library of Congress Cataloging-in-Publication Data

Names: Blanc, Eric, author.
Title: We are the union : how worker-to-worker organizing is revitalizing labor and winning big / Eric Blanc.
Description: Oakland, California : University of California Press, [2025] | Includes bibliographical references and index.
Identifiers: LCCN 2024025392 (print) | LCCN 2024025393 (ebook) | ISBN 9780520394902 (hardback) | ISBN 9780520394919 (paperback) | ISBN 9780520394926 (ebook) Subjects: LCSH: Labor movement—United States—21st century.
Classification: LCC HD4802 .B63 2025 (print) | LCC HD4802 (ebook) | DDC 331.0973—dc23/eng/20240912
LC record available at https://lccn.loc.gov/2024025392
LC ebook record available at https://lccn.loc.gov/2024025393

Manufactured in the United States of America
GPSR Authorized Representative: Easy Access System Europe, Mustamäe tee 50, 10621 Tallinn, Estonia, gpsr.requests@easproject.com

33 32 31 30 29 28 27 26 25 24
10 9 8 7 6 5 4 3 2

For Galit and Eli

Contents

List of Illustrations   ix

Prologue   xi

Introduction   1

PART ONE: ANALYSIS

1. Defining Worker-to-Worker Unionism   35
2. Organizing on a Dispersed Terrain   50

PART TWO: EXAMPLES OF VICTORY

3. Three Worker-to-Worker Wins   67
4. Many Ways to Win (Beyond First Contracts)   91
5. Starbucks Workers' Big Breakthrough   117

PART THREE: HOW TO WIN BIG

6. Which Model Can Win Widely?   153
7. Tactics to Win Big   175

PART FOUR: DRIVING FORCES

8. Government Policy   207
9. Digital Tools   222
10. Youth Radicalization   241

    Conclusion   263

Acknowledgments 267

Appendix: Survey and Interview Methodology 269

Notes 273

Bibliography 301

Index 313

Illustrations

FIGURES

1. Inequality and union strength in the US 2
2. US monthly Google searches for "How do I form a union?" 17
3. Employees of US labor unions, yearly 19
4. US private sector non-agricultural workforce, 1939–2022 54
5. Morrisha Jones shortly before being suspended 72
6. BVWU workers campaign for a contract 73
7. Colectivo union comms 77
8. Colectivo union connects workers to Spot Coffee organizers 79
9. NewsGuild training material 86
10. NewsGuild benchmark tracker 88
11. Trader Joe's United picket in Brooklyn 102
12. Yearly newspaper coverage of unionization 105

13. Frat boys supporting Rutgers faculty-grad strike, April 2023   108
14. Strike with Pride in St. Louis, June 2023   125
15. A "Union Yes" drink order in Vernon, Connecticut   133
16. Total US employment by workplace size, 2022   160
17. Emergency Workplace Organizing Committee homepage   237
18. Political identification of survey respondents   243
19. Divides that drives confronted   245
20. Education levels of worker leaders   247
21. Movement influences on worker leaders   254
22. Celebrating a union election   264

TABLES

1. Staff-to-worker ratios, 1930s vs. today   37
2. Main worker-to-worker organizational forms   41
3. Grassroots unionism, then vs. now   48
4. Largest US employers (by workforce size), 2022   56
5. Recent staff-to-worker ratios   167
6. Top tactics used by respondents in worker-to-worker drives   181
7. Five driving forces of worker-to-worker uptick   209

Prologue

STARBUCKS BARISTA SALWA MOGADDEDI was diagnosed with stage four Hodgkin's lymphoma in January 2022. Deciding to "live my life like I wanted to," Salwa proceeded to unionize her store.

Between biweekly chemotherapy sessions, she spent countless hours driving around her town—Vernon, Connecticut—to talk with coworkers about their fears, their hopes, and what it might take to turn things around. "I'd get these weird bursts of energy right after the chemo from the steroids they'd give me," Salwa recalled. Because she was on sick leave from work, most of these discussions took place in her car, masked up to prevent her weakened body from catching Covid.

When I asked whether it was stressful to simultaneously fight cancer and a multinational corporation during a global pandemic, Salwa replied that she was more worried about how to pay for the hospital bills. Here's how she described it:

> Concerns about the chemo or about retaliation weren't really at the forefront of my mind, because I was already doing it. It's hard to explain to people who've never been through cancer, but you don't have a choice, right? It's either do or die. And I guess I came to feel the same way about the union drive—you know, "whatever happens, happens." You kind of stop being so concerned with your individual fate, because anything could happen. So might as well do something good.

Beyond her personal courage, Salwa's story is important because she and her coworkers demonstrated the viability of a new form of organizing—*worker-to-worker unionism*—that can serve as a model for working people and social movements everywhere.

In contrast with many staff-intensive labor drives, nobody had to persuade Salwa to unionize. Like numerous other young workers today, Salwa—twenty-six years old in 2022—was already ardently pro-labor. Raised by Afghan immigrant parents who were subjected to "unfair and precarious" jobs, by the time she was of voting age she had become "very left-wing." As she put it, "I'm a Bernie [Sanders] fan."

There had been ongoing problems at her store since she began working there in 2016 while attending community college, eventually transferring with a scholarship to Eastern Connecticut State University. "Things got real bad with the pandemic," she recalled. But despite deteriorating conditions, Salwa hadn't seriously considered trying to unionize. "I had read all about labor history, but didn't think anything like that could happen again today," she explained. "It just didn't seem possible."

That changed once baristas in Buffalo filed to unionize in the fall of 2021. She and a pro-union coworker named Mark began following closely on social media: "It was just the biggest inspiration for us—honestly, we were shocked that a tiny little store in North New York was able to win against such a huge corporation."

Salwa decided to reach out to the union to find out more. Had Starbucks Workers United been a staff-intensive campaign, at this point she would have spoken with a full-time organizer. That organizer would have faced a tough decision: Was this store strategic enough, were these workers committed enough, and were enough resources available for the union to dedicate staff to help them unionize? Conventional wisdom in the labor movement, based on decades of hard-won experience, is that staff organizers are needed to help closely guide worker leaders step by step through a grueling battle in which all cards are stacked against them. Like a good sports coach, the organizer would help train and encourage leaders like Salwa, who in turn would be tasked with winning over skeptical coworkers and steering them through the arduous fight.

But this was not a traditional union effort. Instead, Salwa got connected to a barista from Buffalo who, over Zoom, gave her an overview of how they had won, some organizing first steps, and the encouragement to "go for it." She and Mark took up the challenge, deciding that "if they could do it, we could do it too.'"

When it came to organizing the store and overcoming their coworkers' fears, the two didn't try to reinvent the wheel. For the most part, they adopted the tactics passed on to them through further discussions with Buffalo baristas, national online trainings, and digital chats with Starbucks workers nationwide. These included building an organizing committee, mapping their store to understand who knew who, identifying workplace leaders, holding one-on-one conversations with coworkers, assessing their level of support on a 1–5 scale, and inoculating them against management's anti-union talking points and scare tactics. "We created *so many* different Excel docs for tracking everything," Salwa recalls. Systematic organizing like this is not particularly sexy, but it *is* generally effective.

Because of high turnover rates and a generalized fear of retaliation, it took over a month before they had a strong majority of workers on board. On May 12, 2022, fifteen Vernon workers signed a public letter to CEO Howard Schultz declaring their intent to unionize; other baristas supported the effort but asked to remain anonymous because they were worried about getting fired. Their missive deserves to be quoted at length, as it articulates widely shared grievances:

> Many of us were on the frontlines during the peak of the Covid-19 pandemic, continuing to serve Starbucks customers while placing our own health and the healths of our families at risk. In return, Starbucks has forced many of us to work while sick, potentially putting the lives of our coworkers and customers at stake, solely for the sake of maximizing profit.... While Starbucks has boasted record profits, unprecedented growth, and increased demand, partners [i.e., Starbucks employees] in our store are facing labor hour cuts, insufficient staffing, and incomplete to subpar training.

The letter particularly laid into corporate hypocrisy:

> Starbucks claims to be a progressive company, yet proudly boasts their 2021 annual gross profit of $20 Billion (a 28.43% increase from 2020) while paying poverty wages to their employees. For a company whose profits would not be possible without its partners, such contradictory actions leave us with only one avenue: unionization. . . . Despite our concerns and pleas for help, we are met only with opposition or radio silence. Free Spotify and a 30% discount on food and beverages are no longer satisfactory as "fringe benefits" when we have partners who live paycheck to paycheck and are receiving government assistance.

And it concluded with a radical flourish: "To the workers all they produce. Strength to all partners, everywhere."

Organizing at the Vernon store ramped up over the next two months, as did management intimidation and union-busting. By the eve of their election in early July, the store's partners had deepened their internal cohesion and tapped the solidarity of customers, elected officials, as well as other labor unions.

On the day their election votes were counted, Salwa "live action texted the results" to everybody at work—"we were all losing our shit from excitement." The Yes vote was nearly unanimous, with only one worker voting against unionization. For an impromptu celebration, Salwa bought donuts and drove over to deliver them to her jubilant coworkers at the store. "We were just so inspired, we were so motivated—it felt like anything was possible," she recalls. "It was like David beating Goliath." And because their effort was so bottom-up, Salwa knew that it was more likely to inspire others: "All of this creates momentum for more. If a regular person like me can do this, then anybody can."[1]

Through two more years of sustained organizing, Salwa and thousands of her coworkers nationwide eventually forced Starbucks to the bargaining table. This history-making campaign—like recent efforts in media, higher ed, auto, and beyond—provides a roadmap for workers to win at scale in a society dominated by sprawling corporations.

To defeat the billionaires and their political enablers, many more people will have to follow in Salwa's organizing footsteps. How to make that happen is the subject of this book.

INTRODUCTION

IT'S HARD TO OVERSTATE the stakes of turning labor into a powerful mass movement again. Inequality soars when organized labor is weak, because unions are ordinary people's main tool to counter corporate greed. And if you look at most other dire social problems—racial injustice, climate change, right-wing authoritarianism, sky-high military spending—you'll find that they too have deep roots in the power imbalance between workers and bosses.[1]

Labor's decline over the past half century has devastated working-class communities, undermined democracy, and deepened the grip of big business over our work lives, our political system, and our planet. To turn this around, we need tens of millions more people forming, joining, and transforming unions. José Sanchez, a graduate student worker involved in unionizing Duke, put this point bluntly on the eve of their victory: "If there's a silver bullet for getting out of the fucked up-ness of contemporary life, it's the union movement."

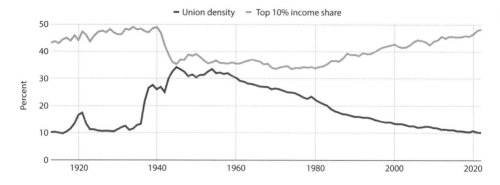

Figure 1. Inequality and union strength in the US. Sources: Historical Statistics of the United States; Bureau of Labor Statistics; World Inequality Database.

By analyzing the recent unionization surge and telling the stories of the worker organizers driving it forward, *We Are the Union* makes a case for how to overcome business-as-usual in both corporate America and organized labor. My argument is simple: a new unionization model is necessary because the only way to build power at scale is by relying less on paid full-timers and more on workers. Though staff-intensive organizing is often very effective, and often does a great job at training people to lead their coworkers in struggle, it costs too much to grow widely. The good news is that recent struggles have built from rank-and-file oriented traditions to develop a scalable approach to worker power capable of fueling exponential union growth and changing the world. As United Auto Workers (UAW) president Shawn Fain explains, "We don't win by telling workers what to do, what to say, or how to say it. We win by giving working-class people the tools, the inspiration, and the courage to stand up for themselves."

This is a book about workplace organizing, but its lessons are broadly relevant for any egalitarian struggle. Labor is hardly the only contemporary movement in serious need of being supercharged by democratically organized volunteers. A major limitation of most progressive efforts from the 1980s onwards is that they've either been well-rooted but small, or poorly rooted and big. Think of a nonprofit you know that provides important services to low-income communities (small but deep) or a huge march you attended that had no follow-up (wide but thin). Both are helpful, but neither can win the types of changes our country so urgently needs.

To build power widely enough to meet today's deepest crises, we must find ways for unruly upsurges to feed into sustainable, democratic organizations—and vice versa. Reviving the bottom-up spirit that enabled US unions to make their big breakthrough in the 1930s, worker-to-worker initiatives from 2021 onwards have shown how this can be done in our atomized, suburbanized society.

Courageous shop-floor organizers have dared to take on corporate behemoths, from Amazon to Starbucks to Volkswagen. Waves of unionization have begun to spread across multiple industries, including higher education, journalism, food service, auto, social services, retail, tech, and museums, as well as nonprofits. And not only are workers fighting back—they're winning.

Despite widespread assumptions among labor leaders and pundits that lightly-staffed organizing can't compel employers to collectively bargain, workers *have* won first contracts in a wide range of industries and companies, including at deep-pocketed chains like Apple.[2] Grassroots workplace fightbacks have also wrested major concessions for millions more workers. No less importantly, these struggles have empowered and transformed their protagonists. In a society where people are conditioned to quietly obey bosses—and at a moment in history marked by pervasive hopelessness—joining together with your coworkers to fight back can be an ecstatic, liberating experience. For a glimpse of what this feels like, here's how one Kickstarter tech worker recalled the night of their union election victory:

> We were about to sing "I Want It That Way" by Backstreet Boys [when the karaoke machine cut out]. . . . Then we just continued a capella for like the

whole song. No backing track, nothing—we just kept going and we got all the way through. So many people were singing along. And that was a magical moment because, I don't know, there were just a dozen of us belting out this song together like without any guardrails like there wasn't anything to hide behind. . . . Sorry, I'm getting poetic now, this was like a little representation of what it was like to unionize, right?

And the fact that their drive was so worker-driven made the victory all the more sweet:

A year and a half of so much work, so much psychological drama, so much uncertainty, so much risk-taking, so much camaraderie that I had never felt before. . . . There was no guidance, I mean there was a little bit of guidance I guess—but ya . . . it's so amazing that we saw it through and got to celebrate together. . . . I will cherish that forever.[3]

These types of struggles have recently snowballed and captured the public imagination, leading to a significant uptick in workers looking to unionize. Labor's most astute opponents have clearly identified the threat posed by this growth in worker-to-worker organizing. Littler Mendelson, the country's most notorious union-busting firm, sounded the alarm in a 2022 report:

There has been a shift in how people are organizing together to petition for representation. What was once a top-down approach, whereby the union would seek out a group of individuals, has flipped entirely. Now, individuals are banding together to form grassroots organizing movements where individual employees are the ones to invite the labor organization to assist them in their pursuit to be represented.[4]

Lamenting that "the ability to encourage activism has never been easier," the report stressed that this "is especially true with the younger workforce . . . [that is] more progressive thinking." And because digital tools have dramatically lowered communication costs, it's now easier for rank and filers to initiate organizing drives and to get trained by other workers nationally. As Littler Mendelson notes, social media enables employees to "begin organizing on their own in a grass-roots fashion . . . [and] allows local organizers to use the collective knowledge of the best organizers around the country."[5]

One of worker-to-worker unionism's key merits is that it's relatively cheap and, therefore, *scalable*—there's no inherent limit to its scope. Scalability is a somewhat cold and technocratic term, normally used more by corporations than their challengers. But here it refers to something simple, visceral, and righteous: building an organized mass movement of ordinary people taking back control over their lives and their workplaces.

Epochal economic changes have made it particularly challenging for unions to scale up. At the time of US labor's meteoric rise in the late 1930s, workers lived in dense, work-adjacent communities, and the economy revolved around large, centrally located establishments like steel and auto factories. Employers were no less viciously anti-union back then, but organizers could focus their limited resources on a relative handful of big, geographically concentrated targets. That's no longer the case.

America's top private employer, Walmart, has 4,600 stores, averaging a few hundred employees each, scattered across the country. Other top private employers—Home Depot, Starbucks, Kroger, FedEx, Target, UPS, Amazon—also have huge numbers of dispersed workplaces, whose workers usually live many miles away from work and from each other. And the same is true within the much-expanded "care economy," which by its nature must have schools, hospitals, and nonprofits dotted across the nation to provide services to local populations.

It's no longer possible to write, as one author did in 1939, that "the most obvious remark we could make at this time is that today in the United States people and industry are highly centralized within a relatively small fraction of the nation's total area."[6] Because of decades of decentralization, building working-class power at scale—at the widest scope necessary—is significantly more difficult.

Given how spread out workplaces are today, Salwa's biblical metaphor, if anything, understates the challenge. At least with Goliath, David only had to concentrate on fighting one giant antagonist. But with a company like Starbucks you have to wage countless separate union battles in every corner of the US. In that sense, mass unionization today is more like confronting the Borg from *Star Trek* or the Mind Slayer in *Stranger Things*, hive minds that act through numerous separate bodies. Fortunately, recent campaigns have developed worker-to-worker structures that can wage precisely that kind of many-fronted battle.

The problem with staff-intensive organizing isn't that it is ineffective. As countless workers can attest from personal experience, heavily-staffed organizing at its best can win major concessions and empower its participants. Indeed, worker-to-worker unionism is largely a development and expansion of its most rank-and-file oriented traditions. But a staff-heavy approach in all its different forms suffers from one basic limitation: it's incredibly expensive.

Up against intense employer opposition and weakly enforced labor laws, current best practice is to hire at least one staffer for every hundred workers to be organized. And it routinely costs over $3,000 to unionize one single worker today, a dramatic increase from the roughly $88 (inflation-adjusted) that it took to unionize each steel worker in the 1930s.[7] As noted in a 2004 balance sheet of the labor movement's then-recent (and ultimately unsuccessful) efforts to bring in large numbers of new members, "effective organizing consumes huge resources—money, staff time, intellectual and legal talent, and so forth. To organize a few thousand workers can take years, cost millions of dollars, and exhaust the capacity of already-stretched union staffers. Can the modest benefits of any single campaign really justify such enormous costs?"[8]

The high cost of staff-intensive organizing means that its scope is inherently limited. As I'll demonstrate in chapter 6, even were US unions to ambitiously use 30 percent of their liquid assets on new staff-intensive unionization efforts, this could only get them back to 2015 levels of strength.

The irony of this cost dilemma is that since the mid-1980s many unions have searched for ways to lean more on members than staff. If you go to any decent union organizing training today, it will rightly insist that the key to successful union drives is for worker leaders to take ownership of the effort by building a strong organizing committee capable of driving the effort forward from below. Moving in a less staff-heavy direction, however, has proved to be much easier said than done—at least until recently.

WORKERS TAKING RISKS

Exorbitant organizing expenses help explain why most unions focus so little on bringing in new members and why they frequently say no to workers when they reach out for support. Rob Baril—president of 1199NE, one of a minority of unions steadfastly committed to new organizing and rank-and-file militancy—lamented to me that organized labor was generally missing the moment:

> We've got 25 million people in the streets after George Floyd's murder, workers have been ground up like a hamburger during the pandemic, and most of the labor movement is doing exactly what they were doing before. . . . The lack of imagination and observation among those of us in positions of leadership in organized labor—it's stunning. The truth is workers are ahead of us.

Take the case of young Chipotle workers in Lansing, Michigan. In the summer of 2022, they won over a majority of their store and then started looking for a union to affiliate with. "We reached out to about a dozen different unions and the sad thing is that a lot of them literally never even called us back—and others said they weren't interested in taking us on," recalled Atulya Dora-Laskey, a twenty-three-year-old worker organizer. "I guess they thought we were too risky an investment and that we were up against too big a corporation. To be honest, it was really discouraging to get rejected so many times."

This type of experience is frustratingly common. Countless other fledgling drives have bumped up against unions' hesitancy to take on new campaigns. As one full-time organizer in the hospitality industry explained to me (anonymously, as with most staff interviews for this book), "Yeah, I'm cautious about just handing out authorization cards [to trigger a union election]. Our members fund organizing through their dues, and it's our responsibility to use these funds wisely."

Given the high costs and high risks of organizing against ruthless employers, this caution is reasonable. The right to unionize—federally codified by the 1935 Wagner Act—has become so whittled down that it often feels like it exists more on paper than in reality. Companies fire union supporters in at least 34 percent of union drives, and in an even higher percentage they're charged with breaking the law.[9] Even if workers manage to overcome this intimidation and win their union election, intransigent employers can then stonewall contract negotiations through endless delays, taking advantage of the National Labor Relations Board's inability to compel companies to bargain in good faith. Bringing employers to the table usually comes down to exerting pressure from below, but this is made difficult by legal restrictions on the right to strike, to boycott, and to organize solidarity actions.

To get a sense of the human impact of our broken labor law system, consider the experience of Moira Madden. In 2018, Moira got a job in Buffalo as a case worker for the Adoption STAR agency, helping expectant parents who were considering placing a baby up for adoption. "A bunch of our organizing committee members were themselves adopted, and we all worked extremely hard for the sake of these children and their parents," she recalled. "But the workplace itself was abusive, they really ground us down. It's a nonprofit, but functions more like your average private company."

She and a coworker began in early 2022 to systematically reach out to others to talk about unionizing. Moira knew that doing so was a personal risk, since she and her partner were trying to have a kid and needed her health insurance. "It was an incredibly stressful and intense time," she recalls. "But I gave the unionization effort my all." Unfortunately, a colleague squealed to management right before they went public. Moira and three co-organizers were immediately fired, with management barely giving any semblance of a legal pretext. Expectant mothers in the system were overnight literally left with no staff support. And with her own health care taken away, Moira and her partner had to put a pause on trying to get pregnant. Despite all this, she didn't regret having taken the initiative: "The owners were—they *are*—so greedy and arrogant. Whether it's a small employer or Starbucks, they all act the same, they could care less about labor law."

Faced with a legal system that does relatively little to uphold worker rights, it's understandable that most unions are hesitant to support new organizing. But this risk aversion is a recipe for continued decline. Atulya concluded that "unions should be better about saying yes to workers when they're organizing." And union hesitancy to onboard eager workers is just the tip of the iceberg. The deeper problem is that labor does so little to proactively reach out to and support the countless people who could initiate organizing campaigns if given the proper encouragement and tools. Movements, unlike protests or one-day sick-outs, don't grow spontaneously—it takes a lot of work and know-how to turn a groundswell of anger, hope, and momentum into ongoing mass struggle.

Unwilling to wait for union leaders to step up, or for politicians to change labor law, a growing number of workers have taken their fate into their own hands and they have inspired others to do the same. Building on labor's best organizing traditions, and leaning on the novel affordances of digital tools, they and a small cohort of left-leaning unions have been pushed by the needs of the moment to pioneer new forms of organizing that can extend widely enough to confront systemic ills. Stephanie Basile of the NewsGuild notes that their innovative member organizing program was born from necessity, not a predetermined plan: "We *had* to develop into a member-led movement because frankly we just didn't have enough staff to take on all these campaigns otherwise."

To be clear, my argument has nothing in common with right-wing claims that established unions are a third party antagonistic to the interests of ordinary workers. Even the average bureaucratic union improves workers' conditions and is orders of magnitude more democratic than non-unionized companies—authoritarian regimes where your only options are to follow orders, quit, or get fired. On this score, I agree with West Virginia teacher leader Jay O'Neal, who in January 2018 posted the following note on Facebook as a response to his colleagues' claims that unions were worthless: "One thing to remember though—unions are very democratic institutions—WE ARE THE UNION. . . . If we want to see real change in our unions, WE'VE got to make it happen."

Jay was proven right. One month later, after intense rank-and-file pressure and multiple one-day walkouts, West Virginia's K-12 unions called a statewide strike, which was won after educators ignored union officials' attempt to return to work prematurely.

A WORKERS' GROUNDSWELL

With most unions doing relatively little to reach the unorganized, workers have stepped up to organize themselves. In the process, they've caught everybody by surprise. "There's just this organic sort of, I don't know what to call it. More like an uprising"—that's how Republican State Senator Mitch Carmichael struggled to describe the grassroots educators' strike that swept West Virginia in February 2018.

Inspired by West Virginia's example, teachers in Oklahoma, Arizona, and beyond followed suit that spring. America was suddenly swept up by its first strike wave since the 1970s.

As I chronicled in my first book, *Red State Revolt*, in early 2018 tens of thousands of rank-and-file educators founded viral Facebook groups to overcome their unions' risk aversion and unite across far-flung regions. With the benefit of hindsight, it's now possible to see that this strike wave heralded the onset of a new model of bottom-up unionism. The biggest difference from past forms of worker-driven activity was that digital tools enabled a far broader geographic scope. In a pre-digital era, rank and filers could only regularly coordinate and deliberate with coworkers who lived close enough to meet in person. But with the advent of social media, they were now able to discuss across wide spatial expanses on the cheap via digital tools.

These K-12 walkouts also presaged other dynamics common to worker-to-worker unionization from 2021 onwards: they were usually initiated by young, radicalized workers; they often relied on time-tested deep organizing tactics at work as well as in the community; they were responses to (and rejections of) decades of neoliberal economics; and they propelled themselves forward through contagious momentum, with attention-grabbing fights inspiring more attention-grabbing fights.

The next big wave of bottom-up workplace activism erupted in response to Covid-19. Virtually overnight, the pandemic exposed employers' willingness to put profits over their employees' health; it made clear the indispensability of "essential workers;" and it clarified to millions of workers the dangers of having no meaningful voice at work. When I surveyed worker leaders about whether their employer's response to the pandemic was a major factor leading them to unionize, 59 percent of respondents answered affirmatively.

"I think the pandemic was pretty much the straw that broke the camel's back at the warehouse—all the other issues had already been there, but that is what really set off the movement [at JFK8 on Staten Island]," recalls Amazon worker organizer Michelle Valentin Nieves:

> Everyone started catching Covid inside. A few coworkers died, management tried to keep it very quiet. They would only tell us later that "someone working Tuesday tested positive," but they wouldn't tell us their name or shift or department. It could be literally the person that was working next to you—and there's basically no ventilation, no windows, they're not really cleaning the equipment, and there's about a thousand of us in there every shift, it felt a ticking time bomb.

Countless Covid-related skirmishes soon swept across American workplaces. I'll give an example from the first campaign I ever took on for the ad-hoc worker support project that eventually became the Emergency Workplace Organizing Committee. On Saturday, March 27, 2020, I picked up a call from Enrique, a worker at the Maid-Rite Specialty Foods meat processing plant in Dunmore, Pennsylvania. "Nos tratan como animales, especialmente a los Latinos," he told me. *We're treated like animals, especially the Latinos.*[10]

Enrique explained that he and many of his two hundred coworkers had begun organizing themselves via word of mouth and a WhatsApp group. They were afraid to go into work, where the production line obliged them to work virtually shoulder to shoulder, well short of the six-foot distance required by law. Not wanting to lose pay or have a point deducted in the company's unforgiving assessment system, a coworker had come into work for a week with Covid symptoms. And his test had just come back positive.

With help from a labor lawyer I knew, Enrique and his crew drafted a letter to management insisting that the company start taking some serious safety precautions. In one of the countless, normally unnoticed acts of working-class bravery that marked the early pandemic, Enrique and coworkers refused to go into work on Monday, March 31. That morning, masked up, he hand-delivered their signed collective letter to management. It concluded: "Until such time as such changes are made as to ensure the safety of all workers and the public at this facility, this group of workers will not be coming to work." Without the resistance of workers like Enrique, many thousands more would likely have died across the US.

Covid-19 was not the only factor creating a groundswell of workplace direct action. An exceptionally tight labor market since 2020 has given workers unprecedented leverage. A new National Labor Relations Board (NLRB), the most pro-labor since 1937, has done everything in its power to boost unionization. And these factors have mixed explosively with longer-term processes like the rise of digital tools and the radicalization of young people.

Once the worst of the Covid-19 crisis had begun to ease, it was clear to those who bothered to look that the US had entered its ripest moment for new workplace organizing since the early 1940s. In October 2021, grassroots labor struggles broke back into the mainstream of US politics. Echoing earlier strike dynamics in West Virginia, over ten thousand John Deere factory workers—coordinated nationally over rank-and-file Facebook groups—forced a strike by rejecting a tentative contract agreement that their union leadership had reached with management. Two weeks into the walkout, workers rejected yet another agreement. Only after a full month of striking did management finally cave to workers' demands for major raises.

A few weeks later, Starbucks baristas (euphemistically dubbed "partners" by the company) at the Elmwood store in Buffalo voted to unionize. To their surprise, they received an avalanche of requests for organizing help from workers across the country.

Soon after, to the shock of organized labor and corporate America alike, a ragtag crew of young multiracial warehouse workers managed to defeat Amazon in an April 2022 union election. "It's the best feeling in the world," declared worker leader Chris Smalls, popping champagne in front of the NLRB's Brooklyn office. One of the many workers inspired by this win was Vince Quiles, a twenty-seven-year-old Home Depot employee in North Philadelphia, who in the spring of 2022 decided to unionize his store after working there for six years:

> You know, I saw what Chris Smalls did and it showed me, "Wow, if you really put your mind to it, you can unionize anywhere." It just takes someone to step up to the plate, to put themselves out there and build an organizing team—to take the risk to do it. So seeing Amazon and Starbucks and all that, I figured it might as well be me.

Labor finally had real momentum nationwide. And this began changing the organizing dynamics on the ground.

A NEW CONTEXT FOR ORGANIZING

"I've never seen this number of workers reach out to our union before," notes Alan Hanson, who was organizing director of United Food and Commercial Workers (UFCW) Local 400 before recently becoming a staff organizer for the UAW. "The amazing thing is when they reach out [to Local 400], they've already done all the things staff organizers normally have to train people to do: map out their workplace, ID leaders, build a representative committee. I've had more worker-initiated campaigns in the last few months than I'd had total since I started organizing in the late '90s."

As Hanson indicates, the breadth of worker self-activity today constitutes a major difference from the bleak decades following Reagan's election. As union strength plummeted, various national unions in the 1990s moved towards new organizing and rank-and-file participation. Some significant gains were made. But faced with intense employer opposition, worker resignation, and accelerated economic decentralization, these unions found that it was exceedingly hard to scale up. Partly this was because of labor's deep-rooted routinism and risk aversion—most local and national unions refused to seriously fund external organizing. And those that did were bogged down by its steep costs.

By the mid-2000s, even those union officials who had dabbled with new organizing concluded that it was just too risky and too expensive to pursue widely until national labor law reform could even the playing field. Henceforth, if unions have done anything beyond narrowly bargaining for their existing units, their external efforts have tended to focus on political lobbying or on getting out the vote for mainstream Democrats.

For its part, the Service Employees International Union (SEIU)—which led some of the most inspiring worker-intensive organizing in the 1990s and which continues to think big—concluded that organizing at scale required spending less time and money campaigning worker by worker, workplace by workplace, company by company. Searching for more scalable alternatives, SEIU's Fight for 15 and UFCW's OUR Walmart sought to garner publicity and spread labor's reach by eschewing cost-intensive deep organizing, focusing instead on winning widespread policy changes and raises by mobilizing scattered worker activists through one-day walkouts and press conferences.

In short: rank-and-file organizing and scalability appeared to be contradictory objectives, at least for the foreseeable future. Labor's powerful approaches haven't been scalable and labor's scalable approaches haven't been very powerful.

Fortunately, effective organizing is context specific. And contexts change. A convergence of factors—the pandemic, a tight-labor market, a vigorous NLRB, the growth of digital tools, and youth radicalization—has opened up new possibilities to build a type of unionism capable of scaling up precisely because it depends on an exceptional degree of worker leadership.

Without intense staff guidance, tens of thousands of workers are now learning the ABCs of organizing through mentorship from other workers over Zoom, through open trainings like Jane McAlevey's

Organizing for Power, through how-to handbooks, and through a fair share of trial and error. As Samantha Smith from the Lansing Chipotle recalls, "We got lots of compliments from the Teamsters when they realized how organized we were. They point blank told us we had already done most of their work for them." How had these Chipotle workers learned what to do? Atulya explains: "For the most part we just followed the instructions that we'd read [in the Labor Notes book *Secrets of a Successful Organizer*] about how to unionize—and it worked."

People can reach deep inside themselves when connected to a big cause worth fighting for. For some radically inclined young workers, a hope to inspire copycat efforts became in itself a powerful organizing incentive. "We knew that if we were successful in this, it would most likely lead to other locations organizing as well," notes Claire Chang, one of the employees who led the successful drive at New York City's SoHo REI. "I think people normally feel hopeless, that nothing is going to change.... We're helping change that." And, sure enough, their March 2022 election win spurred ten other REIs across the US to follow suit.

Working-class people across the country are beginning to see that non-union jobs can become union jobs, and that they personally have a role in making that happen. In the process, workers in all industries have begun to change themselves and their coworkers. Purnell Thompson, a stablehand who helped unionize his Medieval Times castle in Lyndhurst, New Jersey, explained how the unionization process brought them all together:

> We definitely got closer. A good example is the queens never really used to talk to us stable hands—I don't think it was from any mean-spirited place, but like I've been working there for two years and I know a couple of queens who just constantly forgot my name, even though it's printed on the back of my shirt. But now we're all grown pretty close, we know each other very well, and we stand up for each other. With all the crazy union-busting [management has] thrown at us, we've had to trauma-bond.

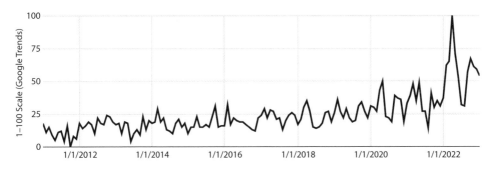

Figure 2. US monthly Google searches for "How do I form a union?" Source: Google Trends.

Even though employers have continued to trample on labor law, momentum steadily increased in the wake of the pandemic. So too has media and popular attention. To cite just two examples: Antiwork—a misleadingly named Reddit group focused on exposing bad working conditions and promoting unionization—shot up from 80,000 members in early 2020 to 2.3 million members by late 2022. And the worker-focused media outlet More Perfect Union, founded in the wake of Bernie Sanders's 2020 presidential campaign, has received over 350 million views on its videos. In the battle for public opinion, labor is finally landing some serious blows. Billie Adeosun, a Starbucks barista in Olympia, summed it up well: "I love that we've made unionizing sexy."

Everything now hinges on translating broad popular support for unions into organization and power. And we're starting to see this happen. Doug Thompson—a baker for Colectivo in Milwaukee—recalled the personal support he received when deciding to unionize: "My immediate friends . . . were like, wow, I can't believe you're doing this, it's amazing. And it really takes a lot of courage. No one said to me, why would you do this? Why would you put your family in jeopardy?"[11]

Put simply, the available evidence suggests that there exists a vast reservoir of untapped potential for union growth. Figure 2, for example, registers a dramatic surge of interest in self-initiated unionization in 2022.

Worker-to-worker unionization drives have also recently won elections at some of the largest corporations in the world—Amazon, Starbucks, Apple, Google, Chipotle, Microsoft. Organized labor has for decades generally avoided trying to unionize such large companies, believing that they were simply too powerful to defeat. In contrast, there were three drives at non-union Fortune 500 companies in 2021 and seven more in 2022—a dramatic break from every other year since the Fortune 500 was founded in 1955.

OBSTACLES AND POTENTIAL

Though labor's uptick is inspiring, its limitations and challenges are also sobering. Corporations remain very powerful, labor law remains very broken, and most unions remain very complacent. That's why it's not surprising that union density—the percentage of workers in unions—continued its slow decline in 2022–23, falling to 10 percent.

But the fact that about two hundred thousand new workers joined unions over these past two years is actually a promising sign when you take into account that labor's funding for new organizing is currently at a historic low. As you can see in figure 3, the total number of union staffers—a suitable enough proxy here for labor's organizing commitment—has plummeted since the early 2000s.[12] What makes this so exasperating is that labor's coffers are bigger than ever, soaring in 2021 to a record-high $13.4 billion in liquid assets.[13] Workers are unionizing by the hundreds of thousands even though most union leaders are barely supporting new organizing.

So while we shouldn't exaggerate the breadth of recent advances, or paint worker-to-worker unionism as a magic bullet, there are many good reasons to believe that labor *does* have the potential for a big nationwide breakthrough. But to have a fighting chance at turning around their decades-long decline, unions need to start seriously funding new organizing—and doing so through a worker-to-worker model.

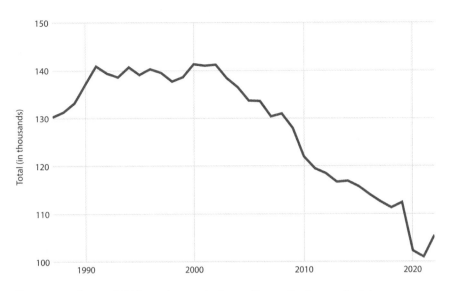

Figure 3. Employees of US labor unions, yearly. Source: Current Employment Statistics survey.

Let me be as clear as possible: this book's argument is not that resources and staff are unimportant. It's that they need to be deployed in a way that's scalable. In other words, unionizing millions will require an *absolute* increase in staffing and financial support for organizing, but a *relative* decrease in the staff-intensivity of most campaigns.

In addition to hiring many more organizers, why don't unions reach out to each of their 14.3 million members nationally to ask them to invite a family member or friend to a training on how to organize their workplace? Why don't they invest in training tens of thousands of young people to get jobs at strategic workplaces to help unionize them? And why don't they adopt the worker-to-worker organizing approaches that—as we'll show below—have been so successfully used by the NewsGuild, Starbucks Workers United, and United Electrical?

Such initiatives would generate countless new leads and drives. The fact that unions are able to coordinate hundreds of thousands of volunteers to get out the vote for Democrats suggests that they could do something similar to grow their membership. Why not use labor's access to a huge amount of voter data to call or knock the doors of every voter who works at Amazon, Walmart, and FedEx to generate leads for ambitious national unionization campaigns at these companies? Unfortunately, most unions continue to think small and act small when it comes to growth, assuming that little can be done to scale up rank-and-file organizing other than lobbying politicians for labor law reform.

It's way past time for organized labor to raise its ambitions. In today's sprawled-out socio-economic conditions, unionizing millions will require a massive influx of resources. This is in many ways a dispiriting reality, since hunkered-down, risk-averse union leaders have shown remarkably little interest in pursuing wide-scale organizing, even though conditions have been exceptionally favorable since 2020.

On the other hand, there's a glass-half-full way to look at the fact that so many of labor's obstacles to growth are internal. Because most unions aren't seriously funding organizing, we've barely begun to scratch the surface of what's possible. It's *not* the case that union density has been declining for decades despite valiant, all-in efforts by the labor movement to turn things around. The attempt has yet to really be made.

And that's a key reason why worker-to-worker unionism is so promising and so different from the revitalization strategies that have prevailed for decades. Rather than focusing on the sisyphean task of gently asking gun-shy officialdoms to take bold organizing initiatives (an approach that's been attempted over and over with limited success), the new model provides tools for workers to start organizing *now,* enabling them to transform organized labor from the bottom up through the sustained pressure of positive organizing examples as well as insurgent contestations of union leadership elections.

Along these lines, a deeply corrupt and moribund United Auto Workers has been radically re-oriented from below, through a worker-initiated campaign to kick out the union's old leadership, through worker-initiated strikes at John Deere, and through worker-initiated drives by grad students who affiliated with the UAW. After electing billionaire-bashing, "Eat the Rich" T-shirt-wearing Shawn Fain as president in March 2023, the UAW went from zero to 100 in a matter of months, successfully striking the whole Big 3 that fall. Riding high off of record-breaking contract gains, including 33 percent pay raises, the UAW immediately proceeded to lean on momentum, worker-to-worker structures, and digital tools to actively encourage workers to self-organize in *all* non-union auto and battery plants. Under the reformed UAW, workers proceeded to make history in April 2024 by turning Volkswagen in Chattanooga into the first big auto plant in the South to go union.

Though there are no guarantees that this ambitious $40 million organizing campaign will achieve its lofty objectives, the reformed UAW is beginning to show how even a seemingly resigned workforce such as Southern auto workers can be roused to action when unions decide to take risky actions, massively invest in new organizing, and trust rank and filers to lead. To paraphrase Che Guevara, the labor movement needs "two, three, many UAWs."

LESSONS FOR OTHER MOVEMENTS

Recent worker-to-worker union drives are full of lessons for anybody looking to challenge systematic injustice. You don't have to be a workplace organizer to understand the urgency of building organized people's power far more extensively. Ordinary people can't outspend the billionaires, but we *do* outnumber them—and the main way to translate this numerical strength into a sustained force for change is *organization*, that is, crystallized solidarity.[14]

The need for broad social transformation has perhaps never been greater. Yet the ability of non-elites to reach their goals has been growing steadily weaker because we're less organized than we used to be. Numerous scholars have documented how a steady decline in mass membership organizations since the 1960s has fueled rampant inequality, hollowed out political democracy, paved the way for right-wing extremism, and hobbled efforts to prevent climate disaster.[15] Countering such deep-set problems is off the table for a progressive ecosystem that remains dominated by rooted-but-small organizations, on the one hand, and big-but-thin protests, internet campaigns, and advocacy groups, on the other. In other words, when powerful, our forces are too little—when large, they're too weak.

This associational decline reflects deep socio-economic changes. But our side's strategic choices also can take a fair share of the blame. It used to be an axiom of progressive politics that people power required organizing people. Far from being solely the purview of unions, this conception also guided the civil rights, anti-war, and women's movements. Ongoing popular involvement was what made these *movements*, not just episodic protests.

But such an organizing tradition no longer holds sway. Instead, we've seen the proliferation of nonprofits locally and nationally. Though they provide important assistance to working-class communities—and can, at their best, develop new community leaders—their dependence on foundation funding, their constricted legal status, and their general reliance on staffers precludes most nonprofits from scaling up to fight for transformative change.[16]

We've also seen huge mass mobilizations sporadically erupt in the US over the past two decades around big-picture problems—the war in Iraq (2003), immigrant rights (2006), Occupy (2011), the Women's March (2017), and Black Lives Matter (2013, 2020). While changing the national conversation and winning partial concessions, these outpourings have lacked the institutional staying power necessary to win their ambitious aspirations. People briefly come out to the streets and then return home.

These problems—ephemerality, power deficits—are even more acute for digital-only "clicktivism," which equates movement-building with posting something on social media or signing an online petition. And while the large advocacy groups that proliferate in Washington, DC, are not plagued by ephemerality, these "advocates without members," as Theda Skocpol describes them, are similarly lacking in system-shifting power.

All these efforts are missing one crucial thing: large numbers of members.

The ensuing progressive cul-de-sac has spurred a search for new models, such as "momentum organizing," which inspires and onboards people through moments of mass effervescence, as well as "distributed organizing," which leverages new technologies to enable volunteers rather than staff to coordinate work locally.

These models have demonstrated their strengths in Bernie Sanders's two presidential campaigns, the Sunrise movement for a Green New Deal, and anti-Trump groups like Indivisible. But these initiatives have also all demonstrated a significant limitation—they haven't built durable structures for sustained struggle. A major reason for this shortcoming is that none were democratic membership organizations. In other words, none broke fully from the top-down, staff-driven norms and structures of post-1960s progressivism. It's hard to convince volunteers to keep sacrificing their scarce free time, and it's hard for them to develop as leaders, when they don't consistently feel that a collective structure depends on their efforts, their financial contributions, and their critical thinking capacities.

Democracy at its fullest is a practice of developing the individual and collective agency of ordinary people. This is certainly a challenging ideal to operationalize in practice beyond small groups; most large-scale efforts inevitably fall short, especially in periods of low mobilization. But without democracy as a north star—as a core means and ends—it's difficult to build or sustain the types of organizations needed to win a better society. As the title of a Labor Notes book on this topic puts it, "Democracy Is Power."

A thoughtful balance sheet of the Sunrise Movement by two of its founders thus concluded that though they were able to "wield a distributed volunteer army to expert effect," Sunrise's surprisingly rapid decline reflected an inability to "build rooted and resilient local hubs for the long term, and offer our members more tangible experience to develop as organizer-strategists."[17] Worker-to-worker unionism shows how to fuse the strengths of distributed and momentum organizing—their ambition, their digitally enabled scalability, their eye for creating and seizing whirlwind moments—to the project of building democratic membership organizations.

Today's new unionization model, like any good form of labor organizing, has another important contribution to make: it shows how to break beyond the echo chamber. Because workplaces bring together a wide range of people whose only necessary commonality is having the same employer, effective worker organizers are exceptionally focused on winning over those who don't already agree with them. Tamar Samir, a YogaWorks instructor who helped turn her company into the first unionized yoga chain in the US, notes how different this experience was from her previous participation in self-selecting environmental rights work:

> Before I had maybe a notion of activism that was a bit unclear—like I knew the things that I believed in, but I didn't really know how to organize to get them. And I feel like having the experience of unionizing and learning how to have organizing conversations, how to listen well, how to overcome resistance—that really changed my skills, my activism intelligence in a way. And I think it restored my faith in people as well. You see that people *can* change.

Persuasion is a skill sorely lacking today among US progressives, who often struggle to engage with people who don't share the totality of their views and who generally spend more time discussing with (or criticizing) each other than they do reaching out to the unconvinced.

Recent bottom-up labor struggles provide an outwards-facing ethos as well as a slew of tips for talking to, and winning over, people who aren't already on board. "You have to put the hay where the goats can get it," explains Quichelle Liggins, a worker leader at the Hyundai plant in Montgomery, Alabama. As Jane McAlevey once told me, organizers "wake up every morning asking how to engage the people who don't agree with us—or who think they don't agree with us."[18]

I've written this book because labor organizing is broadly instructive *and* because it is uniquely placed to overcome systemic injustice. Prospects for transformational change will remain dim until large numbers of workers cohere themselves *as workers*. Non-managerial wage earners have an exceptional degree of numerical strength—upwards of three-quarters of working-age Americans. Uniting around our shared economic interests is crucial for overcoming racism, xenophobia, and all forms of scapegoating. No less importantly, the structural position of working-class people pits us against big business, whose unchecked control over the economy and politics is at the root of so many social ills. Finally, we have unique leverage because every private company and public institution depends on our labor. As the union anthem "Solidarity Forever" puts it, "without our brain and muscle not a single wheel can turn."

ARGUMENT, DATA, METHODS, AND STRUCTURE

We Are the Union's central argument is that worker-to-worker organizing is the only plausible path to scaling up union power. In other words, it can help organized labor extricate itself from the impasse of big-but-weak or small-but-powerful campaigns.

Though they're scalable, labor's largest initiatives—thin PR-oriented mobilizations and getting out the vote for Democrats—can't consolidate the degree of people power needed to unionize millions, transform national labor law, or win big structural change. For such heavy lifts, you need to create crises for economic elites by combining air-war tactics—back-room pressure, media exposure, etc.—with a strong ground war of rank-and-file intensive organizing.

Many staff-heavy union drives have shown on a small scale what this alternative looks like. Via time-tested organizing tactics culminating in (or at least credibly threatening) disruptive mass action, they've beaten the bosses, won material gains, and empowered worker leaders. Their accumulated lessons on winning over a majority of coworkers, building toward strikes, establishing community support, and pressuring politicians constitute a crucial reservoir of knowledge for present and future labor struggles.

But even if we leave aside the challenges of maximizing democratic practices and workers' capacities in staff-intensive efforts, any model that requires something close to one staffer for every hundred workers can't possibly lead enough organizing drives to transform America. In other words, staff-intensive organizing can win battles, but not the war. For that, we need a movement. And to build such a movement, we need an organizing model that can scale up worker power.

While recent worker-to-worker efforts have developed from current best practices and left union traditions, they aren't just more of the same. Pushed by circumstances to rapidly expand rank-and-file responsibilities, they've forged something new in the heat of battle. "There's no blueprint for what we're doing," notes Daisy Pitkin, a national staff organizer for Starbucks Workers United. By trying to make sense of this emergent organizing model, I hope to provide, if not a blueprint, then at least a road map for other workers, unions, and social movements to follow in their footsteps.

We Are the Union is simultaneously a book of social science and an activist intervention. The book's duality partly reflects the fact that I'm both a professor of labor studies and an active participant in the labor movement. If the methods used are typical for a social scientist, the questions I ask come out of two decades of work with and within unions. In addition to being a proud member and strike captain of my faculty union, Rutgers AAUP-AFT, I was part of the group of organizers that at the onset of the pandemic launched the Emergency Workplace Organizing Committee (EWOC) to support worker-to-worker organizing. Ever since, I've helped coordinate EWOC's free online trainings, which have taught a few thousand people how to build collective power at work. It was this concrete movement-building experience that forced me to start grappling with the big strategic questions addressed in the following pages.

While I'm under no illusions that neutrality is either possible or desirable in a society riven with injustice, I began this project with a commitment to make my research and analysis as rigorous as possible. More specifically, I've sought to avoid three common mistakes of labor scholars and organizers.

First is a tendency to overgeneralize from a relative handful of examples (or from personal organizing experience), thereby confirming one's analytical priors by relying on fragmentary evidence. I think a more open-minded approach has paid off, since the process of gathering the data for this book has significantly altered my views on more than a few issues—for example, the challenges of scalability and economic sprawl now loom much larger in my analysis.

Painting one's preferred organizing approach as a panacea is the second mistake I've sought to avoid. Worker-to-worker unionism makes building widespread working-class strength easier, but it does not guarantee it. To overcome some of the most powerful companies in the world, organizing efforts also need a major influx of resources. They need to make smart tactical and strategic choices. Plus they need economic and political conditions to be relatively favorable.

Worker-to-worker unionism, in short, is not a cure-all. Even the best models can still lose. And nobody has all the answers for what, if anything, can turn around labor's decades of decline. But, as I hope to demonstrate, this new organizing model *is* workers' best bet to win widely.

Finally, by specifying the precise mechanisms, methods, and dilemmas of worker-to-worker unionization in today's decentralized conditions, and by grounding my analysis in a sober appraisal of postwar social fragmentation, I avoid a tendency of other calls for bottom-up unionism to flatten contextual and organizing differences between our current era and labor's big breakthrough during the 1930s.

To make sense of recent bottom-up insurgencies, I've gathered what is to my knowledge the largest existing dataset on contemporary US worker leaders and their organizing experiences. With the help of my research assistant Jacob Robinson, I reached out to every union drive that went public in 2022—resulting in over two hundred interviews with worker leaders and over five hundred responses to my anonymous survey asking about their drives and personal backgrounds. To round out the picture, I interviewed over a hundred staff organizers and elected union officials, while also digging deep into the quantitative data on socio-economic shifts, organizing costs, and union staffing, both historically and today. (See the appendix for further discussion of my data and methods.)

Much of *We Are the Union* narrates post-pandemic worker-to-worker unionization struggles, with all their heroism and solidarity, their crushing lows and ecstatic highs. By telling the stories of a growing number of workers who are daring to fight for a collective voice at work, I aim to encourage others to do the same, while providing a slew of how-to organizing tips and ideas. In an era where doom is the pervasive political mood, labor's recent wins are a rare source of hope and inspiration. As Colectivo baker Doug Thompson put it, "The only advice that I could give is: you got to follow your heart, and you gotta do what you think is right. . . . Go for it [unionization] because the win felt so good. . . . I've been happy for all kinds of things, but this alone, I can't compare to any other success that I've had in my life. Nothing. Not graduation. Not marriage. Nothing felt like this."[19]

At the same time, one of the unique strengths of worker-to-worker organizing is that it can build bottom-up power *widely*. Making a credible case for scalable power requires exploring a series of topics that at first glance might seem less than titillating, such as organizing costs, staff-to-worker ratios, and national peer-to-peer organizing structures. I hope to convince readers—including staffers and leaders of deep-pocketed unions—that these questions are pivotal and that there are concrete steps they can take to seize the moment by going all in on worker-to-worker unionism.

The book's basic structure and argument proceeds as follows.

PART 1: ANALYSIS

- Setting the analytical stage, chapter 1 defines what I mean by worker-to-worker unionism and how exactly it's different than heavily staffed approaches.

- Pushing back against assumptions that it's possible to closely replicate the tactics of labor's big breakthrough in the 1930s, in chapter 2 I examine how the decentralization of industry and housing since World War II has dramatically changed the organizing terrain. Because dense workplace-based communities have been pulled apart, new organizational and tactical approaches are needed to scale up today.

PART 2: EXAMPLES OF VICTORIES

- Since the main knock against the new model is that it romanticizes bottom-up organizing and doesn't have the punch to force companies to grant first contracts, part 2 focuses on recent examples of success. I start by looking at three examples of victorious worker-to-worker unionism: Burgerville in the Pacific Northwest, Colectivo in the Midwest, and the NewsGuild nationally. Each of these illuminates key differences between staff-heavy and worker-to-worker unionism. And, contrary to the skeptics, each *has* already won first contracts.

- While good contracts are pivotal, they're not the only important type of union victory. In chapter 4, I show that worker-to-worker unionism is also forging large numbers of workplace leaders, transforming public opinion, reforming stagnant unions, and winning big concessions from employers through direct action.

- Chapter 5 tells the story of the successful years-long campaign by Starbucks baristas to force one of the largest corporations in the world to the bargaining table. Overcoming such a powerful and sprawling company took an exceptional degree of worker initiative, perseverance, and chutzpah, plus lots of union resources.

PART 3: HOW TO WIN BIG

- Case studies of victories can be illuminating, but they don't necessarily provide a compelling argument for the generalizability of a given organizing model. That's why chapter 6 examines the available data on organizing costs to show that even once unions start seriously investing in new organizing, only a worker-to-worker model can build working-class power at scale.

- What tactical approaches are needed to win widely? Chapter 7 addresses this question and argues that worker-to-worker unionism is uniquely positioned to spread and develop the most effective organizing tactics, both in normal periods as well as when momentum is exceptionally high. I show that while deep organizing methods are essential in most times and places, these should be supplemented (or occasionally tweaked) in whirlwind moments when fear is suddenly replaced by hope and determination.

PART 4: DRIVING FORCES

- A rigorous analysis of how we got here and where we might be going requires examining the roots and driving forces of the recent surge of worker-to-worker unionism. Chapter 8 shows how bottom-up organizing has been boosted by state policy, via a tight labor market and a surprisingly effective NLRB.

- Though I make no predictions about the longevity of the post-pandemic uptick—momentum comes and goes—there are compelling reasons to believe that the new worker-to-worker model will remain a central driver of good organizing over the decades to come. Along these lines, chapter 9 argues that one key driving force—digital technology—has irrevocably altered the unionization landscape by, first, lowering organizing costs, making it easier for workers to organize with less staff support, and second, by enabling lightly-staffed unionism to operate beyond a local level for the first time in history.

- In chapter 10, I examine another relatively long-term factor: the politicization of Millennials and Gen Z. Young workers—spurred by post-2008 economic frustrations, Black Lives Matter, and Bernie—are pulling the labor movement into a more ambitious, democratic, and politically independent direction. Even if labor's current momentum is kneecapped, it's unlikely that the genie of digitally enabled, generationally rooted worker-to-worker organizing can be put back in the bottle.

Two last points before we begin. Worker-to-worker unionism is probably crucial for labor revitalization internationally. But since I'm a social scientist whose research was limited to my own country, this book focuses on the United States. I'll leave it to readers and organizers abroad to assess the extent to which my analysis is relevant to their distinct national contexts.

Finally, readers should keep in mind that worker-to-worker organizing is not just a tool for building new unions, it can also be used to initiate collective actions like unauthorized strikes or to reform and strengthen existing unions. Throughout the book I touch on all three forms of worker-to-worker organizing and show how they are mutually reinforcing. By providing ordinary people with tools to change their lives and the transformative experience of actually doing so, this new model helps create more democratic unions grounded in the creative capacities of rank-and-file workers. That said, to keep the book at a readable length I focus on labor's hardest and most pressing task: organizing the unorganized.

PART ONE

ANALYSIS

1

DEFINING WORKER-TO-WORKER UNIONISM

> If we're going to build a movement, we have to give workers the tools they need to take on all parts of workplace organizing.
> KRISTINA BUI, former *LA Times* worker organizer

WHAT EXACTLY IS WORKER-TO-WORKER UNIONISM? To answer this, it's useful to start with a bit of historical background on how rising organizing costs over the past century have transformed the labor movement and constrained its growth.

Labor organizing didn't used to be anywhere near as staff-intensive as it is today. Lightly-staffed unionism in the early twentieth century was most colorfully expressed by the syndicalist-leaning Industrial Workers of the World (IWW), which organized over 150,000 members through scrappy and joyous workplace militancy. But even the IWW's moderate craft union rivals in the American Federation of Labor (AFL) were remarkably light on staff by today's standards.[1] Neither form of unionism, however, succeeded in unionizing the large mass production industries that came to dominate America's economy from the late 1800s onwards.

Labor's big breakthrough during the 1930s was also driven forward by rank and filers. Leaning on the structural leverage and densely packed geographic concentration of mass production workers, union density doubled from 1934 to 1939. The formation of almost every major new industrial union was the same: workers initiated drives themselves and eventually linked up with the national apparatus of the Congress of Industrial Organizations (CIO) to organize the rest of their companies and industries. And while staff support *was* pivotal to the ultimate success of this upsurge, it was minimal compared to today's norms.[2]

We have good enough data to estimate how much things have changed. As labor scholar Kate Bronfenbrenner's research has detailed, the rule of thumb since the 1990s for a sufficiently staffed union drive has been one full-time staff organizer for every targeted hundred workers.[3] Compare that with the Steel Workers Organizing Committee, which hired about 275 full-time organizers to organize an industry of 480,000 workers. That's a ratio of one staffer for every 1745 workers—in a campaign that was by all accounts the *most* staff-heavy, top-down effort of the 1930s. And bottom-up unions like United Electrical (UE) organized 650,000 workers from 1936 through 1945 despite never having over 293 organizers on staff.[4] In other words, union drives today routinely hire about twenty times as many staffers per worker as efforts a century ago.[5]

How then did labor become so top-heavy? Militant movement unionism was quashed by an employer counter-offensive begun in 1938, popular backlash against disruptive strike militancy, and an anti-labor, anti-Communist political assault led by Republicans and racist Southern Democrats, with the fratricidal backing of AFL leaders. This reactionary wave culminated in 1947's Taft-Hartley law—which dramatically undermined labor rights and outlawed a slew of effective

TABLE 1
Staff-to-worker ratios, 1930s vs. today

Union	Staff-to-worker ratio	Years
SWOC	1 to 1,745	1936–1942
UE	1 to 2,218	1936–1945
Staff-intensive best practice	1 to 100	1990s to today

tactics—followed by the McCarthyite mass expulsion of leftists from unions in the 1950s.

With labor's momentum decisively checked during the post-war economic boom, unions' internal life became dominated by full-timers. As West Coast Teamsters head Dave Beck put it, "Why should truck drivers and bottle washers be allowed to make big decisions affecting union policy? Would any corporation allow it?"[6]

Such a shift towards bureaucratized service unionism took place during, and was facilitated by, the slow-but-steady suburbanization of postwar America. It was further boosted by our country's decentralized labor relations and weak welfare state: because US labor law treats each separate workplace or company (rather than a whole economic sector) as the assumed terrain for collective bargaining, an army of staffers was needed to organize, bargain, and service thousands of separate, intricately detailed contracts.

The resulting mushrooming of professionals was exacerbated by the absence of a national health insurance and pension system, a vacuum partially filled by the construction of "private welfare states" by each company. In unions, as in government, increased atomization generally equals increased bureaucracy. By the early 1960s, there were over 60,000 full-time union staffers in the US, one for every 300 union members—in contrast, there was only one for every 2,000 members in Britain and one for every 1,700 in Sweden.[7]

Under this American "service model," new organizing became very staff intensive. Similar to traveling salesmen, organizers would make a unionization sales pitch to workers individually or at plant gates.[8] If enough workers were convinced by the spiel, they had a decent shot at voting in a union and winning a first contract, since union-busting (outside of the South) tended to be significantly less intense than would later become the norm. Though union density peaked in 1955, union membership continued to rise until 1979.

Then came the 1980s. Labor was thrown into an existential crisis by Reaganism, deindustrialization, the onset of neoliberalism, and full-throttled union-busting. As union membership in the private sector began to plummet from 1981 onwards, many labor leaders—with SEIU in the lead—began promoting a new approach, seeking to move towards an "organizing model" based on worker involvement and more funding for new organizing.[9]

The plan to win at scale was simple: fund more good organizing. It was on this platform that progressive SEIU leader John Sweeney was elected president of the AFL-CIO in 1995 as part of the New Voices slate. Sweeney's team strengthened the AFL-CIO's Organizing Institute to spread best practices, they pledged to dedicate 30 percent of their national budget to new organizing, and they pushed for affiliates to do the same. True to this spirit, various unions—such as SEIU, the Communication Workers of America (CWA), the American Federation of Teachers (AFT), and what soon became UNITE-HERE—put serious effort into organizing and member involvement. Hundreds of thousands of workers were recruited into unions, often through comprehensive campaigns that creatively combined rank-and-file intensive workplace organizing with "corporate campaign" pressure tactics that used staff and union resources to leverage companies' non-workplace vulnerabilities.

Though post-Reagan organizing orthodoxy recommended deeply involving workers, organizing in practice generally remained staff-heavy and top-down. Labor lawyer Julius Getman lamented that "virtually all unions today regularly talk the talk of grassroots, bottom-up organizing and member mobilization. But that is not how the vast majority operate."[10] In large part this was because conditions were so unfavorable. Faced with intense employer opposition, a decentralized society, and working-class resignation, unions needed large numbers of staff organizers to foster worker agency.

It's worth noting that bottom-up alternatives to the dominant approach failed to take off in this era. United Electrical—the US union with the longest and most consistent commitment to rank-and-file unionism—witnessed huge losses in the 1980s and 1990s among its blue-collar manufacturing base. Its attempts to turn things around, for all their creativity, made little headway when faced with employer threats to pack up their factories and move. For example, UE's Plastic Worker Organizing Committee (1989–93) was a bold worker-driven organizing project with the slogan "It's Time." But after years of making little progress, the joke among worker leaders and staff became, "Well, maybe it wasn't quite time."[11] For grassroots efforts to win widely, conditions have to be favorable. Willpower isn't enough.

Despite sustained efforts to scale up by funding good organizing, New Voices's impasse culminated in a demoralizing split of SEIU and its allies from the AFL-CIO in 2005, followed by an intense melee of raids and jurisdictional fights.[12] Ever since then, the main story within labor is how little new union organizing has even been attempted—at least, until the recent worker-to-worker uptick.

DEFINING THE NEW MODEL

The idea that workers should organize other workers is hardly a new one. Though many union drives fail to put this into practice, since the late 1980s it's been a basic axiom of labor strategy, as reflected in tactics like building strong organizing committees tasked with holding one-on-one conversations with coworkers. To quote UNITE-HERE's unofficial motto, "the organizer organizes the committee, and the committee organizes the workers."[13]

Building off of this foundation, worker-to-worker unionism gives rank and filers responsibility for key tasks that are normally done by paid, full-time staffers. Increased reliance on workers can take numerous forms, ranging in scope from low-level responsibilities like creating a drive's visual logo to ambitious duties like running its social media or researching the company. But three things in particular define the new model:

1) Workers have a decisive say on strategy,

    and

2) Workers begin organizing before receiving guidance from a parent union,

    and/or

3) Workers train and guide other workers in organizing methods.

In other words, workers initiate and/or train an organizing drive, *and* they play a central role in determining its major decisions.

The upshot is that worker-to-worker efforts are generally cheaper and easier to spread widely. Worker organizers can more consistently become strategy-making generals, not only foot soldiers, as is the case in many (though not all) heavily staffed efforts. And because the gaps of power, experience, and authority between workers tends to be lower than between workers and full-timers, worker-to-worker organizing also tends to be more democratic.[14]

This approach is similar to the type of bottom-up unionism that was common in the US before World War II. But at least one component sets it apart: its reach can extend beyond a local level. With the rise of digital tools, it's now possible for workers to reach out to, coordinate with, and train other workers anywhere in the country. And this is not a minor development, since companies and working-class communities have sprawled out so much over the past century.

Readers shouldn't get too hung up on terminology, since *worker-to-worker* and *staff-intensive*, like all categories, are only ideal types meant

TABLE 2
Main worker-to-worker organizational forms

Forms	Example
Worker-initiated drives that don't affiliate with an established union	Burgerville Workers Union
Worker-initiated drives that affiliate with an established union	Colectivo (joins IBEW)
Unions where workers train other workers	NewsGuild

to facilitate analytical clarity. Practice on the ground is always muddier. Some drives are "edge cases" between the two models, and within each model there are varying degrees of staff-intensivity—for example, between the independent and stafferless Burgerville Workers Union and a well-staffed, but still worker-to-worker, effort like the NewsGuild's Member Organizer Program.

In the next chapter we'll examine union campaigns illustrating the three main worker-to-worker organizational forms laid out in table 2. For now, it's sufficient to note that this model refers to a phenomenon much wider than just new independent unions—most worker-initiated drives in recent years have chosen to affiliate with established unions, hoping to lean on their staffing and legal resources. (Oftentimes such decisions are made only after deep collective deliberation: 35 percent of worker-to-worker survey respondents participated in debates and votes about which union to affiliate with.)

Even when they affiliate to a pre-existing union, self-initiated drives differ from standard drives not only in their origin but also generally in their subsequent trajectory and degree of rank-and-file ownership. And regardless of whether or not a particular effort is self-initiated, I consider it to be an example of the new model if—in addition to workers' high strategic sway—the main organizing training it receives is from a worker rather than a union staffer.

It's worth underscoring that the new model does not consist of passively waiting around for workers to spontaneously rise up. Worker-to-worker unionism leans heavily on proactive tactics like seeding drives through mass online trainings and digital tools, and by having workers reach out to other workers in a given company or industry via personal networks or cold calling. It also proactively spreads unionization via "salting"—encouraging organizers to take jobs at strategic workplaces with the goal of unionizing them.

DIFFERENT FORMS OF STAFF-INTENSIVE UNIONISM

What I'm calling staff-intensive unionism covers a wide variety of different (often contradictory) strategies and practices, whose only inherent commonality is that they're relatively reliant on full-timers.

How is worker-to-worker unionism different than what labor organizers call hot-shop organizing? Individuals or small groups of workers in hot shops reach out to a union for help, but they don't generally first start *organizing* on their own—for example, trying to convince skeptical coworkers or launching a collective action like a petition. Nor do they normally have a strong say in the drive's overall strategy.

They also generally diverge in breadth. While hot-shop organizing normally impacts a single discontent workplace, worker-to-worker union drives have tended to be part of efforts to organize an entire company or industry. It's like the difference between founding a boutique shop versus a retail chain. Scale, moreover, is related to cost: fighting for and servicing thousands of separate contracts is incredibly resource-intensive. Hot-shop drives are often initially cheap, because union staffers tend to provide little organizing assistance, hoping that high worker frustration on its own can eke out an election win. But things tend to get very costly on the back end because hammering out and servicing countless separate contracts requires lots of paid negotiators, lots of lawyers, and lots of union reps, especially when rank-and-file organization is weak.

What about the difference between worker-to-worker unionism and what in the 1990s and 2000s was called "social movement unionism"? This is a trickier question to answer, since this term has been given so many different meanings. Most attempts are long, omnibus definitions, such as sociologists Voss and Fantasia's argument that social movement unionism consists of a half-dozen attributes: worker involvement, research on corporate vulnerabilities, activity outside routinized legal structures, broad social justice focus, tactical flexibility, and a long-term vision.[15] The prevalence of catch-all definitions reflects a real strategic ambiguity within the AFL-CIO's New Voices project. Increased rank-and-file involvement was generally seen as just one of many different useful innovations for revitalizing labor, not its *sine qua non*. Similarly, many labor academics of the era argued for combining "bottom-up" and "top-down" approaches—a stance that, while appropriate enough for the question of how to win particular campaigns, had little to say about which models were actually scalable.[16]

The nature of workers' involvement was also left ambiguous in these definitions, as in the prevailing union practices of the period. Were workers only foot soldiers and press conference enhancers in campaigns directed from above? Or should they also be decision-makers at all levels of the effort? Even definitions that focused specifically on rank-and-file involvement tended to elide the difference between increased participation and increased leadership. As such, labor scholars Turner and Hurd argued that "the essence of social movement unionism" is "a new emphasis on rank-and-file participation or mobilization."[17]

My conception of worker-to-worker unionism has the analytical and practical benefit of being much more specific. While it's crucial for labor to uphold the progressive stances and organizing tactics associated with social movement unionism, for these to involve tens of millions, not just tens of thousands, you need an actual mass movement. And a movement is a movement to the extent that it scales popular initiative.

BUILDING FROM (BUT DIFFERENT THAN) LEFT UNIONISM

While most post-Reagan organizing manuals insist that workers are the union and that they should have ownership over the unionization process, prevailing practices in staff-heavy efforts tend to fall far short of this goal. I call such practices *hollow organizing,* since they have the outwards trappings of systematic deep organizing (such as quantitative and escalating benchmarks), while lacking its beating heart: rank-and-file leadership development.

Whereas labor is generally more talk than walk when it comes to worker-intensive organizing, various left-leaning unions in both theory and in practice place a central focus on identifying and developing worker leaders. As Local 1199's influential "Advice for Rookie Organizers" put it, "Tell workers it's their union and then behave that way. Don't do for workers what they can do."

Worker-to-worker unionism should be seen as an outgrowth and extension of this left-labor tradition, exemplified by unions like 1199 New England, National Nurses United, and UNITE-HERE. Both approaches share a bottom-up ethos, but they tend to differ in practice concerning staff intensiveness. Though the former's focus on training workers makes it more scalable than other forms of staff-intensive unionism, it is still significantly more reliant on paid full-timers. For example, the staff-to-worker ratio at 1199NE aims to be around 1 to 125 by the eve of an election. And while both traditions at their best aspire to give worker leaders a decisive strategic say, it's easier to approximate this ideal in practice when workers take on more initiative and responsibilities.[18]

I don't want to overstate these differences: staff-intensiveness is a spectrum, with these two types of rank-and-file oriented unionism often shading into each other. For example, lightly staffed campaigns within unions like 1199NE with very strong rank-and-file ownership constitute "edge cases" that could be reasonably categorized either way. Moreover, the speed and extent to which unions can move towards a worker-to-worker model depends not only on leadership strategy, but also on the degree of self-activity, confidence, and politicization of workers in distinct occupations and industries at a given moment in time.

When we turn from the question of organizing *models* (the division of labor) to organizing *methods* (tactics), the similarities are also significant. Most recent worker-to-worker drives have consciously implemented the longstanding rank-and-file intensive workplace methods advocated by scholar-strategists like Jane McAlevey as well as Kate Bronfenbrenner.[19] Rather than counterpose such tactics to a worker-to-worker model, the latter should be seen as a way to spread the former.

Recent labor debates have been marred by a mistaken tendency to assume that unorthodox models necessarily go hand in hand with unorthodox methods. But unions like the NewsGuild combine innovative worker-to-worker national structures with a rigorous and creative commitment to time-tested tactics. Stephanie Basile from the NewsGuild notes that "building a movement takes a lot of methodical organizing and leadership development—if people just think they're signing a card, you're gonna be toast."

In other words, the difference between staff-heavy and worker-to-worker unionism does not neatly track on to debates over whether to stick with (or move beyond) tried-and-true workplace organizing tactics.

LEANING ON STAFF IN A DIFFERENT WAY

The defining trait of worker-to-worker organizing is that it's lightly staffed. But unlike many previous cases for grassroots unionism, my core criticism of staff-heavy approaches—that they're too costly to scale—does not suggest that full-time organizers and union resources are unimportant.[20] Especially in today's atomized conditions, we should all take seriously the following argument made to me by a staff organizer from a left-led East Coast hospitality union: "I think that there can be an over-romanticization of worker-led stuff. Of course, we can't organize anything without workers, they're the people who *do* everything at their sites, but they're going up against brutal companies and they're working full-time, so they deserve to have experts on their side with the organizing experience and the capacity to help them win."

She's right. Capacity and accumulated experience *are* crucial, and staff are generally an essential vehicle to transmit both. But here's the problem: most unions use this correct general argument to justify their specific (staff-heavy) division of labor, without seriously probing the potential to scale up by deploying experienced full-timers and union resources in a new way. The case studies examined in the following chapters suggest that workers can and should do more than they're normally asked—or allowed—to.

Take the question of capacity. It's obviously true that full-time organizers have more time to support an effort than workers. And if you're a union running a few drives a year, then a staff-heavy approach may pose no major problems. But what if you want to support hundreds or thousands of campaigns? The only way to generate that level of capacity is by distributing responsibilities much more widely to worker leaders; in such a scalable approach, staff still play an essential role—helping formulate industry-wide and company-wide strategy, providing legal support, doing time-consuming logistics, coordinating worker volunteers, etc.—but in a much less intensive way for each particular workplace. Viewed from the angle of building a mass movement, capacity turns out to be a major liability for staff-heavy unionism.

What about the expertise born from accumulated organizing experience? It's true that having battle-tested organizers on your side is invaluable. And it's very helpful for drives to be able to lean on staffer expertise, all other things being equal. At the same time, the recent uptick has shown that:

- full-timers can help train far larger numbers of workers via mass online trainings;
- workers who have unionized their sites are perfectly capable of (and oftentimes best suited for) guiding and supporting other workers step by step through their drives;
- workers themselves can accumulate expertise by participating in or supporting multiple drives; and
- workers rather than staff are best situated for taking the tactical risks that are often necessary to win big in whirlwind moments.

By more fully baking in rank-and-file ownership of the organizing process, a worker-to-worker model can help workers consistently relate to staffers as partners in struggle, not as experts to be deferred to. Of course, if a particular set of workers lack the interest or capacity to take on more responsibilities, there will be instances where good staff-intensive organizing is the most feasible approach. But the only way of testing how far it's possible to go is by actively encouraging worker-to-worker unionism. And unions need to be crystal clear about the urgency of moving in such a direction, since prevailing staff-heavy approaches simply can't build power widely enough.

A NEW FORM OF WORKER-TO-WORKER ORGANIZING

I'm definitely not the first person to make the case that putting workers into the driver's seat is *the* key to building a powerful mass labor movement. Multiple generations of leftists and shop-floor militants have raised this banner, from the IWW and early Communists to today's Labor Notes network. In that sense, *We Are the Union* makes a new case for an old strategy.

TABLE 3
Grassroots unionism, then vs. now

	1930s	Today
Geographic scope	Local	Local, regional, national
Means of coordination	In person	In person, digital
Relationship to working-class culture(s)	Leans on and expands preexisting dense social ties and class sentiments	Rebuilds class ties/culture via deep organizing, media, and electoral politics
Industrial scope	Hard industry	All industries, including service and public sector
Approach to strategic targeting	Concentrates on big targets at heart of industry	Combines targeting with widespread seeding of drives
Union resources needed to scale by the millions	Medium	High

But when I call worker-to-worker unionism a new model, I'm not only referring to its novelty as a widespread phenomenon in our contemporary labor movement. Socio-economic changes since the 1930s oblige (and make possible) significantly new organizing approaches. Table 3 summarizes some of the main differences between effective rank-and-filed oriented models then and now, which we'll examine in detail over the course of the book.

An underestimation of today's unique challenges has led more than a few advocates of militant grassroots organizing to rely too much on examples from the distant past and to be excessively vague about the means to build new unions today. Radical union writer Joe Burns, for example, has explicitly made a case for saying little about organizing methods, arguing that "left-wing trade unionism is not fundamentally about skills; it's about putting trade unionism on a class struggle basis.... Perhaps less organizing would be required if we actually had strategies that made sense to workers."[21] Parallel to this vagueness about the nuts-and-bolts of union growth, leaders and activists grouped around Labor Notes have until recently focused more on transforming existing unions than on building new ones.

Critics of lightly staffed organizing thus generally respond that it sounds good on paper but isn't realistic, since it relies on a romanticization of "spontaneity." Depending on who they're referring to, such criticisms may sometimes be fair, other times not. But either way, we need to replace a blurry image of worker-to-worker organizing with a high-definition picture. Without such clarity, it'll be hard to diffuse a new grassroots model or to counter the claims of its skeptics.

Labor scholar-activist Teresa Sharpe, for example, argues that a fatal flaw in a worker-to-worker strategy "is the implicit assumption that strategic skills and new tactics arise spontaneously"; its "advocates cannot explain how the rank and file creates winning campaigns in the absence of skilled leadership."[22] But the examples I point to in the following pages show that, far from hoping that organizing skills would "spontaneously" appear, these have been frequently taught to new drives by other workers, usually online via mass trainings (with some staff support) or in one-on-one Zoom conversations.

Contrary to what union strategist Sam Gindin has recently claimed, the relevant debate is not over "spontaneity vs. organizing."[23] The real question is: What *form* of organizing has the potential to win widely enough to beat the billionaires? Since so much rides on the extent to which conditions and tactics have changed since US labor's breakthrough in the 1930s, our next chapter dives into the data to show that a deep, and deeply consequential, socio-economic dispersal *has* taken place. As we'll see, the decline of centralized mass production and dense working-class neighborhoods requires that today's organizers develop distinct approaches to knit workers together across their spatial divides.

2

ORGANIZING ON A DISPERSED TERRAIN

> If you look at old school unions, things were different back then. Like I was watching a movie about coal miners, they all worked at the same place, they lived next to each other, drank at the same bars. So there's an inherent culture that already exists that organizers can lean on. But where I work, and where I live, that's just not there anymore—so we have to find ways to actively build those connections.
>
> KEVIN GALLAGHER, Apple Store worker organizer

WRITING IN 1936, Communist labor leader William Z. Foster made the following recommendation in his pamphlet on how to organize the steel industry: "Meetings should be held especially in popular neighborhood halls, where the workers' fraternal lodges meet, where the workers dance, where their weddings take place, and where they are generally accustomed to going."[1]

The almost complete disappearance of these types of neighborhood meeting spaces provides a small window into how America has been reshaped over the past century, a transformation that has made scaling up union power significantly more difficult and that precludes us from simply importing old organizing methods to today. Of the many factors that have transformed class relations—deindustrialization, neoliberalism, financialization, globalization—here I'll focus on the one that is perhaps the most directly relevant to organizing at scale: economic and residential dispersal.

US labor's leap forward in the Great Depression was rooted in a centralized political economy very different from our own. Industries tended to be clustered in a handful of regions and cities. Workers tended to be concentrated in dense working-class neighborhoods adjacent to their jobs. In the largest corporations, though not necessarily elsewhere, jobs tended to be in massive factories. And due to the tightly bound nature of their assembly line and production systems, strikes by even a minority of well-positioned workers could relatively easily shut down factories and production chains.

Intense employer and state repression made organizing difficult and risky. But in such a context, it was a no-brainer for radicals and CIO organizers to target big, strategic workplaces in large corporations.[2] As shown by the watershed Flint sit-down strike of 1936-37, knocking out a couple "mother plants"—like General Motors Fisher Plant Number One—could shut down production nationwide and set off a chain reaction across the entire region and industry. Along these lines, the CIO single-mindedly focused on unionizing hard industry, rejecting hundreds of requests for union charters in other sectors of the economy.[3]

But in the decades since World War II, America's socio-economic topography has sprawled, making it harder to organize workers and making it harder for organizing victories to spread. Such changes don't necessarily mean the labor movement is less potentially powerful than it was in the past. But they do require that we more rigorously adapt our organizing methods to today's conditions.

An extreme illustration of how things have changed was provided to me by a staff organizer with the Utility Workers of America. He explained their difficulties unionizing wind techs in Texas:

Oh, my goodness, they were spread over—you know, *Texas*. Good luck finding these people, right, they're all over creation. And they have much less affinity toward one another, because they probably don't even know each other. They might work for the same employer, but work hundreds of miles apart. Contrast that to a distinct power plant, where everybody's all right there, and you can see why it's such a challenge.

And even when these Texas wind techs do manage to win a union, the resulting ripple effect will tend to be lower than in the past because they're less likely to live in dense working-class neighborhoods, where the good news of the union can easily spread by word of mouth. If dominoes are stood up too far from each other, knocking one down won't automatically set off a cascade.

US labor revitalization requires a clearheaded map of our terrain and viable mechanisms for deliberately scaling up worker power. Because of the socio-economic decentralization described in the following pages, we should expect that triggering and spreading union avalanches today will require initiatives to scale up that are more proactive, more well-resourced, more geographically spread out, more industrially varied, and more digitally enabled than was necessary or possible in the 1930s.

ECONOMIC DECENTRALIZATION

In the first half of the twentieth century, the US economy was dominated by manufacturing, which was concentrated in a relative handful of cities and regions. In the 1930s, for example, two-thirds of factory workers were employed in 3 percent of the nation's territory.[4] Taking advantage of this industrial concentration and a favorable political context under FDR and the Second World War, a grassroots worker upsurge unionized mass production industries in the late 1930s and early 1940s.

But employers did not wait long to launch a counter-offensive. Politically, unions were race-baited in the South, red-baited everywhere, and hemmed in by new anti-labor laws. Economically, to escape the manufacturing belt's strong labor movements, employers dispersed across the country, especially to low-wage, anti-union areas like the South and the Sunbelt. This flight from union power was made feasible by improved communication and transportation technologies and also by America's federated labor and employment laws, which enable peripheral states and locales to compete for industry through "business friendly" policies.

The old centralized industrial hubs were not just relocated. Different parts of the production process were split up and farmed out to different locations—and oftentimes to different companies. The newly built factories were significantly more spread out from each other, and smaller in size, than the ones left behind. Accordingly, anti-union manuals suggested building new plants two hundred miles apart or more.[5]

Though the extent to which factories could be easily scooped up and sent to China or Mexico has generally been overstated, significant numbers of factory jobs *were* lost to international capital flight. Credible threats of offshoring, moreover, played a major role in scaring industrial workers and union leaders into submission.

Manufacturing jobs have not only decentralized since World War II, they have decreased significantly in number. Figure 4 charts the well-known decline of hard industry and the rise of services.[6] What's often missed about this shift is its spatial consequences: services are even more geographically dispersed than today's factories, to say nothing of prewar manufacturing.[7] In other words, deindustrialization has dramatically accelerated economic dispersal. The reason for this is that most services need to be relatively close to the people to whom the service is being provided. It would make no sense, for example, to cluster hospitals or Walmart superstores in one or two regions of the country.

Large service sector corporations, like their manufacturing counterparts, have also been "vertically disintegrated," with various occupations

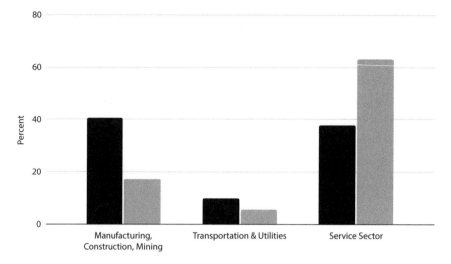

Figure 4. US private sector non-agricultural workforce, 1939–2022. Source: Historical Statistics of the United States; Labor Force Statistics from the Current Population Survey.

that used to be done in house, such as cleaning or sales, farmed out to subcontractors often in entirely separate locations. Similarly, high-wage employees—for example, dispersed tech or white-collar workers at a company like Starbucks—often never interact face-to-face with the lower-paid employees who sell their companies' products.

WORKPLACE SIZE DECLINE

One important result of manufacturing decentralization and the rise of services has also been a significant decline in the size of workplaces, especially within the largest corporations.

A quick word of caution: we don't actually have a good sense of the extent to which workplace size made large factories so strategically central in the past. Other crucially important factors include their close ties with surrounding residential communities, their highly integrated and disruptable production processes on the shop floor and beyond, and the omnipresence of big establishments within big companies (those with the deepest pockets for granting concessions). Size on its own does not necessarily make a workplace easier to organize. In fact, for the past fifty years unions have had consistently much higher win rates at small and medium-sized establishments.[8] But larger workplaces *do* lower organizing costs by concentrating workers and, thereby, increasing their interpersonal ties and making it possible for organizers to have a wider impact.

Scholar-activist Kim Moody's 2017 book *On New Terrain* obscures these trends towards smaller workplaces, especially in the largest American companies. As part of his case that working people have been re-concentrated by "the logistics revolution" into large workplaces in large urban areas, Moody writes that "the nation's workplaces are not getting smaller measured by the average number of workers."[9] He justifies this conclusion by comparing the percentage of large workplaces in 1986 to today. But it makes more sense to zoom out further back in time. The data clearly shows that since the mid-1970s the percentage of thousand-person-plus workplaces in all industries *have* declined, by about 3 percentage points, and that factory sizes in particular have fallen sharply.[10]

And the available data going back to the 1930s, though somewhat spotty, suggests a far more dramatic decline in the centrality of large workplaces. We know, for example, that there's no industry today even closely comparable to pre-war auto: in 1939, 76 percent of auto workers were employed in workplaces that had a thousand or more employees.[11] In contrast, the largest corporations today are generally dispersed into thousands of small and medium-sized establishments (see table 4), making it significantly harder to scale up workplace power.

This mushrooming of smallish workplaces at the heart of the US economy constitutes a dramatic shift from both the 1930s and the 1970s. By way of comparison, GM's 69 plants employed 3,478 workers on average during the Great Depression and US Steel's 121 plants averaged

TABLE 4
Largest US employers (by workforce size), 2022

	US employees	Workplaces	Average workers per workplace
Walmart	1,300,000	4,600	283
Amazon	1,100,000	1,285	856
UPS	443,000	5,452	81
Home Depot	437,000	2,000	219
Kroger	430,000	2,719	158
Target	400,000	1,956	204
FedEx	370,000	11,800	31
Starbucks	258,000	15,873	16

SOURCE: Data provided to me by union researchers in these industries

2,159.[12] Manufacturing is still an economically central part of our economy. But big companies no longer generally depend on big workplaces.

SUBURBANIZATION AND THE NEW WORKING CLASS

Economic sprawl has always gone hand in hand with housing sprawl. As such, the relationship of home to work, and of workers to other workers after clocking out, has been dramatically transformed over the past century.

As one geographer recently explained, "Working class consciousness and organizing has tended to reach highest levels where workers live in dense communities close to their workplaces."[13] Capitalists learned this the hard way when urban working-class explosions rocked intensely concentrated US cities beginning in the mid-1880s. Following in the footsteps of urban planners in places like Paris after 1848's center-city insurrections, America's big employers and city planners reacted by pushing and pulling workers out of downtown, especially from 1899 onwards. This, however, was a slow process: for the first half of the twentieth century, most workers continued to live in densely packed urban neighborhoods.

We shouldn't romanticize that era. Working people a century ago were not homogenous, nor were they united on a class-wide level. Women were all too often marginalized in a male-dominated culture. And deep racial, ethnic, and religious divisions sorted workers of different backgrounds into distinct jobs, blocks, neighborhoods, or states. Uniting these disparate blocs of workers was never easy or automatic. But the compactness of urban working-class life led to the flourishing of clubs and organizations—religious, social, cultural, and sometimes political—among workers of all backgrounds. Within such ethnoracial blocs, workers were far more cohesive than they are today.

Even before the rise of mass trade unionism, solidarity with other workers was more deeply felt than today because it was more deeply rooted in the routines of daily life.[14] Successfully unionizing one node of these tight social networks could more easily set off an organic chain reaction. Unfortunately, there aren't many places today that resemble southern Michigan circa 1936, as described by two sociologists:

> Workers from the many GM establishments—as well as workers from other Big Three plants and myriad suppliers—lived in the same neighborhoods, socialized in the same bars, and played in the same parks. The tightly coupled southern Michigan production culture therefore created enduring personal and community relationships among workers who—in a dispersed production system—would have had few useful relationships unless they deliberately sought them out.... [W]orkers from different factories knew each other, creating a city- and even regionwide interpersonal network that facilitated the type of grassroots organizing utilized by UAW organizers in Flint and elsewhere in the auto production culture.[15]

This type of world was stretched apart by mass suburbanization. There's little empirical basis for Moody's suggestion that the emergence of new working-class neighborhoods have generally made up for the decline of cities' old dense working-class neighborhoods.[16] Even a quick look at the data on population density in urban areas registers a dramatic decrease from 1950 to 2000—a 25.8 percent drop, on average, according to one dataset.[17] Chicago has become almost as sprawled out as Los Angeles, dropping from 17,409 inhabitants per square mile to 12,746.[18]

As car commuting, isolated tract homes, and television became the norm after World War II, working people came to live and socialize further from each other as well as from their places of employment. To quote historian Eric Hobsbawm, the late twentieth century was marked by "the breaking of the threads which in the past had woven human beings into social textures."[19] Though white and white-collar workers were the first fractions to leave the city, suburbanization has become the norm for the US working class as a whole. In many metropolitan areas, a majority of low-income households now live in the suburbs, as do a majority of Americans.[20]

Commute distances provide a good glimpse at how much things have changed. In 1934 Pittsburgh, more workers walked to work than drove. As late as 1950, a majority of US working-class families did not own a car. And even in car-centric Detroit, mid-century UAW shop stewards lived on average only 3.4 miles from work.[21]

Compare that with the average American today, who commutes 20.5 miles to work *each way*—a 27 percent time increase since 1980 (the first year the US Census began tracking the figure).[22] As Robert Putnam explains in his bestseller *Bowling Alone*, "Each additional ten minutes in daily commuting time cuts involvement in community affairs by 10 percent."[23]

It's not just unions that have paid the price. As Putnam details, since the 1960s the United States has witnessed an across-the-board erosion of associational life, strong interpersonal networks, and church attendance. Recent studies have confirmed these findings, including the fact that personal discussion networks have shrunk by one third since 1985.[24] Though sprawl is not the only factor driving this atomization, it *is* clearly a phenomenon that organizers have to acknowledge and find answers to.

WHAT ABOUT LOGISTICS?

Not everybody agrees with the picture of social-geographic dispersal I've painted above. Some authors and organizers in recent years have insisted that the rise of logistics—transportation and warehousing for supply chains—has recreated organizing conditions similar to the 1930s by geographically concentrating large numbers of workers with a high degree of structural power. Like the "clusters of auto assembly plants of yesteryear in Detroit or the steel mills in Gary," writes Moody, today's warehouse and transportation workers, as well as their interlinked white-collar and point-of-sale peers, are "tied together by urban-based concentration" as well as "the modern just-in-time supply (production) chain." Modern supply chains, due to their numerous chokepoints, "have reproduced the vulnerability that capital sought to escape through lean production methods and relocation."[25] In his view, "Amazon can be today what General Motors was for organized labor in the 1930s: the high-visibility site of the spark that inspired millions to strike and join unions."[26]

This analysis suggests a relatively unproblematic and straightforward approach to scaling up: organize logistics workers at the nerve center of contemporary capitalism and detonate a working-class explosion. Take John Womack's case for focusing on employees with the power to disrupt supply-chain choke points:

> Unionizing movements happen in a kind of avalanche. That one rock falls, and that moves other rocks, and eventually the whole side of the mountain gives way. And that's what you want in a company like Amazon or in the Big 3 automobile industries. But Amazon, in particular, depends on those warehouses.... And if [unionists] can organize several of the big warehouses, that, I think, would make a big, big difference.[27]

Much of this is accurate. Organizing logistics workers *is* particularly pivotal because of their economic leverage. (The same holds for manufacturing, as we've seen in the UAW's big recent wins.) It's also true that because logistics workers link together worksites in so many industries—especially retail—they have lots of potential leverage to support other unionization efforts. And logistics workers *are* economically central: three of the eight largest companies are explicitly in logistics (Amazon, UPS, FedEx) and the big retailers on that list (Walmart, Home Depot, Target) are also central drivers of the logistics revolution.

But a closer look under the industrial hood shows why we can't copy the old hyper-concentrated strategy of the Communists and CIO. For starters, logistics doesn't carry anywhere near the numeric weight of manufacturing in its heyday. Whereas manufacturing workers made up 30 percent of the US workforce in 1939, transportation and warehouse workers make up 4 percent of the workforce today.[28]

Nor does logistics play the same magnetic role in the broader community, since metropolitan areas are less dense than they used to be. One of the reasons why the unionization win at a big Amazon fulfillment center like JFK8 on Staten Island was so exceptional is that many workers were obliged to commute hours to work each way, leaving them with less time for off-work socializing and with fewer personal ties with their equally dispersed coworkers. Organizing something like systematic house visits to discuss the union with all employees—a crucial step in the summer 1936 drive leading to the Flint sit-down strike—is much harder in today's suburbanized context.

Inside a warehouse itself, as sociologist Nantina Vgontzas has uncovered in her research on Amazon, a redirectable labor process means that, unlike in an assembly line, small groups of workers refusing to work can't shut the place down. And the "dispersal of the labor process across warehouses" means that no single workplace can paralyze the broader distribution network. There are too many different nodes through which shipments can be rerouted: "In most cases, management can simply block off that warehouse by pressing a 'little red button,' which tells the system to not send any new orders to that warehouse."[29] Due to this optimized-and-dispersed labor process within and between Amazon's many workplaces, "a few strategically placed workers can no longer shut down an entire warehouse or distribution channel, as they could in the golden days of manufacturing."[30]

That's why, like in the rest of the economy, tapping the structural leverage of warehouse and transport workers requires organizing on a wider geographic scale than in the past. No less significantly, effective organizing today requires involving more people and a broader range of occupations. Vgontzas captures this perfectly:

> While the form of power present in today's warehouses can be likened to that in yesterday's factories . . . the scope of its activation will need to be far more diffused. Amazon's fulfillment network will not be shut down by workers strategically placed along the assembly line in several key facilities, as in the interwar strikes that led to the initial unionization of mass industry. It will require a much wider level of coordination within fulfillment centers, across regions, and between nodes in Amazon's network, from fulfillment centers to the tech offices that optimize fulfillment work.[31]

Strategic nodes still exist at the heart of our economy. But in comparison with a century ago, disrupting these chokepoints requires organizing more workers, more widely, more systematically.

IMPLICATIONS FOR ORGANIZING

What does all this social dispersal mean for labor strategy? That's one of the key questions that this book attempts to address, and I won't try to lay out all my answers here. But a few preliminary big-picture points are merited.

It seems clear that economic-residential sprawl has made it harder to unionize at scale. The costs of unionizing a single workplace rise when workers have fewer ties to each other, since this obliges organizers to focus more on fostering relationships between coworkers. And this same dynamic makes any single victory less likely to organically spread outwards via workers' personal networks. One recent quantitative study finds that the impact of strikes on union growth has been declining since the 1880s.[32]

Because economic growth has taken place in such a spatially fragmented way since World War II, tapping workers' shopfloor power is more challenging than ever. But that doesn't mean that it is less strategically necessary than in previous eras.[33]

How then can workers' immense-but-latent power be widely tapped in today's decentralized conditions? Targeting pivotal workplaces and companies is still an important tactic. Some jobs, workplaces, and industries are still more strategic than others, due to their disruptive capacity, economic importance, or social weight. If you're a young person looking to change the world, I'd definitely recommend getting a job at Amazon to help unionize it.

But this type of strategically targeted organizing today needs to be combined with initiatives to let a thousand organizing flowers bloom. Here's an example of what this can look like: Leaning on the momentum generated by its successful strike in late 2023, the newly reformed UAW has used digital tools and light staff support to actively encourage (and provide tools for) *all* non-union workers to immediately start self-organizing. Rather than targeting specific factories chosen ahead of time, the union has cast its organizing seeds widely, focusing on providing the most material support for those plants where fired-up workers have gone the furthest in collecting union authorization cards with little direct staff guidance.

In contrast with the UAW, labor's prevailing way of responding to working-class fragmentation has been either to give up on new organizing or to use more staff to try to fill in the gaps. There's a compelling logic to heavily staffing up: given how dispersed jobs and communities are today, it's unrealistic to expect workers to replicate the organic, bottom-up dynamics that prevailed before the Second World War.

Providing a high amount of full-timer support, the argument goes, can make up the difference. This approach, which has prevailed among organizing-focused unions since the 1980s, received its most eloquent defense in a 2014 article by historian Gabriel Winant:

> The organic integration of the working-class social world is gone.... On the Lower East Side, or in Back of the Yards, where everyone on the block had basically the same job and the same daily routine and experience, marching in sync to the factory whistle, collective experience needed less formal incorporation to survive.... [In today's conditions] a successful organizing campaign needs at least one full-time organizer per hundred workers. In a good campaign, the staff organizer identifies, recruits, and trains leaders from the rank-and-file, who do the work of engaging others and developing their collective voice.... Today, rank-and-file insurgency simply will not form without being fostered. The economic environment is far too hostile.[34]

This is partially right. Compared to a century ago, it will take more resources and more sustained fostering to win widely today. Workplace dominoes today *do* need an extra little push. But unlike the staff-heavy, 1-to-100 model defended above, only worker-to-worker unionism can leverage union resources in a way capable of scaling up working-class power. Part 2 of this book digs into a range of success stories to show what exactly this entails.

PART TWO

EXAMPLES OF VICTORY

3

THREE WORKER-TO-WORKER WINS

> The [IBEW's] financial and organizing help was invaluable, definitely. At the same time, it's true that they had to learn from us about how to organize a bunch of young workers, people who are very online and who tend to do things differently, in an industry they hadn't organized before.
> RYAN COFFEL, Colectivo barista

WHAT DOES WORKER-TO-WORKER UNIONISM look like in practice? In this chapter, I examine three major unionization efforts that have won even in the face of ruthless union-busting. Each corresponds to one of the new model's main organizational forms: Burgerville (an independent union), Colectivo (a worker-initiated drive that joined an established union), and the NewsGuild (a union where workers train other workers). Contrary to the widespread belief among labor leaders and scholars that lightly staffed campaigns can't win first contracts, each of these *has* achieved this exasperatingly difficult goal.

BURGERVILLE WORKERS UNION

One of the most underreported victories of the recent labor uptick has been the years-long effort to turn Burgerville into the country's first unionized fast food chain. The campaign at Burgerville—a Pacific Northwest chain with over forty stores and 1,400 workers—is an instructive test case for worker-to-worker unionism because it secured a first contract through an independent union that had exactly zero union staffers. This is an even more impressive achievement since fast food is an industry famously difficult to unionize, both because its employees are relatively easy to replace and because its workplaces are so dispersed, so small, and so high turnover.

In many ways the Burgerville unionization story starts in East Los Angeles, where Mark Medina was radicalized by having "grown up incredibly poor." Mark, the son of Mexican and Guatemalan immigrants, explained to me that his family was occasionally homeless and forced to squat on a factory floor in East Los Angeles: "I remember when we had nothing to eat, collecting cans with my brother and sister to feed our family."

All this formed the basis for Mark's subsequent organizing trajectory. "I know it sounds cheesy, but I remember thinking when I was a kid that 'I don't want anyone to have to go through I had to go through' and by the time I was in high school I had decided that I wanted to make the world a better place." So he got into radical politics, embracing the dictum that "the working class and the employing class have nothing in common." He soon got a taste of unionism while working as a janitor in Portland, leading a march on the boss and becoming a shop steward in SEIU Local 49.

In November 2015, Mark, Luis Brennan, and a few fellow IWW members began salting four Burgerville stores. Pushing back against the idea that food service workers could only be unionized after passing legal reforms, here's how Mark articulated the drive's overarching strategy in a 2018 interview:

> My goal is to win this campaign and put it to the rest of the labor movement as a way that you can organize this industry on a low-cost organizing model that is member-run, member-led.... We don't have to wait for

politicians to clear the pathway, we can do it now. And if we can win in this campaign, we can demonstrate to larger labor unions that they can do this too.[1]

They began small, building relationships with coworkers, talking during and after work about their complaints and hopes, their lives and hobbies. Those most interested in fighting back were recruited to organizing committees, which pushed for floor mats at one store and against an unfair manager at another. In the spring of 2016, they went public as the Burgerville Workers Union (BVWU).

Choosing to start acting like a union without waiting for recognition by employers or the state, they wore buttons at work saying "I can't afford lunch here. Ask me why." Contrary to stereotypes of fast food workers and the Pacific Northwest, few Burgerville employees were well-off white hipsters looking for a bit of extra spending money. Mark notes that BVWU's membership is primarily made up of "poor people . . . and our recent membership survey showed that 60 percent of our union is Black and brown." Next came regular informational pickets, plus organizing marches on the boss when coworkers were fired or unfairly disciplined. The actions were lively—lots of joyous singing, creative chants, funny signs. "One of our goals is to make fighting back as fun as possible," notes Mark. "People aren't going to want to engage if unionizing is boring."

Social events—regular barbecues, parties, concerts, bowling nights—were pivotal mechanisms for integrating new members, forging a union culture, and giving workers a good reason to stick it out at Burgerville. As worker Claire Flanagan told a reporter, "The union has changed people's relationship with the job and work. It's gone from being a place I go to work to pay my bills to feeling invested in our coworkers and the job in a much deeper way. This is my community."[2]

Whereas paid staff organizers normally drive forward day-to-day unionization tasks, at Burgerville this fell on hyper-committed workers like Luis and Mark. Jokes of collapsing from exhaustion were not uncommon among core organizers, who often found themselves with an inexhaustible to-do list of organizing and logistical responsibilities.

Good organizing never stops, especially in a high-turnover industry. "My message to anyone who wants to do this is it does take planning and it does take preparation and organizing work," explained Luis in 2018. "Those magic, spontaneous moments happen but there's a lot of hard work behind [it] too."[3] What differentiates a drive like Burgerville's from a staff-intensive effort was not its level of "spontaneity," but rather its high degree of worker leadership.

One of the key novelties of BVWU compared to heavily staffed unions was rank and filers' degree of say over the course of the campaign. Weekly meetings, open to any union member, decided on all big questions. At Burgerville, bottom-up democracy within the campaign proved crucial not only for cementing workers' ownership of the drive, but for shifting its strategic path onto a more pragmatic path. More specifically, in its first two years of life BVWU was firmly committed to a "solidarity unionism" approach, in which workers steer clear of state institutions. But the union shifted under pressure from, and through democratic deliberation with, rank-and-file workers unschooled in IWW doctrine. In early 2018, they collectively decided to file for NLRB elections after assessing that they had gone as far as possible without engaging the state.

Experience vindicated their reorientation. In a major boost to BVWU's legitimacy and public profile, all three stores that filed in 2018 won their elections, as did the two that filed in 2019. "For a long time people have dismissed fast food as unorganizable, saying that turnover is too high, or the workers are too spread out," BVWU declared after it won its first election in April 2018. "Today Burgerville workers proved them wrong."

Unlike in most staff-intensive drives, winning a union election at Burgerville seamlessly passed into the fight for a first contract, because the same set of people were driving both. One of the most irrational and self-defeating norms within established unions is that after an election win full-time organizers are usually replaced by full-time contract bargainers ("representatives") who generally have neither the relationships with worker leaders, the organizing skills, the knowledge of the workplace, nor the time capacity to effectively help workers continue to build the power necessary to win a first contract. One union staffer texted me a complaint about his local: "[We] follow the traditional union organizational pattern where the new organizing people and representational organizers not only are in different departments but also hate each other. And yes, the handoff happens after the election but (bizarrely!!!) before the first contract."

BVWU was able to avoid this internal stumbling block since its leadership was not contingent on staffing dynamics. Filing and winning NLRB elections, however, did spur management to dramatically ramp up its counter-offensive. Beginning in 2018, the company went all out to stop the unionization effort: captive audience meetings, management intimidation, and over a dozen firings of pro-union activists, usually on the flimsiest of pretexts. In March 2019, for example, Burgerville retaliated against 90 percent of the Oregon Convention Center store's employees within a week after they filed for a union election. Many workers were "indefinitely suspended" without pay, including Morrisha Jones, a longtime BVWU member who had worked at the company for three years and was eight months pregnant. Her misdeed? Forgetting her name tag at home, an action that normally resulted in a warning, a chance to retrieve it from home, or simply a new tag.

The union responded with a big public offensive in defense of Morrisha, taking its case to Facebook, the press, and community members, who were asked to call corporate headquarters to demand her reinstatement. As BVWU's GoFundMe for Morrisha declared, "Punishing expecting mothers, who are living check-to-check, is inhumane. It is disgusting. Shame on you Burgerville." Hours after being asked for comment on a soon-to-be-published exposé of Morrisha's treatment in a local weekly, Burgerville's lawyers notified the union that it was

Figure 5. Morrisha Jones shortly before being suspended. Source: BVWU.

rescinding all disciplinary charges at the store, with back pay for the suspended workers. "BIG NEWS! BURGERVILLE BACKS DOWN!" exclaimed BVWU online. Mark recalls that this fight "really underscored to us how vulnerable the company was to anything that could tarnish its brand."

Worker leaders understood that they had to create enough of a crisis for Burgerville to make granting a first contract less costly for the company than continuing with the status quo. Walking out was one crucial weapon in their arsenal. "Every time we went on strike—and we struck *a lot*—it was an effort to put their brand at risk," Mark explains. "We knew that the economic costs of taking out five stores [out of 42] were significant, but ultimately less important than overall brand damage."

A year into the contract negotiations, management and its lawyers were continuing to stonewall. So BVWU decided to escalate with its biggest strike yet: an open-ended walkout begun on October 23, 2019, at four stores. Mark recalls that the action was a game changer:

Figure 6. BVWU workers campaign for a contract. Source: BVWU.

We were getting headlines in every newspaper, a ton of TV airtime, there were back and forth op-eds for and against the company, everybody was talking about us. That's what broke them, because all of a sudden on the eve of the strike they started making significant TA [tentative agreement] concessions, hoping we wouldn't walk—and when we did anyways, after two days of striking the company asked us to hold two marathon bargaining sessions, 9 a.m. to 9 p.m., in which they finally began moving on a lot more.

After four days of striking, Burgerville workers jubilantly returned to work, with about 90 percent of the tentative agreement now agreed upon. Though Covid-19 gave the company another long excuse to delay the contract's finalization, workers kept organizing. Victory finally came when BVWU's worker negotiating team signed a tentative agreement with Burgerville on November 11, 2021. The union's Facebook post the following day summarized the wins (many of which were granted to all stores):

We did it!! After 7 strikes, a boycott campaign, 5 elections, hundreds of workplace actions and dozens of picketlines and citywide actions. Upon ratification we will have ended At-Will employment, ended unfair scheduling, won tips for workers that have averaged a 22-25 take home pay . . . and so much more. In addition throughout bargaining the company has conceded and unilaterally applied many of our major demands like free shift meals, 1$ wage increase after our strike in October 2019, 5 paid holidays and in store tipping system.

The core lesson from Burgerville's experience is clear: worker-to-worker campaigns *can* go all the way, even before labor law is reformed, even in an extremely high turnover industry. At the same time, it's worth reflecting on the fact that the full protections of the union's contract and shopfloor organization only covered five stores. In the absence of more staff backup, BVWU leaders had their hands full just keeping things moving locally.

Precisely because most other worker-to-worker drives have perceived a need for more resources, they've generally chosen to affiliate with established unions. And because the spatial divide among worker organizers was limited to Portland, BVWU was not—unlike so many other recent bottom-up drives—obliged to find ways to leverage digital tools to coordinate across a wide terrain. The story would have been different had they tried to immediately unionize every store in the company, like their Midwest peers at Colectivo.

THE COLECTIVO COLLECTIVE

Jokes about unionizing had been occasionally thrown around the Colectivo cafe on Milwaukee's Humboldt Avenue, where barista Hillary Laskonis had worked since the fall of 2017. Then, in March 2020, a lack of a collective voice at work suddenly became a life-and-death matter. With Covid-19 surging, Hillary and a few other baristas began drafting a petition to close Colectivo's stores for a minimum of two weeks with full pay for workers. They did so semi-publicly, over a viral thread on the Colectivo Meme Page, a big employee-run Facebook page normally used to gripe about things like annoying customers. (A tip to readers: don't request milkshakes from baristas on busy days.) The petition was sent off, with hundreds of signatures. On March 16, under public and state pressure, Colectivo agreed to both demands.

Most of this initial organizing took place online because everybody was on lockdown and because workers lived scattered across different cities in Wisconsin and Illinois. Since the Meme Page was not a secure forum, Hillary and her co-organizers launched a new secret Facebook group for the explicit purpose of discussing how to unionize. Operating under the cover of a meet-up to play Dungeons and Dragons, the group's name was D&D Game Night.

These baristas joined forces with a group of Colectivo's warehouse workers who had also begun to self-organize. Next, this core group began systematically reaching out to coworkers, and they began interviewing unions to potentially affiliate with. Talks with the Teamsters fell through because Colectivo's worker organizers were set on organizing at the largest scale possible. As one of the worker leaders involved in these discussions explained to me, "We wanted to organize the whole company, not just the few places that we already had a strong base at. But the Teamsters seemed to think that was too ambitious."

With high turnover, twenty-five small stores, and roughly five hundred employees dispersed across two states, organizing all of Colectivo *was* a daunting organizing challenge. Fortunately, the International Brotherhood of Electrical Workers (IBEW)—specifically Wisconsin Local 494 and Illinois Local 1220—agreed to support the Colectivo workers' bold vision.

Once cafes began opening back up in April and May 2020, the big question became how to win over the majority of stores and coworkers who weren't yet on board. One of the key reasons Colectivo's worker organizers could even pose this as a realistic objective was that, unlike at Burgerville, they had an established union to lean on. By all accounts, over the entire course of the campaign IBEW and its staffers did an excellent job of providing Colectivo worker leaders with resources, legal services, and light-touch strategic support. The extra capacity provided by the IBEW allowed worker organizers to focus the entirety of their energy on the daunting task of building a strong union culture in every single store and warehouse.

Receiving union resources while still being able to fully steer the campaign was in many ways the best of both worlds. And to their credit, IBEW organizers agreed to defer to workers on strategy. "We took the lead on all the things we felt confident about," explains Ryan Coffel, a fifteen-year veteran barista and store manager in Chicago. "It was a real learning experience, and a real collaboration, for both of us; they gave us ideas for what to do, we'd workshop them and then act on the ones that made sense to us. When we didn't think something would work, or didn't see it working when we tried it, they'd say, 'No problem, you know best,' and we'd just move on."

This degree of rank-and-file say over the campaign was significantly higher than in most shallow mobilizations and staff-intensive drives, which often make no effort to involve workers in developing a plan to win. In the Fight for 15, for instance, some participants complained that workers' strategic say was limited to what one described as "rubber-stamping some decisions that are already made."[4] A recent study similarly found that workers at an OUR Walmart rally in Chicago gave speeches pre-written by UFCW staff, leading one young activist to lament that "a lot of times I think an organizer acts in a lot of other ways [like] the bosses act that are problematic."[5]

Along similar lines, Keenan Dailey—a Trader Joe's worker leader in Boulder, Colorado—noted to me that even though their drive was self-initiated, once they affiliated with the UFCW "it felt like we were just along for the ride." Some other staffed-up organizing efforts do a better job involving rank and filers in tactical choices (such as who to reach out to first at a workplace), but workers rarely have a decisive say on *all* major facets of the drive's approach. As Teresa Sharpe notes in her

Figure 7. Colectivo's union responds to suggestions that IBEW officials would dictate everything. Source: Colectivo Collective.

detailed study of a rank-and-file oriented but staff-intensive hotel organizing drive in the Bay Area, "there were moments when workers recognized the discrepancy between the language of democracy ('you call the shots') and the reality of a high level of staff control."[6]

Colectivo reversed these authority dynamics. As is usually the case, worker leaders met with staff organizers to deliberate over next steps. But much of the planning was done also in regular Zoom meetings open only to worker organizers where, as Hillary recalls, "we'd review what was working, what wasn't, and plan our next steps."

For example, IBEW's initial approach was to have their staff organizers give out fliers to workers as they came in and out of work. But the workers' committee assessed that this wasn't particularly effective and quickly insisted that all outreach be done by workers themselves. Ryan explained:

When the IBEW organizers—and, you know, these dudes really do look like big grumpy construction workers—were out there talking it up with folks, it gave the impression that the union was a third party. So we insisted that all outreach be done by us. It put way more work on our plates, for sure, but it's just so much easier to convince people when you're speaking as a coworker. I'm not sure most established unions get that yet.

Though none of the workers were experienced labor organizers, they gave themselves a crash course in organizing tactics through trial and error, by reading Jane McAlevey and *Labor Notes*, and by reaching out to Spot Coffee workers in New York who had recently unionized. Having mapped out which stores they were strong and weak at, Hillary, Ryan, and fellow worker organizers began systematically going shop by shop to talk with those who weren't yet on board. And whenever possible, they would pick up shifts at other locations to build relationships that way.

This one-on-one work was always labor intensive, occasionally awkward, and frequently stressful. Like in any deep organizing effort, it was also the campaign's bedrock: unionization, at its core, is about developing relationships of trust between coworkers via countless conversations to help people see how their problems at work can only be resolved through collective action.

If the tactics used by Colectivo organizers were time-tested, their back-end organizing model was highly innovative. A worker-to-worker drive of this geographic scope—some core organizers lived about 150 miles from each other—would not have been possible without digital tools; only full-time organizers would have had the capacity to drive across the Midwest knitting together local organizing committees and developing cross-state strategy. But platforms like Zoom made it possible for Colectivo workers to lead the campaign even though they didn't live close enough to regularly meet in person. "I've never met in person about half the organizers I met with weekly for years," notes Ryan.

Figure 8. Colectivo's union connects workers to Spot Coffee organizers. Source: Colectivo Collective.

Despite the company's professed commitment to social justice, Colectivo's owners responded by transforming the drive into a knock-down, drag-out battle—what union organizers call a "boss fight." Some forms of retaliation were almost silly. After customers started responding to the union's public request for them to order drinks under the name "IBEWSTRONG," Colectivo's IT department had the word IBEW automatically blocked from orders. Management's most ill-advised move came at a big captive audience session in Chicago, where Ryan was one of over 150 workers they packed into a rented movie theater at the height of Covid:

> The first weird thing is that, with zero context provided, they have this video loop playing of African people chanting and dancing the whole

time. Then finally they connect the dots, sort of, when the [Chief Financial Officer] explains that in 2018 he and the owners travelled to the places their coffee was produced, and he tells us "Rwanda was the most interesting place we visited, we saw the victims and perpetrators of the genocide working together. If they can forgive one another, so can we at Colectivo." It's so bizarre that they actually thought that was somehow going to help convince a bunch of low-wage workers to vote No.

Other union-busting actions were far more serious. The owners began going to the stores to pull workers off the floor for intimidating one-on-one "check-in" conversations. Next they hired the notorious firm Labor Relations Institute (LRI) to lead captive audience sessions in every store and to guide the union-busting campaign. Mass emails soon pummeled employees with anti-union talking points, including the suggestion that unionization would bankrupt the company. Only a few weeks after hiring LRI in October 2020, Colectivo unexpectedly closed down two Wisconsin stores. Most egregiously, five organizing committee leaders were fired, in what organizers and coworkers (and later the NLRB) perceived as clear-cut retaliation.

"I called my other trainer in tears. . . . I was just so shocked," recalled Zoe. "I knew that they were going to fight back, but I didn't think they'd fight back like that."[7] And as Starbucks management would also later do, Colectivo's management (falsely) declared that they couldn't grant raises until the union process was concluded. "It really felt like the walls were closing in on us, they were looking for any excuse to fire us," remembers Hillary. "If there wasn't a broader network of solidarity, I'm sure it would have been too much for me or for any of us."

Despite this employer offensive, workers narrowly won their March 2021 NLRB election. "I'll never forget that day," recalled long-time baker Doug Thompson. "I was elated. We just jumped for joy. I went out to the local the day after and got my 'Proud Union' sign and stuck it in front of my house. And it's still there."[8]

But then the company resorted to bosses' classic tactic for stonewalling first contract negotiations: delay, delay, delay. There are few meaningful legal penalties in the US for companies like Colectivo who try to wait out an elected union through exhaustion, harassment, turnover, and constant legal challenges.

Fortunately, strong rank-and-file leadership, born from their deep sense of ownership of the effort, managed to keep up momentum for the long-haul contract fight. Workers like Hillary and Ryan (until he was fired in retaliation) stuck it out for the sake of the organizing effort. Most new hires were just as pro-union as their predecessors. Plus, the IBEW dealt with the tedious and costly legal proceedings, enabling workers to stay focused on the organizing. They did so rigorously, following best practices for high-participation contract campaigns: systematically surveying members to find out their bargaining priorities; holding open trainings to encourage as many workers as possible to join bargaining negotiations; ensuring regular one-on-ones and phone trees to keep people up to date; collectively drafting contract proposals; and setting up a shop steward system ahead of time.

All that was essential. But organizers also understood from day one that an outpouring of external solidarity would be required to put the campaign over the top. Social media was one important avenue to publicly expose the contradiction between Colectivo's liberal words and its union-busting deeds. The union's robust digital output was generated by two barista volunteers, Zoe and Kait (who continued to co-lead union comms even after being fired). Memes, photos, videos, songs, articles, and petitions were evocatively wielded to capture the community's attention.

No less importantly, Colectivo workers reached out directly to their customers, friends, families, neighbors, and comrades. Getting support from community members is important in most labor struggles, but it's particularly crucial in the service sector, which depends on a loyal customer base to keep on buying products. The average American today has much more of a direct relationship with a company like Colectivo, Starbucks, or Amazon than they did with US Steel or the Phelps Dodge mining company—a dynamic captured by *The Onion*'s satirical article, "Starbucks Fights Unionization Effort by Hiring Pinkertons to Order Exhausting, Hyper-Specific Drinks." Whatever its periodic annoyances, this dependence on consumers (or service-receivers at schools and hospitals) creates lots of potential for outside leverage.

Demanding that owners start bargaining in good faith, Colectivo workers organized petitions and joint rallies at cafes with these supporters, elected officials, labor leaders, and members of the Democratic Socialists of America (DSA) and its youth branch, Young Democratic Socialists of America (YDSA). Members of the YDSA club at Shorewood High School in Milwaukee had a particularly noteworthy impact, since they plastered up pro-union posters—listing the names of Colectivo's owners, with the demand they start bargaining—in their neighborhood and at their school, which two of the Colectivo owners' children happened to attend. YDSA's actions set off a public scandal when the owners' spouses replied with a flurry of mass emails to community members and district admin, claiming the school poster campaign was a form of "bullying" their kids and demanding the club's faculty sponsor be disciplined, all while not-so-subtly noting the Colectivo owners' "generous financial support for [school] endeavours and the district as a whole."

Escalating public pressure—combined with sustained rank-and-file organizing and consistent NLRB decisions in favor of the union—was the straw that finally broke the owners' backs in the spring of 2022. The company caved and met most of the employees' core demands. In June, workers ratified their first contract by a 95 percent margin, which codified paid sick leave, better scheduling rules, a 6.7 percent pay raise, and "just cause" job security for *all* workers, from the warehouses and drivers to administrative employees.

Colectivo was now the largest coffee chain in the country with collective bargaining. "History has been made," proclaimed a press release issued by the Wisconsin AFL-CIO. To celebrate, it quoted Hillary—the only original member of the voluntary organizing committee still employed by the company:

> This contract ratification is the culmination of the efforts of hundreds of workers over the past three years. We could not have made it to this point without their bravery, the tireless work of the folks at the IBEW, as well as the vocal support of thousands of customers and members of the community. I am beside myself with gratitude for all of them this week.

In some ways, Colectivo was a fairly by-the-books victory. Hardly seeking to reinvent the tactical wheel, its organizers leaned on all the tried-and-true tactics of deep organizing. Yet this dynamic, combined with the drive's affiliation with an established union, masks two crucial novelties.

First, Colectivo worker organizers had an exceptionally high amount of leadership over the campaign—a degree of ownership reflecting the drive's self-initiated origins and its continued reliance on a worker-to-worker infrastructure even after affiliating with the IBEW. Second, by leaning on digital tools to connect physically distant worker leaders, Colectivo's drive demonstrated how worker-to-worker drives can now, for the first time in history, coordinate themselves beyond a local level. Before the digital era, worker organizers would have had to depend on full-time staffers to oversee their regional campaign. Now they could take the lead themselves.

THE NEWSGUILD

While worker-initiated organizing is one hallmark of the new model, another is that workers train other workers. And no union has done this more systematically, widely, or successfully than the NewsGuild.

It's strange that so many people have suggested that worker-to-worker unionism can't win first contracts, since the NewsGuild for many years now has proven this to be false. Reversing decades of decline, the union won seventy-one first contracts between January 2021 and February 2023. And many of these have not been easy fights.

The Guild has triumphed even in the face of extremely hostile and powerful employers such as the hedge-fund controlled McClatchy Company, which runs twenty-nine daily newspapers in fourteen states. With the backing of member organizers, and after two years of company stonewalling, journalists at the *Fort Worth Star-Telegram* went on an open-ended strike in late 2022 that lasted twenty-four days and ultimately forced the company to grant them a great first contract—the first at any newsroom in Texas. Similarly, it took thirty-two months of struggle at the *Dallas Morning News* for workers to win a first contract in 2023.

Rather than narrate one particular drive, let's take a close look here at the innovative structure lying behind this cascade of victories: the Guild's Member Organizer Program (MOP). At the MOP's foundation, explains NewsGuild national organizer Stephanie Basile, is the idea that "workers are capable of learning how to do everything a staff organizer knows and does."

Its roots go back to 2016, when a journalist in Springfield, Illinois, named Dean Olsen took the initiative to cold call journalists across the country who worked at the same parent company, GateHouse. Having unionized his paper four years earlier, Olsen would call people up, ask how things were going at their job, then pivot to explain why he and his coworkers had gone union and why others should consider doing the same. In a period when the NewsGuild was still largely a stagnant, sleepy union, the result of these efforts was two successful 2016 drives at papers in Sarasota and Lakeland, Florida.

Newly hired as the Guild's national organizer, Basile sought to expand this bottom-up dynamic by asking a few worker leaders from recently organized shops in Florida and California to travel with her when she trained new drives. This side-by-side initiative was strongly encouraged by Communication Workers of America (CWA) national organizing director Sandy Rusher, reflecting the CWA's long tradition of relying as much as possible on members themselves to organize new workers.[9]

A side-by-side training approach worked well as long as only a few new shops were engaged. But once the numbers of leads began to exponentially expand, Basile realized they needed a bigger, more formalized structure capable of onboarding more volunteers and training more drives. A crucial step towards making that possible came in 2019, when Jon Schleuss—a rank-and-file leader of a victorious self-initiated *LA Times* drive in early 2018—ran for union president and unseated the NewsGuild's long-time incumbent. Had it not been for this insurgent reform campaign, the MOP may very well have been still-born.

Now with vigorous union backing, the MOP was built up by Basile and other NewsGuild staffers together with worker leaders like Andrew Pantazi from the *Florida Times-Union* and Kristina Bui from the *LA Times*. Though building on the CWA's rank-and-file traditions, the MOP developed these in an ambitious new direction: by leveraging digital tools, large numbers of workers nationwide would get skilled up in all aspects of organizing, including those tasks normally only done by full-timers. In the process, they would not only learn and implement new skills, but learn how to teach these to others, a competence normally monopolized by staff. As NewsGuild instructional materials explain, "The strength of our union is tied to our commitment to developing others."

The Member Organizer Program revolves around three interlinked nationwide structures—trainings, mentoring, and pods—none of which would have been possible beyond a local level in a pre-digital era.

How do we define leadership?
Learn, Do, Teach

Leadership isn't about taking on the tasks of our union ourselves. It's about developing others to participate by providing the resources and opportunity to do so. The strength of our union is tied to our commitment to developing others! **How have you seen this play out in your union?**

The Learning Pyramid shows how much we retain based on various learning methods. Teaching others is the most effective way to develop and learn yourself.

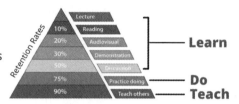

Your union is taking action one week from now. Twenty people need to be called and invited. What do you do?

- Call them myself because no one else will do it well → **NOPE**

- Send a text message to our unit's group chat asking others to do it. → **GETTING THERE**

- Identify two coworkers who I think would be good, make the first call together with them, assign out people to call, and then schedule a debrief. → **GREAT**

> **REMEMBER**, a task is not just something to get done. It's an opportunity to grow your union by developing fellow members. A task absent of development loses much of its value. Make the most of every opportunity! Learn, Do, Teach!

Figure 9. NewsGuild training material. Source: The NewsGuild.

Monthly National Organizing Trainings

The purpose of these Zoom trainings is to frontload the teaching of essential skills—from the ABCs of launching a drive to more particular responsibilities like running a good meeting—rather than resort to the inefficient practice of having staffers teach these separately to each new drive one by one (or having staffers do it themselves, instead of workers). MOP trainings are presented by member organizers to other media and nonprofit workers, which helps cement their skills and expands the Guild's overall capacity. And unlike in many unions, these trainings cover contract bargaining and beyond, not just winning a union election.

As Kristina Bui explained to me:

> These trainings are great because they give so many workers a chance to learn and teach new skills. And we give back-end support to whoever is leading the trainings, but this approach has really freed up staff to focus more on other things. Since many of the steps necessary to build a strong union—winning people over, inoculation, facilitating a good meeting, contract bargaining, all that—are almost identical for any drive, why not give all these tools to different workers all together?

"Pods"

The heart of the MOP are its "pods" of member organizers: regular meetings of workers from different geographic areas and different stages of union drives and contract campaigns (or post-campaign union building) to share experiences and brainstorm next steps. Though their number fluctuates, there are normally around eight hubs of ten to twelve members each, meeting on a monthly basis. And member organizers who lose their jobs are still encouraged to participate, further increasing the MOP's overall capacity and social movement dynamics.

	A	B	C	D
1	Benchmark	Step 1: Learn it!	Step 2: Do it!	Step 3: Teach it!
2		Co-facilitated with another organizer and/or was prepped by an organizer	Led facilitation	Prepped another organizer to facilitate
3	**Long Term Goal:**			
5	**Training Benchmarks**			
6	Organizer Training	☐	☐	☐
7	Affirm, Answer, Redirect training	☐	☐	☐
8	Inoculation training	☐	☐	☐
9	Shop Steward training	☐	☐	☐
10	Contract Campaign training	☐	☐	☐
11	Record keeping, list work	☐	☐	☐
12	Project management, tracking your work	☐	☐	☐
13	Meeting prep - create an agenda, do turnout	☐	☐	☐
15	**Campaign Benchmarks**			
16	Facilitate a meeting	☐	☐	☐
17	Have one-on-ones organizing conversations with coworkers	☐	☐	☐
18	Work through a challenge with an OC member	☐	☐	☐
19	Stage 1 - Contact - have initial info calls and early discussions with workers interested in organizing	☐	☐	☐
20	Stage 2 - Committee - train and build an Organizing Committee, attend weekly meetings, work with them through building to a super-majority of support	☐	☐	☐
21	Stage 3 - Campaign - go through the process of going public, fighting for and winning voluntary recognition, or filing for an winning an NLRB election	☐	☐	☐
22	Stage 4 - Contract - go through a contract campaign through contract ratification	☐	☐	☐

Figure 10. NewsGuild benchmark tracker. Source: The NewsGuild.

Effectively distributing responsibilities downwards has obliged the Guild to develop more extensive training materials and organizing support than I've seen in any other union. To systemize the organizing tasks of pod members, for instance, the MOP has developed an elaborate online tracking system consisting of a campaign tracker (listing out every step a drive can take from day one up through contract ratification) and a benchmark tracker (listing out every skill a member organizer should learn, do, and teach). "The tracking really helps," notes Schleuss. "But good God, there are so many Google Docs."

The nationwide deliberative space of the pods also makes it possible for worker organizers to experiment with tactics and to share the ones that work—a national diffusion mechanism one rarely finds within the siloed structure of autonomous locals that prevails elsewhere in organized labor.

National Worker-to-Worker Mentorship

In the MOP, member organizers—with some staff support—are in charge of fielding new leads who come in and, if these pan out, helping guide their drives. "Workers who've organized their own workplace are the best people to spread the [organizing] gospel and to train new shops," argues Schleuss. "They've been through it already and they know the industry, so they can speak from personal experience and connect on that level with anybody going through it the first time."

Many volunteers do such tasks for free, while others who take on bigger responsibilities get paid for five hours of work a week to provide the steady, personalized encouragement and support that most new drives need to meet their potential. And because the guidance they are getting is from another worker rather than staff, the interpersonal power and authority dynamics are less likely to lead to unhelpful patterns of deference.

Increased bottom-up ownership over union strategy serves a crucial pedagogical function: workers learn more—and can therefore teach more to others—when they're fully included in all key decisions of a drive. This approach solidifies a democratic culture and frees up Guild staffers to help formulate overall campaign strategy at a company and industry-wide level, research corporate vulnerabilities, and provide backend support for member organizer structures. And in the same way that digital tools allow workers to train workers anywhere in the country, so too do they allow seasoned staffers to offer their hard-won two cents more widely.

CONCLUSION

The victorious campaigns explored in this chapter took place in different regions, in different industries, and among different layers of the working class. They also had divergent levels of resources and divergent relationships to established unions, ranging from a shoestring independent project in fast food to a well-resourced drive in journalism.

But behind these distinctions lies a crucial commonality: each was a lightly-staffed worker-to-worker effort in which workers democratically set the strategy and either self-initiated the drive or received organizing guidance from other workers. Not only can these types of struggles win widely, they've shown that they can overcome relentless union-busting and that they can force intransigent employers to grant first contracts.

That said, worker-to-worker unionism—like any organizing model—has limitations, especially in its most DIY iterations. For instance, even if independent unionism may often prove to be effective on a local level, it's unclear how low-resource efforts like BVWU could scale up sufficiently on their own to beat the largest corporations.

Even in those drives that do affiliate with established unions, relying less on staff can sometimes lead to suboptimal tactical choices. And worker-to-worker unionism *will* almost always translate into a less tightly run ship. But this, in my view, is a necessary price to pay for involving far more people, more widely, and more deeply. Stephanie Basile from the NewsGuild captures the dynamic well:

> I think the big drawback is that you don't know what's going on everywhere and maybe a member is not doing it as perfectly as an experienced staffer. But building a movement is always going to be messy and I think the strengths far outweigh [the drawbacks]. If we really want as many people as possible out there leading and building power, I shouldn't know what every member organizer is doing—and we need to have confidence in them, right?

4

MANY WAYS TO WIN (BEYOND FIRST CONTRACTS)

> Normally, when you work a job like this, you grow kind of numb to the bad [company] behavior. But then when you realize unionizing is an option, that you can get involved . . . it just kind of wakes you up from what you've been dealing with.
>
> SHREYA CHAUDHARI, Starbucks worker organizer

MANY LABOR LEADERS AND SCHOLARS think that winning a first contract is the only way to achieve significant changes via workplace organizing. And there's more than a grain of truth to this assumption. Union contracts *are* the best mechanisms for cementing workers' interests and voice at work. Precisely because of this, winning a first contract generally requires building a higher degree of sustained power than is needed for other types of actions, like a petition or a one-day sickout.

But accurately assessing the impact of worker-to-worker unionism—and charting a strategic path forward—requires a broader conception of what victory can look like. In this chapter, we'll see that there are many ways to win other than first contracts.

Worker-to-worker organizing has wrested major employer concessions through direct action and pre-contract unions.

Rank and filers have also transformed themselves, the public, and organized labor. Each of these types of wins is crucial, each mutually reinforces the other, and each sets the stage for millions of workers to eventually win the contracts they deserve.

DIRECT ACTION WINS

"Spontaneous" direct action—activity initiated and organized outside of established institutions—has since 2020 been wider in scope, and more successful, than is usually acknowledged.

Some sense of the explosive growth of grassroots workplace activism during the initial months of Covid-19 can be gleaned from the website Coworker.org, a platform to support self-initiated worker actions like petitions to management. From February to March 2020, there was a 3,800 percent increase in worker campaigns and a 4,043 percent growth in actions.

Worker-initiated strikes also multiplied once the pandemic hit, particularly among those forced to work in person. A research assistant and I tracked every strike in this period. What we found is that in the first eight weeks of 2020 (that is, before the pandemic) there were twenty-seven strikes. Of these, only 7 percent were unauthorized, meaning they were either of non-union workers or of unionized workers who struck without leadership permission. But in the second eight weeks of the year—from early March through the end of May—we found seventy-six strikes. Testifying to the grassroots nature of worker action during the worst of the pandemic, 70 percent of these walkouts were unauthorized. This exceptionally high rate of wildcat activity continued up through June 2020, when fourteen of twenty-one reported strikes were unauthorized.[1]

Meat packing was a major center of strike activity in this period. Some strikers were non-union, like at the Perdue plant in Kathleen, Georgia, where a packer named Kendaliyn Granville explained why she and her coworkers had walked out on March 23: "We're not getting nothing—no type of compensation, no nothing, not even no cleanliness, no extra pay—no nothing. We're up here risking our life for chicken."[2] Other strikers were unionized, but workers took action without waiting for permission from union leaders. For instance, about a thousand workers at the JBS meat packing plant in Greeley, Colorado, refused to come in to work on March 30. *The Denver Post* reported that local UFCW officials were just as surprised by the news as management.[3]

Other blue-collar occupations witnessed similar dynamics. Auto factories saw numerous wildcat actions.[4] And in Pittsburgh, a sanitation strike was livestreamed directly by a worker involved, Fitzroy Moss, in a Facebook video that went viral locally. Despite a legal ban on striking, Moss and his coworkers refused to drive their garbage trucks on the morning of March 24 when they learned via word of mouth (not management) that two coworkers had tested positive.

Schools and hospitals were also hotbeds of labor action. At Detroit's Sinai-Grace Hospital—owned by for-profit, Texas-based company Tenet Healthcare—non-unionized night-shift nurses held a short sit-in on April 2 to protest extreme understaffing in a Covid epicenter. But according to a subsequent lawsuit, preventable deaths continued to mount, including of a young man who died because staff were too overloaded to notice that his ventilator had come loose. Around midnight on April 19, after pleading for hours with management to bring in more help, nurses decided to occupy their breakroom to demand increased staffing. One of the striking nurses, Salah Hadwan, took to Facebook Live to make their case: "Tonight was the breaking point. Because we cannot safely take care of your loved ones out here . . . we had two nurses the other day who had 26 patients with 10 vents." At this point, a fellow striker yelled out "Unacceptable! We want the public to know we're fighting for y'all and y'alls loved ones." Hadwan and three other nurses were fired, but their efforts were not entirely in vain. Extra nurses were finally hired in May.[5]

Over the coming months and years, workers all across the economy waged innumerable battles for PPE, hazard pay, paid sick leave, and safe return to work policies. As bad as things got, without this type of bottom-up resistance it's likely that many thousands more would have died.

That year witnessed another eruption of grassroots struggles after police murdered George Floyd on May 25, 2020. Minneapolis's bus system was shut down when drivers refused to help the police transport arrested protestors. A particularly high-profile BLM worker action came in August, only minutes before tipoff in Game 5 of the NBA playoff's first round. Upon seeing a viral video of police in Kenosha, Wisconsin, shooting Jacob Blake seven times in the back, the Milwaukee Bucks went on a wildcat strike, canceling the game, as well as the day's other playoff matches. BLM solidarity even spread to the decidedly unwoke fields of Major League Baseball, where multiple teams refused to play that day. It took the joint pressure of Michael Jordan—now an NBA owner—and Barack Obama to get the Bucks and others to agree to resume the season. But the players had made their point to millions and, in the process, demonstrated the power of withholding your labor. As Miami Heat forward Andre Iguodala put it to the press: "You have to be willing to sacrifice corporate money for people to realize there's a big problem out there."[6]

Across the country, employees put up signs at work, wore BLM buttons and masks, and went with coworkers to marches. They also took this fight directly into their companies and institutions. "Throughout 2020, social justice issues showed themselves in the workplace more than in the past few decades," noted Littler Mendelson.[7] Workplace actions were not the main avenue of BLM struggle. But they were a stream feeding into the broader river of protest that succeeded in convicting killer cops like Derek Chauvin, lowering the incidence of lethal force by police, and in bringing about numerous-if-modest police reforms.

Beyond BLM and Covid-related demands, "spontaneous" workplace resistance from 2020 onwards has wrested countless partial victories related to pay, staffing, and working conditions. Here's one small example: In the summer of 2022, a group of teenage camp counselors at a Jewish day camp outside of Chicago worked a field trip that lasted into the evening, well past working hours. Ignoring labor law, the camp didn't pay them for their extra hours worked. A nineteen-year-old counselor, Gabe K., took the initiative to get his coworkers to sign a collective letter demanding they get paid. Afterwards, Gabe wrote to me about the experience:

> There was a lot of fear, especially from the counselors who had worked there multiple summers. Lots of them, including people who signed, told me that there was no way this was going to work. . . . [But] the camp eventually agreed to pay about half of what they owed. I think this shows how directly organizing around specific issues can be a powerful tool, particularly since lots of us work temporary, part-time jobs as young people, and we're some of the easiest workers for companies to take advantage of.

Gabe is right. Direct actions *can* win significant external changes. And as we'll see below, workplace fightbacks can also win workers a greater sense of dignity and power, both individually and collectively.

FROM ACTION TO ORGANIZATION

Labor fights are rarely just about pay. Talk to a worker about why they're organizing and you'll likely hear as much about respect and dignity as you will about dollars and cents. Joselyn Chuquillanqui—who unionized her Starbucks store in Great Neck, New York—explained to me, "I was terrified [by what management might do], especially since I depended on the job for health insurance and college tuition. But it was worth the risk because we deserve to be treated humanely."

Precisely because direct actions can be so empowering, they often lay the groundwork for workers to build or join unions. Winning a social media-fueled push for guaranteed housing, for example, helped generate the momentum and organizing relationships that culminated in the unionization of 5,500 minor league baseball players in October 2022. Bosses are well aware of the contagion threat of *any* contestation at work, which is why companies like Whole Foods prevented employees from wearing BLM face masks. A leaked high-level internal company email explained that such actions might be "opening the door for union activity."[8]

My survey of worker leaders confirmed that a large number of their drives were preceded by ad-hoc actions like a petition or walkout. Sometimes small wins propelled workers forward. At Kenyon College in rural Ohio, the success of a student petition to win back pay for undergrad workers pushed off campus in March 2020 paved the way for a subsequent student worker unionization drive. And this drive, in turn, helped spur a subsequent wave of undergrad unionization nationwide. Similar ad-hoc efforts and partial wins paved the way for almost every higher-ed grad student drive of 2022 and 2023.

Other times it was management's refusal to meet basic demands that propelled workers to form a union. That's what happened with the strippers at Star Garden in Los Angeles, who successfully unionized after initiating a petition and weekly pickets for eighteen months to demand security measures for dancers in the face of belligerent customers. Similarly, sixty tech workers at Raven Software (the producer of top-selling games such as *Call of Duty*) walked out in December 2021 to protest layoffs; half a year later, they successfully unionized.

Even a failed petition or walkout can be a win if it develops new leaders and builds up workers' confidence in their collective power. That's the deeper strategic meaning of the labor slogan "When We Fight, We Win."

Take the case of Massachusetts's Milford Regional Medical Center. Hundreds of nurses self-organized a worker-community petition in late March 2020 for better staffing, more PPE, and hazard pay. When they attempted to deliver the petition, a hospital exec refused to accept it. Soon after, the workers' organizing committee reached out to the Massachusetts Nurses Association to affiliate. Nurses overwhelmingly won their February 2021 NLRB election, and in November 2022 they celebrated again by ratifying an excellent first contract.

To win first contracts at scale, labor will have to more widely foment and connect with the types of bottom-up actions that paved the way for unionization at places like Kenyon, Raven, Star Garden, and Milford. Though it may make financial sense for local unions to only give organizing support to workers they're trying to unionize, this dramatically constrains their range of intervention and undermines the emergence of ever-larger numbers of worker leaders and fightbacks. What might be individually rational for a particular union is collectively irrational for labor as a whole.

PRE-MAJORITY UNIONISM (AND ITS WINS)

Where winning a contract or a union election is not in the immediate cards, pre-majority unionism—acting like a union before formal recognition—is a necessary path forward. This is relevant for workers who are legally barred from collective bargaining, such as gig workers or public sector workers in many red states. It's relevant for workers in many big workplaces and big corporations, where unionization is often necessarily a marathon. And with the growing threat that Republican authoritarianism will further constrict labor rights, a pre-majority approach might soon become increasingly relevant for large swathes of the American workforce.

My interviews with staffers and elected union leaders unfortunately indicate that most unions today only put resources into drives they think can lead relatively straightforwardly to a first contract—a cautious approach that, while understandable, significantly constricts labor's willingness to support all workers interested in organizing. Unions like UE and the CWA, with their consistent support for pre-majority efforts, have long been the exceptions that prove the rule.[9]

"What makes a union a *union* is workers organizing collectively for their rights," argues Hayden Lawrence, a software engineer at Google and a worker organizer with the Alphabet Workers Union–CWA, a union of over 1,400 Google workers, both blue-collar and white-collar. "We don't have to wait for a NLRB election to start acting like a union." One major way they make their pre-contract union a reality is by having every member (except those in exceptional hardship) pay 1 percent of their salaries in dues. This financial approach helps ensure both the campaign's financial sustainability as well as the ranks' democratic ownership of the effort.[10]

The recent breadth of wins outside the bounds of formal collective bargaining suggests that far more unions should be saying yes to and seeding organizing efforts even when winning a contract may not be immediately feasible. What's surprising about the nascent, pre-contract union drives at mega-corporations like Google or Amazon is not that they haven't yet won contracts; by way of comparison, it took multiple decades of organizing to win first contracts at GM and Ford. The remarkable thing—arguably the most underreported story of labor's recent uptick—is how much these unions have *already* won for millions of US workers, despite not yet having unionized anywhere close to a majority of these companies' workplaces.

Employers have coughed up serious dough following union election wins. Apple, for example, gave all its retail workers a 10 percent wage increase soon after a June 2022 worker-to-worker union election victory in Towson, Maryland. Similarly, REI gave major raises after their SoHo store in Manhattan voted to unionize that March. Saying that you're listening to your employees, and partially addressing some worker concerns, is a key page in the playbook of most union busters.

Even credible threats of a union election win have wrested major policy changes. In July 2022—on the eve of Trader Joe's NLRB elections in Massachusetts and Minnesota (both of which were won by the union)—the company granted significant wage increases nationwide, doubled workers' store discount, increased paid time off, and added extra pay for working Sundays and holidays. Similar across-the-board concessions were made after workers at Home Depot, Lowe's, and La Colombe filed for union elections, to name just a few such examples.

Protests and public shaming campaigns have more bite when they're tied to pre-contract unions with a credible threat of spreading. Google, for example, quickly raised wages to $15 an hour when subcontracted quality assurance workers organized a petition and bicoastal pickets through the AWU.

Such fightbacks put employers in a bind. Change nothing and play into worker criticisms—or grant concessions and risk encouraging more people to join the nascent union. Companies will, of course, deny making changes in response to collective demands, but the timing of these concessions usually undermines their case. And while it's true that tight labor markets have also put upwards pressure on wages, leaked memos have explicitly confirmed that some improvements *are* a response to union drives. As Josh Eidelson reported in April 2023,

> Wells Fargo & Co. leaders are privately expressing increased concern that a years-long effort to unionize the bank's employees could soon start notching victories—and have made plans to spend millions addressing the "pain points" that can fuel organizing efforts. The lender has seen "an increase in organizing activity" by employees working with the Communications Workers of America, according to an internal PowerPoint presentation viewed by Bloomberg News. That comes amid what it called a broader "resurgence" of US union activity.[11]

In any case, when it comes to granting concessions, the subjective assessments of top executives matter less than those of workers. Felix Allen, who founded Lowe's Workers United at his store in New Orleans, recalls coworkers' responses when corporate bumped up everybody's salaries to at least $17 an hour shortly after their union drive went public:

> [Management] came in and they put up a flier that said something like Lowe's is investing in its associates by giving billions in raises for all frontline associates. They claimed that it was because of an online survey we take every year, not because of the union effort. But at least everybody in our store saw that was bullshit, people saw it as a direct result of our organizing. Everybody at work came around to thank me for the raise—old ladies were trying to buy me food.

What about at Amazon? Here the material concessions were even more dramatic. A few months after the Amazon Labor Union went public in 2021, the company announced it would spend $1.2 billion to create a new advancement pathway by training three hundred thousand low-wage Amazon workers for higher-skilled jobs at the company and beyond. After ALU won its election at the JFK8 warehouse in April 2022, Amazon reversed its no-cell-phones-at-work policy and declared it was giving $1 billion in pay raises over the following year. Then in September 2023, Amazon conceded close to half a billion dollars in raises to subcontracted delivery drivers.

These types of material and transformative wins are ubiquitous with pre-contact unions. Consider, for example, how Michelle Valentin Nieves—a conveyor operator at JFK8—describes the impact of their election win on warehouse dynamics:

> It feels much different now. Managers have changed, they're not as cocky as they were before. You don't see as much of the "I'm going to write you up or terminate you because you get on my nerves, just cause I feel like it." So the managers have changed, and workers have changed—people are not as scared as they used to be.

This shift, she added, took place in herself as well:

> Before, I would just see myself as an individual and not as part of a collective. Like it used to be that if one of my work friends was wrongfully terminated, I'd be like, "Oh man, poor Jason, I hope that he gets another job real soon—farewell and good luck, I'll buy you a drink Friday night." You know what I mean? But now if that happens I'm grabbing a bunch of people to go together to speak with human resources, we'll rally, send out a mass text, pass out fliers, all that.

In worker-to-worker union drives, personal metamorphosis is the norm, not the exception. "This has been an incredible learning experience," explains Beth Maslinoff, a ballet dancer who unionized her company in Memphis. While trainings and guidance are pivotal, there's no pedagogical tool quite like throwing yourself into a struggle that depends not only on your time, but also on your intelligence. Leaders develop by leading, organizers develop by organizing, strategists develop by strategizing.

"The funny thing is I have pretty serious social anxiety; even in terms of [pre-shift] huddles at the store, I would not really engage with them because I get anxious," noted Jamie Edwards, a worker who helped lead the first successful unionization drive at Trader Joe's in Hadley. "But the organizing has pushed me to speak out a bunch, including in front of audiences as big as 2,000 people. Unionizing has forced me out of my comfort zone."

Faced with a lonely, atomized society, one of the most immediately felt union wins is a newfound sense of belonging to a collective bigger than yourself. For Carly Hamilton, a public defender leading an effort to organize her profession despite having no legal right to unionize (or strike) in Colorado, "connecting with other defenders in the system all over the state has been so truly magical. It's something that we don't get to do very often in this job—it's been just really rewarding to see people get excited, building that solidarity." Divisions at work also tend

Figure 11. Trader Joe's United picket in Brooklyn. Source: Eric Blanc.

to diminish over the course of a good organizing effort. "It's such a beautiful thing to see people of all different backgrounds together on the picket line, fighting for each other," observes Mark Medina at Burgerville.

Pre-contract gains are not just crucial to help sustain momentum and worker morale. Improving work conditions also lowers turnover, which, in turn, makes organizing easier. Bad jobs lower workers' expectations and tend to keep people moving out of the company faster than organizers can bring them into the union. In that way, concessions that might in the short term inhibit unionization (by making the boss seem responsive) can eventually rebound to the benefit of a long-haul organizing drive. Few people today realize that US labor's 1930s upsurge was preceded over the course of the 1920s by expectations-raising "welfare capitalism" and a major drop in turnover rates—a shift that was partially due to employer concessions and changes in work culture made in response to labor militancy during and immediately following World War 1.[12] Similarly, unions have everything to gain by lowering the 150 percent turnover rate at Amazon and in fast food, whose astronomically high churns are roughly three times the national private sector average of 47 percent.

Bottom-up drives also tend to forge worker leaders who are more likely to stay in a job for the sake of the organizing effort. Jamie Edwards, who is now the president of Trader Joe's United, explained to me that, "if it wasn't for the fact that I played a big role in this then I might just step away [from Trader Joe's] sooner rather than later. But since I brought in most of the people from our local, I have a responsibility to stick with this to the end." Claire Chang at REI sounded a similar note: "There are moments where I'm so sick of working here, I hate dealing with management and I know that they've been trying to fire me for a while now, but I just haven't given them like a good enough excuse to can me. I really want to see a contract ratified, I want to see this through."

SHIFTING PUBLIC OPINION

Capturing hearts and minds might sound less important than capturing cold hard cash, but that's not quite true—at least not for movements trying to build the momentum and power necessary to win widely. After decades of economic decentralization and bipartisan abandonment of working people, laying the groundwork for widespread union growth is inseparable from rebuilding a baseline level of working-class culture and consciousness. Apple worker Kevin Gallagher—whose Towson store won a contract in July 2024—observes that the absence of such a culture has obstructed the spread of their union nationwide:

> I think that over the next years, maybe the next decade, what's going to be the most important shift is that if we keep organizing, union values will start seeping their way into the structure of daily life, right? It needs to become mainstream, part of our culture in general. Once there's more social pressure to organize your workplace, once it's trendy everywhere, only then are we going to see a really big swing [towards unions].

Many workers in the US still don't know that they personally have the ability to join a union, let alone start one. A still-common misconception, for example, is that unions are only for blue-collar workers. *New York Times* tech worker Vicki Crosson explained to me that one of the biggest obstacles in their organizing drive was the assumption that "unions are just for coal miners or something, not for us." Many others assume that jobs are either union or non-union by nature, for reasons unknown.

And even workers who might want to start a union rarely know how to get started. This sad state of affairs was described by Manny A., an operator and former Navy sailor who initiated a worker-to-worker drive at FuelCell Energy in Danbury:

> I think one of the greatest obstacles [to unionization] is just knowing even there was an option to unionize, honestly. Because we don't get that information on it, unless you look for it or are presented that information—it's not like there's a union organizer outside of most of our shops saying, "Hey, you know, you can unionize." I had to spend a ton of time digging around online to figure out what to do. But most people don't seriously consider that they have an option.

Though they have a long way to go, worker-to-worker drives have done far more to bring "the labor question" back to the center of American political life than the hundreds of millions spent by labor unions on expensive messaging consultants, lobbying campaigns, and press-savvy top-down mobilizations. As seen in figure 12, in 2022 press coverage of unionization skyrocketed.[13]

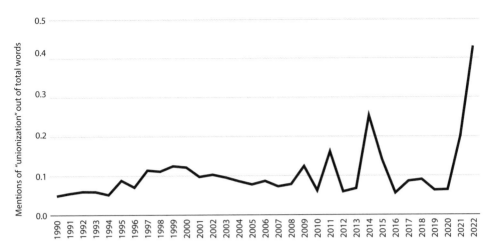

Figure 12. Yearly newspaper coverage of unionization. Source: Newspapers.com, an archive of over 22,000 local US newspapers.

Part of the reason for this attention explosion is that recent bottom-up drives—in a dramatic break from labor's prevailing risk aversion—have taken on some of the largest corporations in the world. NLRB General Counsel Jennifer Abruzzo underscored to me the nationwide importance of waging prominent fights: "The organizing that is done with the more high-profile organizations [like Starbucks and Amazon] gets the word out, right? Because it's in the press, that's what people see or read about or what have you—and that's education in and of itself, it's outreach in and of itself, so I think it's really important that [they] keep doing that."[14]

To be sure, there's always a danger of focusing on getting attention and media hits at the expense of deep organizing. Nevertheless, earned media *is* crucial for shaping popular opinion. And it turns out that worker-to-worker organizing is the best way to get it.

What has this looked like in practice? For starters, the labor beat has been resurrected from the dead, as mainstream newspapers have finally begun hiring labor reporters again to cover compelling stories of ordinary workers fighting back, especially against mega-corporations.

Unsurprisingly, worker-to-worker drives—led by Starbucks Workers United, followed by the Amazon Labor Union—overwhelmingly dominated the press surge of 2022.[15]

Even before the summer 2023 Hollywood strikes brought scores of celebrities onto the picket lines, our pro-labor zeitgeist had already broken into the rarefied heights of mainstream popular culture. To reach the furthest corners of US society, it makes a difference when someone like Britney Spears shares a call on Instagram to "redistribute wealth, strike" at the onset of the pandemic.

Various worker leaders I spoke with explained how popular culture had inspired them to unionize. Organizers at Colectivo and Trader Joe's, for example, both noted that their introduction to the idea of unionizing their shops came from watching the NBC sitcom *Superstore*. "My wife and I were binging *Superstore*, which has this long unionization plot, and I'm sitting there on the couch thinking like 'I could do that,'" notes Maeg Yosef from the Hadley TJs. "It was a bigger impetus than I usually like to admit."

Attention on its own will not turn things around for unions. But why would millions of workers risk their livelihoods for a cause they barely hear or think about? Word of mouth is still crucial, but traditional outlets and social media can boost unionization at scale.

Coverage of morally reprehensible union-busting also tarnishes company brands, while increasing pressure on elected officials to enforce and improve labor law. We saw that in the 1930s and we're seeing it again today in response to high-profile, worker-driven campaigns.

As Felice Ekelman of the prominent union-busting law firm Jackson Lewis lamented at an October 2022 industry summit, "*The New York Times*, *The Wall Street Journal*, every newspaper reports on every union win . . . when an unfair labor practice charge is filed, when there are challenges to elections. When did this become first page news?" To this, one of her colleagues replied: "And guess who's reading it? My kids. Literally. I have an 18-year-old, my kids are into it." Though professional union busters are not yet publicly shamed at any level close to what they deserve, Julia Rock's investigative report on this summit at least found that they are now complaining that their teenage children are embarrassed to be publicly associated with them.[16]

Even more importantly, watching ordinary workers taking on billionaire CEOs tends to spur copycat attempts. During the Big 3 strike, UAW president Shawn Fain's Facebook Live video updates became so popular among auto workers in a few non-union Southern plants that, as various participants reported to me, you could hear everybody's phone playing the feed when the assembly line got quiet.

My survey of worker organizers nationwide found that 55 percent of them cited other union drives since 2020 as a major spur for their decision to unionize. And by far the most influential campaigns were at Amazon and Starbucks, despite the fact that neither had yet won a first contract.

When workers break ground in new regions and industries—media, tech, higher ed, gaming, cultural institutions, recreation, social services, as well as auto and fast food—this goes a long way to showing that unions are for all. A greater media spotlight has also undercut the longstanding myth that unions are just for white men in hard industry. Attention on worker leaders like Jaz Brisack from Starbucks or Chris Smalls from Amazon helps show that the new face of labor is far less "pale, male, and stale" than in the past. As seen in my survey results, today's grassroots worker leaders are as racially diverse as the overall US workforce and they are disproportionately female and non-binary, with men making up only 35 percent of surveyed worker leaders.[17]

Whereas it was common until recently to look at unions as a narrowly self-interested group, or as the cause of inflation, today they are receiving across-the-board popular support even when they're squarely focused on winning better economic conditions for their members. Only 9 percent of the population sided with Big 3 auto bosses over workers in the fall 2023 UAW strike.[18] That said, it certainly helped the

Figure 13. Frat boys supporting April 2023 Rutgers faculty-grad strike. Source: Eric Blanc.

action's national appeal that it was framed as expansively as possible. As Shawn Fain declared on the eve of the strike, "It's a battle of the working class against the rich, the haves versus the have-nots, the billionaire class versus everybody else. . . . It's time to decide what kind of world we want to live in and it's time to decide what we are willing to do to get it."

UNION REFORM WINS

All these wins demonstrate the impact of bottom-up workplace action. That said, their breadth still falls far short of what's needed to turn things around for working people in this country. Because union resources are crucial for enabling existing drives to scale up and for seeding countless new ones, we need many more labor unions to start acting very differently.

What's a realistic mechanism to get stagnant, risk-averse unions to move in this direction? And what kind of organizing should they promote if and when they do? Recent experience shows that the answer to both is worker-to-worker unionism. That's why organizers should be thinking about union reform as much as reformers should be thinking about new organizing.

Some of the most significant wins of the recent labor uptick consist of changes made not to employers, but to unions. Rank-and-file union members have come together to vote out their moribund leaderships. And workers empowered by bottom-up drives have pressured unions into doing more (and more bottom-up) external organizing.

A comparison with labor's last attempt at revitalization is instructive. As labor scholar Richard Hurd noted in 2004, "The ultimate limitation in the AFL-CIO's Changing to Organize is that it does not require organizational change beyond resource reallocation, but rather implies that union revitalization is simply a matter of adding members and spreading the labor movement as it exists."[19] Part of the problem with this approach is that members of weak, hollowed-out unions are generally unwilling to volunteer their time to recruit new members. Nor are other workers eager to join unions with bad reputations and feeble contracts. Union busters at Trader Joe's and Tyson Foods, for instance, recently issued leaflets citing the lower pay of workers in UFCW shops and plants.

During the New Voices era, union democracy was not infrequently dismissed in the name of focusing on bringing in new members—or on overcoming do-nothing local bureaucrats through top-down mechanisms like trusteeships. Yet without significant rank-and-file ownership of the turn to organizing it was relatively easy to continue with business as usual. Quantitative research has shown that the more power was concentrated by top union officials, the less funding was given to organizing.[20] National and local union leaderships mostly ignored the AFL-CIO apparatus's exhortations and modest carrots to start seriously funding new organizing. As movement veteran José La Luz lamented, "Only a handful of . . . unions reached the mark set by [AFL-CIO organizing director] Richard Bensinger to devote 30 percent of the entire union budget to external organizing. The hard truth is that the majority of the unions didn't even get close to the 10 percent that was set as a minimum goal."[21] And even in those unions that did make a more concerted effort at new organizing, a staff-driven approach fell short of aspirations to build a sustainable organizing culture.[22]

In fairness to these initiatives, conditions in the 1990s and 2000s were far less favorable for grassroots organizing than today. There wasn't much working-class effervescence at the time for leaders to lean on. Be that as it may, one of the most important components of today's worker-to-worker uptick is that it is advancing a more viable path of labor revitalization: do-it-yourself union reform.

In the wake of the 2008 economic crisis, the "troublemaker's wing" of the labor movement saw big breakthroughs when rank-and-file K-12 teacher caucuses in Chicago, Los Angeles, and beyond took back their unions and transformed them into powerhouses capable of leading huge city-wide strikes against austerity. The organizing prehistory of these walkouts too often gets overlooked because, as the *New York Times* noted in 2020, "nobody pays much attention to [internal] labor union elections."[23]

An increased number of rank-and-file workers over the past five years have charted a new direction for labor by electing fighting leaderships in a wide range of industries. Jon Schleuss at the NewsGuild is a perfect example. Born into a conservative family in rural Arkansas, Jon first got politicized through LGBTQ issues and eventually landed a journalist post at the *LA Times*. In 2018, at the age of thirty-one, he led a successful worker-initiated union drive at the *Times*, and one year later he ran an insurgent campaign to unseat the Guild's sixty-one-year-old incumbent president.

"The reason I ran was because back when I was telling my colleagues at the *Times* to sign union authorization cards, I would always say that the NewsGuild is a great union," Jon recalls.

> At the time I felt like I was lying to them when I said those words, because I knew there were serious problems and deficiencies: it didn't have organizing in its blood and we personally weren't getting great advice [for our drive]. The only way I could make peace with what I was doing was that I promised myself and a few people on our OC that if we won, we would do everything we could to fix the union—to make it more focused on organizing, more focused on building rank-and-file power. And it turned out that most of the longtime leaders who remained also believed in that vision and were quick to move it.

Jon's run was a long shot, counting only on the backing of his co-workers, his own meager bank account, and a couple reform-minded locals. Even his boyfriend doubted whether it was worth the effort: "I remember actually having this fight with him—he was pro-union, but was trying to tell me their problems are too entrenched to fix. My feeling was 'I have to at least try.'" But after successfully forcing through a national revote after an initially undemocratic election, Jon won the presidency and, ever since, has helped transform the union into a vanguard of new organizing:

> When we were in the hardest parts of [the *LA Times*] campaign, there was a thing we repeated to each other: "We have more power than we know." And whether you're a worker struggling against an employer who is fighting you every step of the way, or if you're a rank and filer pushing against a deadweight union leadership, you can remind yourself that you have more power than you know. Workers can accomplish so much—that's where the power is, it's the rank and file.

Even greater reform wins have recently taken place among blue-collar unions like the United Auto Workers. For those who've spent decades trying to help rank and filers transform their unions, the election of Shawn Fain as UAW president in March 2023 felt like a dream come true. Fain, who joined the union in 1994 as an electrician at the Kokomo Casting Plant in Indiana, explicitly credits Labor Notes for his political trajectory, noting that its 1991 *The Troublemaker's Handbook* was one of his two "bibles." What it taught him, he explains, was "faith in the membership, faith in the working class."

How was it possible to elect Fain and likeminded reformers to head such an important union? For starters, the US Justice Department legally intervened in 2020–21 to oblige the corruption-riddled UAW to initiate a democratization process. But it took three streams of overlapping worker-to-worker organizing to take advantage of this opening. Most important was the small-but-determined Unite All Workers for Democracy (UAWD) caucus, founded by rank-and-file autoworkers in 2019 to bring the union back to its democratic, militant roots. Noting that he's "a proud member" of the reform caucus, Fain explains that "I wouldn't be standing here today as president of the UAW if it wasn't for the badass members of UAWD." After campaigning successfully for the direct election of officers in the union's 2021 referendum on this question, the caucus ran a slate for union leadership under the banner "No Corruption, No Concessions, No Tiers." These insurgents were very few in number. But Fain eked out a 69,487 to 69,010 win, since UAWD's platform resonated widely and since voter turnout in the moribund UAW remained so low (only 14 percent in the 2023 elections).

The second factor was the rank-and-file strike revolt at John Deere in the fall of 2021. Well over 60 percent of Deere workers voted for Fain, with their largest and most outspoken local—Local 838—voting for him by a 70 to 30 percent margin. Third was the uptick in self-initiated graduate student worker drives that chose to affiliate with the UAW. As in the NewsGuild, small pockets of newly organized, radicalized young workers played an outsized role in union reform. A cohort of lefty higher-ed organizers played an important backend role as volunteers and as full-time UAWD staffers. And though 97.5 percent of Fain voters in the 2023 election were not graduate students, the latter did vote for him overwhelmingly and, as such, were another key tipping point in an extremely tight election.

From the moment of their election onwards, UAW's new guard has given a masterclass on how to fire up a previously cynical and checked-out workforce by championing accountable leadership, raising expectations, tapping into anger at corporate overlords, and showing that workers can win big through mass militancy.

Within two months of launching their national organizing campaign in November 2023, over ten thousand workers across the South had already signed union cards. To envision and execute this ambitious national organizing campaign, UAW's reformed leadership from day one has hired a crew of left-leaning organizers and comms people from the NewsGuild, Labor Notes, Bernie 2020, Justice Democrats, and beyond. As is usually the case, union transformation has brought in top-notch staff, not vice versa.

In April 2024, inspired by the new UAW and supported by a new guard of staff organizers, Volkswagen workers became the first to achieve a feat that many skeptics believed would never happen: unionizing a large auto factory in the South. "When we saw the Big 3 contract wins, it's all anybody was talking about," recalls Chattanooga Volkswagen worker organizer Zach Costello. "I even saw some anti-union people flip themselves, I didn't do nothing."

The UAW's ambitiousness stands in marked contrast with most established unions, which remain hesitant to build up such a large cohort of empowered, volunteer worker organizers. As one long-time labor activist puts it, "Why don't union leaders make a strong effort to inspire their members to become volunteer organizers? The answer is that many of them don't want to. They're scared that once the rank-and-file is activated, they won't be able to control them. They might be nurturing candidates who will try to take away their jobs."[24]

Though any union can adopt worker-to-worker methods, it's likely that organizing extensively along these lines will require that many more unions undergo transformations like the NewsGuild and the UAW. This will often be a lengthy and uneven process, as seen in the decades of work put in to transform the Teamsters. But fortunately there are additional ways for rank-and-file workers to pressure and transform unions in the meantime.

Self-initiated union drives can push organized labor to take new organizing more seriously. For example, attention-grabbing union election wins like that of the independent Amazon Labor Union have put serious pressure on established unions to ramp up their own efforts at Amazon. And it's harder for unions to continue underfunding organizing when more and more organizing committees knock on their doors to affiliate. Flight attendant Jonnie Lane, for example, notes that the recent nationwide unionization effort at Delta was initiated by a small group of rank and filers led by her colleague Christina Simonin: "The unions were hesitant since past efforts had failed. But Christina coordinated so much grassroots campaigning—she even self-funded it, she'd go to FedEx and print out thousands of [union] authorization cards herself."

Many of the young workers entering organized labor are bringing with them a distinct spirit and distinct organizing approach. "We first of all have to stand up to our employer. But when needed, we also have to push unions as an institution," explains one of the worker leaders at REI whose drive voted to affiliate with the Retail, Wholesale and Department Store Union, a branch of the UFCW. Another REI worker organizer explained to me that they wanted to stay as a rank and filer rather than go on staff, since doing the latter would make it harder to pull the union in a new direction.

At REI, as in so many other drives, a significant obstacle to effectively organizing at scale has been that national labor unions are often composed of "little fiefdoms," to quote Faye Guenther, president of UFCW Local 3000, which is spearheading a national push to reform the

UFCW.[25] Across the country, workers have taken the lead on building national coordination at big companies and within industries. For example, worker-initiated drives won ten elections at the national chain Half Price Books and chose to affiliate with their closest UFCW locals. But after these locals insisted on pushing for separate contracts rather than coordinating a company-wide campaign, rank-and-file leaders took the initiative to set up biweekly Zoom calls and an online Discord to directly coordinate and develop strategy. "The union wasn't making those links, so I felt like we had to," explains David, a worker who unionized his Half Price store in Minneapolis.

Overcoming labor's atomization is an even more urgent task *between* unions, which all too often engage in turf wars instead of joining forces against employers. On this question, again, it's been up to rank-and-file activists to push in a different direction. For instance, the Apple workers who won union elections in Maryland (with the Machinists) and in Oklahoma (with the CWA) have taken the initiative to regularly coordinate their bargaining strategy. As Kevin Gallagher in Maryland explains, "There's a really great working relationship going on—Michael [an Apple worker leader] from Oklahoma City and I text daily. We're in different unions, but we're very much connected." These kinds of bottom-up coordinating initiatives have taken on an increasing urgency since almost all unions these days operate beyond their historic industrial jurisdictions. Nine different unions, for instance, organize graduate student workers.

Rather than having unions compete in organizing workers, it would be more reasonable to adopt the approach of the early CIO: different unions pool their resources for big joint organizing projects in a given industry or company. This not only avoids wasteful and counterproductive competition, but provides the campaign with enough institutional autonomy and legal firewalls to take bigger risks.

Worker-to-worker efforts, in all their many different guises, are crucial for transforming unions into organizations dedicated to developing and unleashing rank-and-file power. Reform can take the classic model of insurgent grassroots slates for union office, but it also can look like worker-to-worker campaigns pulling big established unions in a new direction. As we'll see next, that's exactly what happened in the case of Starbucks Workers United.

5

STARBUCKS WORKERS' BIG BREAKTHROUGH

> I kept up to date with politics, but I was the type of person who's like, "I gotta go to work and school, I don't have time for activism." But after Buffalo, I dove headfirst into organizing my workplace because it was so close to home—I felt like I could fix something in my control, whereas everything else feels outside my reach.
>
> BRANDI ALDUK, Starbucks worker organizer

THE ONLY THING HARDER than winning a union election against a megacorporation is winning a first contract. So it's not surprising that countless skeptics suggested that Starbucks workers wouldn't be able to muster enough power to force management to the bargaining table. Thankfully, partners and organizers ignored their critics. And after over two and a half years of relentless battle, it appears that they're coming out on top.

On February 27, 2024, Starbucks raised a white flag by reaching a deal with the union to finally begin bargaining in good faith and to stop illegally denying equal benefits to unionized workers. To be sure, the struggle is far from over—it'll take lots of organizing to keep management from backtracking and to unionize the thousands of remaining stores. But as we go to press, all signs point to a simple if still hard to believe conclusion: Starbucks workers are going to get a union contract.

If this agreement holds, workers will have not only defeated one of the world's largest corporations; they'll have done so by overcoming a scorched-earth union-busting campaign of unparalleled intensity and breadth. In the process, they've inspired a labor effervescence that has the potential to upend the service sector and beyond. It's been close to a century since workers have successfully stormed the anti-union fortresses at the heart of America's political economy. You have to go back to the 1930s to find a similar breakthrough.

Given the importance of this campaign, we should take a close look at how Starbucks partners have won widely through worker-to-worker unionism. Though deep union resources proved crucial for sustaining and spreading the effort, hundreds of worker-initiated and worker-trained drives got it off the ground. And it took rank and filers' continued ownership of their union's comms, strategy, culture, and politics to eventually force management to the table.

BUFFALO ORIGINS

Movements often look spontaneous and inevitable from the outside. But more often than not you can trace their roots to someone daring to take an organizing initiative. In this case, the impetus came from a small crew of "salts"—people who purposefully take a job in order to unionize the workplace—in Buffalo, with support from a very small regional unit of a very small union, the Rochester Regional Joint Board of Workers United.

Salting is an old tactic, yet it remains surprisingly underused by most unions despite the recent emergence of a young generation of leftists inclined to believe that billionaires should not exist and eager to make that belief a reality through the labor movement. Even more rare is the type of salting done in Buffalo. In typical staff-intensive efforts, salts normally take a job for just a few months, with the goal of mapping the workplace and passing on information to staffers about who the influential workers are. In contrast, Buffalo's crew—with the guidance of longtime unionist Richard Bensinger—became "inside organizers" who immersed themselves in the job to directly help unionize their coworkers. "Compared to a staffer, you just have more credibility with people when you're in the trenches with them and experience all the problems with them directly as a coworker," notes Casey Moore, one of the group of about ten young radicals who started salting Buffalo Starbucks stores in early 2021.

Understanding that good workplace organizers have to be good workers, it took this cohort many months and lots of flash-cards-tested effort to memorize countless recipes and become proficient baristas. James Skretta recalls working so hard at mastering the job as quickly as possible that, four months in, one coworker thought that they might be working undercover for management.

Building relationships at work—another key salting task—was easier: the stores are small, the job requires close coordination in close quarters, and their class backgrounds, age, and personal dispositions were similar to Starbucks baristas. These were the types of low-wage jobs the salts were used to working, so there wasn't much of a cultural gap to be bridged. And the accumulated grievances and progressive sensibilities of their coworkers were high enough that nobody thought it was strange when they began not only to complain about problems like understaffing (griping was already a common activity), but to raise the possibility that they might be able to fix them collectively.

Starbucks founder and CEO Howard Schultz later claimed that the unionization effort was nothing more than "outsiders trying to take our people." But this conspiracy theory can't explain why so many partners took up the effort as their own in Buffalo and beyond. Indeed, in the face of escalating union-busting—including a November 9, 2021, citywide captive audience meeting with Schultz himself—there's no way that the union could have flourished had it not been for the leadership of longtime Buffalo baristas like Gianna Reeve, Lexi Rizzo, and Michelle Eisen. By the time the initial crew came out as salts to their co-organizers in December, they had developed such a degree of camaraderie that it was an uncontroversial afterthought.

SEIZING THE (NATIONAL) OPENING

Nobody had originally planned to organize Starbucks nationwide. The Buffalo push was part of an ongoing regional campaign to unionize coffeeshops in upstate New York. But to the surprise of everyone involved, requests for organizing support erupted after Buffalo's baristas filed for a union vote in August and won their first election in December. Michelle Hejduk—a partner in Mesa, Arizona—was one of the first workers to reach out: "Before Buffalo, it didn't dawn on me that you could *start* a union. I thought it was more like you had a job that was union or you had a job that wasn't."

Part of the reason for this outpouring of interest was that Buffalo's effort was discussed so widely online and in the news. "If you were on social media and worked at Starbucks there's no way you weren't seeing what was going on in Buffalo," recalls Billie Adeosun in Olympia. Press coverage provided an opening to talk at work. Sara Mughal, who organized the first store in New Jersey, notes that "there's an unspoken rule that if you speak about unionizing, you're gonna get in trouble, maybe fired. But the Starbucks [campaign] was so widespread in the news that it made it something that we could talk about at work without any sort of suspicion."

Faced with so much unexpected interest, most staff-intensive efforts would have stuck with their original, locally targeted, game plan. It seemed like borderline lunacy to undertake such a daunting and unprepared-for national battle, especially with so few resources. But Buffalo's worker organizers were confident enough in their coworkers' fighting capacities to take the risk.

It was at this juncture that a relatively traditional and modest campaign morphed into something qualitatively different, a worker-to-worker explosion embodying the spirit of Napoleon's military adage "on s'engage et puis on voit"—basically, jump into battle and then figure it out.

Casey Moore describes what this entailed after they won their first election in Buffalo:

> So when things all of a sudden went national, it was kind of like an all-hands-on-deck thing. Even had we wanted to be more staff driven, we couldn't have been, because there just weren't enough [full-time] organizers to follow up with everybody reaching out to us. I was taking stores in Florida and Tennessee and Texas and different places—like I literally didn't have a life at that time, because I was working at Starbucks, helping organize stores and also doing a lot of the media for the campaign. But that's the way it grew exponentially.

As Casey notes, there is no way Starbucks Workers United (SBWU) could have filed 251 union elections in the first four months of 2022 had it relied on a traditional staff-intensive model in which at least one full-time organizer is needed to closely guide every workplace drive from inception to victory. Given the tiny size of Starbucks workplaces and their dispersion across the country, a traditional approach was basically off the table. Instead, with momentum suddenly on their side, SBWU leaned on its existing worker leaders and digital communication to spread as widely and as quickly as possible.

This barista upsurge from December 2021 through May 2022—when 1.9 union petitions were filed on average every day—was *the* defining moment of the campaign, imprinting a worker-to-worker DNA onto its entire subsequent trajectory. Brian Murray was one of the Buffalo baristas tasked with responding to the unexpected outpouring of national requests for organizing support. Here's how he described the onboarding process:

There was never a national plan that workers had to follow. When I spoke with new stores, it was more like, "Here's the NLRB process, here are some helpful talking points with coworkers, here's why it's important to have a strong OC that covers every shift." The basic message was, "Here are some organizing tools, take these and run with them. If you have any questions, or if you want to brainstorm, we're here as resources, as other workers at Starbucks, to help you with that." We told workers explicitly, "This is your union you're building from the ground up, and whatever you want that to look like, it's up to you." And that's what they did in terms of how they organized their stores, how they organized regionally, or the actions they took, like creating their own logos or deciding to walk out and then afterwards telling us about it.

ROOTS OF AN EXPLOSION

Given that Starbucks has a reputation for being a good place to work, corporate execs and outsider observers were taken by surprise by the unionization surge. But in many ways it was precisely because workers believed that Starbucks was a decent employer that their raised expectations crashed so hard on the rocks of understaffing, stagnant pay, hard-to-access benefits, and the absence of a voice at work.

Like so many baristas I spoke with, Sarah Pappin—a nine-year partner at Starbucks in Seattle—had been a true believer in the company's ethos: "Before the union drives started popping off, I thought the company really cared about me and other employees, which is one reason I had stayed there so long. And so when we went public and marched on [Starbucks's] headquarters, it was very emotional and overwhelming for me to be at that building that I had thought stood for so much. I could only get through a third of my speech at the rally because I got too choked up, it just felt like a very heavy sense of loss."

What set the stage for these types of ruptures? The pandemic—both its initial outbreak and the winter 2021–22 Omicron surge—was one important factor. Maggie Carter in Tennessee, who turned her store into the South's first to unionize, had a small kid at home and she was terrified of getting him sick: "Risking his health to serve coffee just didn't feel right." When I asked her if she considered quitting, she replied that "being a single parent is honestly what tied me to the job. The most stuck I've ever felt in my life was at the beginning of the pandemic at Starbucks."

An exceptionally tight labor market also gave partners more confidence to speak up. "The fact that bosses in this industry are just so desperate for workers gives us a lot of leverage," notes Lua Riley, who unionized their Philadelphia Starbucks store. "If they happen to fire some of us for organizing, we all know that it's not hard to find another shitty barista job out there." And, as we'll dig into in chapter 8, an exceptionally vigorous and pro-union NLRB, despite its trademark slowness, also played a crucial role in helping their efforts get off the ground.

A generalized politicization of young people was another key precondition. Moe Mills, a St. Louis Starbucks partner, recalls that "what really woke me up to Starbucks's progressive BS was that when George Floyd was murdered, partners came into work and got in trouble for wearing Black Lives Matter stuff. Starbucks sent out to everyone that political attire was against dress code and partners would be sent home. We were outraged—and it was only after Starbucks got canceled on Twitter because partners spoke up about this that they retracted the policy."

Pay concerns, combined with understaffing during the pandemic's peak, were front and center for Thanya Cruz Borrazás, a twenty-two-year-old barista in Nottingham, Maryland, who started working at Starbucks as a high-school senior. Deciding to unionize her store was no small decision because she and her family were immigrants from Uruguay: "It was definitely scary. Especially because it's Starbucks, it's like a giant, anti-union corporation. When I first started and I would come home, I talked to my parents about it. They were really scared for me because, being international, they think we'll get deported for anything." Nevertheless, Thanya plunged ahead: "It seemed like it's worth the risk because if we win, the benefit will be worth it. Honestly, I felt like this was the only way out—joining a union seems like basically the only ticket for people like me to join the middle class."

While it is true that Starbucks offers somewhat better benefits than its competitors, this doesn't negate how hard the job can be at its worst—and how frustrating it was for employees to lack a say in how to make things run more smoothly. For instance, Maggie Carter began to organize her Starbucks cafe in Knoxville in December 2021 after management repeatedly ignored suggestions from she and her coworkers about how the store's layout could be improved to deal with peak customer surges. "Do you know what it feels like to be consistently ignored by higher-ups who aren't even on the floor or in your store working every day?" she recalled. The most Starbucks has been able to manage in terms of industrial democracy has been to include an empty chair at every corporate meeting, meant to symbolically represent workers. "Why isn't that seat filled?" noted Buffalo shift supervisor Gianna Reeve. "It's kind of laughable [for Starbucks] to brag about that."[1]

A disconnect between workers' expectations and management's constrained practices of inclusion has been no less deep regarding LGBTQ rights. For many years now, the company's reputation for inclusivity has attracted large numbers of queer workers, especially in relatively conservative areas. "Our store has been a sort of 'safe haven' in Trump country, almost all of us are gay or trans," explains Aneil Tripathi, who successfully unionized his Starbucks cafe in Anderson, South Carolina, in May 2022. But this was not outweighed by the many ways the corporation treated them as cheap, disposable labor: "There are worse places to work if you're gay, sure, but it's also the case that Starbucks consistently brushes our concerns under the rug and treats us as coffee robots."

Figure 14. Strike with Pride in St. Louis, June 2023. Source: Moe Mills.

The unionization surge made it clear that many partners were not satisfied with management's narrow conception and practice of social justice. "Be Gay, Do Strikes," a slogan coined by Billie Adeosun, has in a variety of iterations become an unofficial motto for SBWU across the country.

Starbucks's queer-friendly culture ultimately rebounded against management. Sarah Pappin explains that "people like us who are marginalized are used to having to fight for our right to exist in a space. We know that our rights are not gifts from above and shouldn't be taken for granted. And so I think that's why you have a lot of scrappy worker-to-worker energy and also a lot of joy in our union. LGBT communities have long traditions of making shitty situations fun somehow—we're going to party as we fight because they can't take that away from us." As anybody who has attended an SBWU strike can attest, these are not dour affairs. "I've supported so many picket lines now, my car is covered in glitter for the rest of its life," Sarah told me. "But at least people are happy."

EARLY WORKER-TO-WORKER ORGANIZING

From December 2021 through the summer of 2022, Starbucks Workers United surged forward on momentum and an exceptionally high degree of worker initiative, with most partners organizing their stores through a combination of intuition and light-touch guidance from other baristas regionally as well as nationally. The fact that these were such small workplaces with relatively cohesive workforces made it significantly easier to move quickly. Every new store that filed encouraged others to do the same, creating a self-propelling feedback loop.

Though a handful of staffers supported in this period, the extent to which workers initiated the organizing on their own or received guidance only from other workers was extraordinarily high. Brian Murray summarized the prevailing thinking at the time on the limited role of staff in the campaign: "You really need workers to make the strategy, to own the big decisions that are being made. But at the same time you've got to balance that out somehow with staff support, so they can do all the boring, busy work stuff that leads workers to more quickly burn out."

What unionization looked like on the ground varied widely by region. In areas where there was no joint board of Workers United—for example, the Pacific Northwest, Texas-Oklahoma, and Massachusetts—the degree of self-organization went furthest, as workers filled the vacuum by creating elaborate regional structures to onboard, train, and support new drives. "It was chaotic, absolutely," recalls Casey in Buffalo. "But it was *fun*. There were so many worker-driven initiatives, people were trying different things in different regions. If it worked, great, let's adopt it. If somewhere else it didn't work, okay, let's not do that again."

What the campaign in this period lacked in systematicness, it made up for in chutzpah. After giving a few specific organizing tips to a partner on an early December 2021 Bernie-hosted online panel, Buffalo partner Gianna Reeve insisted that the main thing to understand was that they were *powerful*: "You have power within yourself to do things that you could not imagine you could do."

Organizing knowledge and how-to tips were passed on through regional Zoom calls and online trainings. When I asked how they organized the West Coast's first Starbucks strike, Billie explained: "We started off completely in the dark, but we got so much support from partners everywhere that by the end we were ready to do it again. And each time we've gone on strike, or helped others plan one, it gets easier. It feels good to be able to learn one, do one, teach one, or whatever that saying is. I learned how to do it and then I did it and now I can teach somebody else and empower somebody else."

In this same DIY spirit, all of SBWU's social media and comms output—both locally and nationally—was done by workers. Indeed, the campaign's very first national structure was the Comms Committee, led early on by Casey Moore, Sydney Durkin in Seattle, Brick Zurek in Chicago, and Nabretta Hardin in Memphis. Grabbing headlines and social media hits was crucial for spreading organizing to new stores, but also for compromising the company's liberal brand. "We knew from the beginning that to bring the company to the table we'd have to damage their image enough to make them scared they'd lose a whole generation of Gen Z customers," Casey recalls. All media was important, she added, but the campaign's reach was widest online. "Social media is a way to engage directly with the broader public in a way that most unions haven't been doing very well. And while of course getting articles in the *New York Times* helps, we've found that viral TikTok videos end up reaching a lot wider group of people."

Throughout this early upsurge, the dominant mood among worker organizers was a heady mix of exhilaration and fear. "I wish I could go back to that point in the process again," recalls Maggie. "It was terrifying, but so much fun—I knew that if someone was going to get fired at my store, it'd be me. And I'm the only provider for my son. But, still, it was an experience I'll cherish for the rest of my life."

Though unionization tactics used on the ground varied widely, there was one common thread: drives were won by workers talking to their coworkers about what they wanted to see changed, what they were scared of, and what collective action could achieve. The campaign spread like wildfire through thousands of such conversations, held during breaks or after work in parking lots, whispered on the floor (or during night shifts) so managers couldn't hear, or over the phone and online when no other options were available.

As exciting as this upsurge was, there's no need to romanticize it. Though the union's win rate in elections remained remarkably high—well over 80 percent—more systematic guidance in organizing methods might have helped even more stores succeed. In Marin County, California, a drive led by two high-school juniors—Ella Clark and Emma Orrick—lost by one vote in part because they went public too early and because they didn't focus enough on winning over older workers. Here's how Ella explained the loss:

> Looking back, I think it was a mistake that I talked about the union with my manager—I thought he was way more progressive than he turned out—so there was a lot of union-busting before we could talk to everyone.... And it didn't help that both of us are in high school. We didn't really have the respect of everybody [at work], most of them are over twenty [years old].

Some stores won their elections despite extremely unorthodox and risky tactics. Brandi Alduk's store in Queens, for example, got all workers together for a meeting at a coworker's house and gave everybody a veto over the decision to unionize. A more common problem was that in numerous stores that won their votes, it proved hard to sustain a majoritarian union presence if the drive had organized too quickly or if it had won without the support of influential workers that others look up to ("organic leaders"). But these drawbacks only became clearer once the initial upsurge was kneecapped by illegal union-busting.

UNION-BUSTING ON STEROIDS

On March 29, 2023, Starbucks founder Howard Schultz was forced to testify in the US Senate about his role in overseeing what the hearing's chair, Bernie Sanders, rightly labeled "the most aggressive and illegal union-busting campaign in the modern history of our country." Two days later, the company fired Lexi Rizzo, an eight-year company veteran who was central to launching the unionization effort in Buffalo. Forced to apply for food stamps and Medicaid to survive, Lexi posted the following video message to Schultz on TikTok:

> I have given every ounce of everything that I have to this company, there is no one that has worked with me that will not tell you that I do not love and care for this place and my partners and my customers. My heart is broken. You know that you're a heartless monster—and I don't know how you sleep at night, I don't know how you look at yourself in the mirror. You have hundreds of thousands of people giving everything that they have so that you can make another dollar and then you treat us like we're dirt. It's disgusting. You know what kind of person you are. And everyone else is going to find out.

Lexi was just one of thousands targeted by Starbucks's scorched-earth campaign, which was dramatically ratcheted up when Schultz returned as CEO in April 2022. Countless partners were harassed, over two hundred unionists were fired, and—most consequently—union stores were illegally denied equal benefits and pay in May 2022. By February 2024, the NLRB had already issued 133 formal complaints against the company, which was alleged to have violated labor law 2,482 times. All in all, Starbucks shelled out an estimated $240 million for this union-busting offensive.[2]

What these numbers point to is the fact that Starbucks executives—aided by their hitmen at Littler Mendelson—spent well over two years attempting to systematically terrorize their idealistic young employees into submission. "After they fired me, I cried for like four days straight," recalls Tori Tambellini, a three-year partner who had led a successful drive at her Pittsburgh store in the spring of 2022. Despite her outspoken organizing role, she had assumed management wouldn't touch her since she had won various internal Starbucks awards—Partner of the Quarter as well as district Barista Champion—and had recently administered Narcan to a customer, saving their life. Nevertheless, on the flimsiest of time and attendance pretexts, management fired her on July 17, obliging her to survive off an emergency GoFundMe set up by her coworkers.

Though Tori kept on organizing other stores for SBWU and got her job back a year later thanks to the NLRB, the damage had already been done. Looking back, Tori reflected on the Board's relative powerlessness to stop this illegal campaign:

> The sad thing is, Starbucks really broke people down. Firing me terrified people at my store. And the same thing happened over and over across the country. And it's not just the firings—what was even worse was that they denied the same benefits to unionized stores, which really undercut our momentum. Starbucks thinks it's above the law and has calculated that the costs of getting hammered with a bunch of ULPs [unfair labor practices] are outweighed by the advantages, since the punishments are pretty minimal.

Often it was the most vulnerable workers who were impacted by union-busting. The first prominent mass firing of worker organizers, for example, targeted a multiracial group of seven partners in Memphis in February 2022. Many more were to come. Joselyn Chuquillanqui, a seven-year partner in Great Neck, New York, lost her health insurance and college tuition reimbursement to Arizona State University when management fired her in the wake of their store's unionization effort. "Getting fired was really, really stressful because I had a bunch of outstanding bills and because I provide for my niece," she recalled. "But as long as they keep putting profits over people, it feels like we have to keep on organizing."

As retaliation for unionizing, many LGBTQ partners and women had their hours cut to less than twenty a week, thereby denying them access to gender-affirming care and abortion benefits. These issues came to a head for Gwen Williamson, a trans shift supervisor who initiated the unionization drive at her store in Bellingham, Washington. When Starbucks fired her in February 2023, she lost her ability to make ends meet and receive gender-affirming treatments. But when I asked her if she regretted having gotten involved in the union, she replied: "Not at all. If I had to go through it again, I would, because this struggle is so important not just for me, not just for Starbucks, but for the working class across the entire nation—and hopefully across the world."

This spirit of self-sacrifice and solidarity stands in sharp juxtaposition with the moral rot that pervades Starbucks summits, the pristine suites of Littler Mendelson, and the cramped offices of the corporate hierarchy's foot soldiers. In fairness to lower-level managers, they were put between a rock and a hard place. But ultimately everybody *did* have a choice on how to respond, as could be seen in the decisions of honest managers in San Antonio, Memphis, and beyond to quit rather than persecute low-wage employees attempting to exercise their constitutionally protected right to unionize. In Pittsburgh, Pennsylvania, for instance, a manager decided to resign rather than bust his store's union drive, even though this meant losing health insurance for himself and his newborn baby.[3]

ORGANIZING ON A HARDER TERRAIN

Relentless intimidation ultimately had its intended effect. Fear, demoralization, and exhaustion spread across the workforce. The number of new leads suddenly plummeted in the summer of 2022. And in the stores that had already won, notes Bek from Ithaca, "they just really started trying to make our lives a living hell, to force those organizers they hadn't fired to quit." How, then, did SBWU manage to persevere?

A big part of the answer lies in the community and solidarity forged between workers. To quote Dylan Lux in Tumwater, Washington: "I've never really personally had until now—until the union—a real sense of community." It's these personal bonds that glue together a long-haul organizing effort not only in the face of union-busting, but through a no-less-daunting obstacle: the tedium of trying to outlast a stonewalling employer.

Outside observers normally only see union efforts at their most exciting, during NLRB elections, strikes, or protests. But the bulk of good organizing consists of mundane, often-exhausting tasks like following up with flaky coworkers, trying to find a time to meet with new hires, endless planning meetings, and picking up shifts at other locations in the hope of finding new leads. It's hard work. And to sustain yourself as an organizer you normally need a close crew of union siblings. As G. Gamache in St. Louis notes, "I've had to shelve everything else in my life, but no matter what they throw at us, we're not going to give in until we get that damn contract, we're in this together—so many of us are hyper-committed to [seeing this] through to the end."

Much of SBWU's community building happened organically through the organizing process itself. But it also took some proactive effort. In Seattle, workers hosted Spaghetti Nights and the Pacific Northwest regional organizing structures held biweekly Zoom "smoke breaks." Billie explains: "Burnout is a real danger, especially after Schultz went ballistic and we hit what felt like a plateau. So we needed to just have a regular kickback where we're not talking about work or organizing, just a chance to hang or play an online game together."

Workplace actions—especially work stoppages—were also key to sustaining momentum and forging solidarity. The centrality of strikes within SBWU's tactical repertoire stands in sharp contrast with the US labor movement's continued hesitancy to lean on this tactic. In addition to periodic nationwide mobilizations, many Starbucks strikes were begun locally by workers as responses to grievances at their

Figure 15. A "Union Yes" drink order from a supportive customer in Vernon, Connecticut. Source: Salwa Mogaddedi.

stores. Alydia Claypool in Kansas City, for instance, explained to me that her store had organized five strikes (only one of which coincided with a national day of action), on issues ranging from short staffing to illegal firings. These work stoppages served to keep up economic pressure on the company, to keep SBWU in the public eye, and to provide workers with a shot of agency in between the long slog of day-to-day organizing and management harassment.

Countless workers recounted to me the invigorating feeling of shutting down their workplaces. Other stores succeeded in partially paralyzing operations, and they reveled in the incompetence of the corporate scabs who attempted to fill in. "Watching executives and upper management trying to make frappuccinos is so entertaining, they almost never have any idea what they're doing," Billie laughed.

Workplace organizing—especially when it's youth-led—can tap into a particular joie de vivre. "One of the things I drill into partners before they go on strike is that you need to figure out ahead of time how you're going to have fun on the picket line," explains Sarah Pappin. "Like don't just have a playlist, have a *jamming* playlist. I love all our labor traditions, but please god I promise you that 'Solidarity Forever' is not going to get you the same amount of energy as Blink 182, trust me."

Partial victories along the way were no less crucial for sustaining morale. Though winning a NLRB union election doesn't guarantee a first contract, it *can* be a tremendously empowering experience capable of energizing its protagonists for months and years to come. Here's how Maggie described the day of her Knoxville store's election:

> Oh my gosh, it was a beautiful feeling to know that we did it, we showed up for each other and we didn't allow these corporations to continuously abuse us. It felt like victory, but also just sweet liberation. You know they kept telling us, "We want you to vote No, we want you to be a partner with Starbucks." And it's like, "I've been that for three years, bro. This is the most I've ever felt like a partner right now, today, when I won this election."

Conversely, the NLRB's standard refusal at Starbucks to allow decertification elections—which enable union workplaces, often under management pressure, to quit the union—was an additional factor preventing management from creating a public narrative that the tide was turning.

The union also did a great job of fighting for and highlighting partial concessions from management along the road to a first contract. After listing out "some of the incredible things workers have fought for and WON over the past year," a SBWU Twitter thread in November 2022 noted that "these are all things that we accomplished even without a contract!" It concluded: "Starbucks doesn't want us to organize because they know that when we organize, we win." Savvy organizing can turn employer carrots into pro-union weapons.

The company conceded on crucial demands, many (though not all) of which were granted to all stores nationwide. Such concessions include the introduction of credit card tipping (resulting in major take-home pay bumps); the ability to pause mobile orders when slammed with customers; a starting wage of no less than $15 an hour; major investments to upgrade failing equipment; quicker sick time accrual; looser dress codes; and the removal of multiple executives, including Schultz himself in September 2023.

This brief outline of national impacts, moreover, fails to capture the countless pre-contract changes won by unionization efforts locally. Wherever workers band together, a workplace rarely remains the same. The following examples provide a window into the local wins:

- In Buffalo, filing for a union election finally got management to remove a dangerous beehive stuck for months inside the back of a cafe.
- In Memphis, over a year's worth of organizing, and multiple legal battles, forced Starbucks to rehire the "Memphis 7" fired in early 2022.
- In Boston, a sixty-four-day strike won workers' demands around scheduling and removed an abusive manager.
- In Oklahoma City, a three-day strike reversed illegal hour cuts for shift supervisors.
- In Brooklyn, after unaddressed mold problems and a bedbug outbreak, a forty-six-day strike forced the company to address the health issues as well as pay for home bedbug inspections.
- Logan Matthews—a Starbucks worker since 1997, who helped unionize his Jonesboro, Georgia, store—was fired two days after their election. Logan's coworkers immediately struck, SBWU raised hell nationally, and within days he was rehired.

Worker organizers were justified in being proud of their accomplishments. Shreya Chaudhari, a barista who helped organize her store in Denton, Texas, explained in 2023 that, "It's felt really invigorating to know that we've able to make change happen—even if these haven't been given yet to union stores. If it hadn't been for our unionizing, there's no way Starbucks would have granted credit card tips or a $15 minimum wage."

At the same time, it's remarkable that so many leading worker organizers persisted in their efforts despite receiving *worse* pay and benefits from May 2022 onwards as punishment for having unionized their stores. The numbers willing to persevere would certainly have been far smaller had it not been for the youth radicalization that lay behind and sustained so much of the organizing.

Though a desire to improve your personal economic situation is often a central motivating factor for initiating a union drive, it's not usually enough to motivate someone to stick out years of a brutal boss fight. Most partners I interviewed were driven not only by a desire to win a first contract at Starbucks, but by a moral-political conviction that they were part of a long and righteous tradition of resistance to capitalist injustice. It's not a minor data point that 52 percent of Starbucks workers in my survey considered themselves to be political radicals, with progressives coming in second at 28 percent. Visions of thoroughgoing social transformation and a sense of historical perspective can be intensely motivational, especially when shared among a tight-knit group of organizers.

Many partners were already leftists and saw unionization as an effective way to put their ideals into practice. For Max Yusen—who turned his St. Louis Starbucks store into a union bastion—the Bernie campaign was his main outside inspiration for unionizing:

> Growing up, unions were not a huge part of my family, I didn't have any relatives in them or anything. But labor was a big part of Bernie's message and being around union members while canvassing and inside DSA really made me see how important they are. So when I moved back home to

St. Louis, I decided on my own to get a job at Starbucks with the goal of unionizing it.

Many other partners, however, were liberals or progressives pulled towards anti-capitalist politics through the fight itself and the union-building process. Here's how Billie—who was raised in a conservative Jehovah's Witness family—describes her personal transformation:

> I didn't know anything about labor before January [2022]. But I've grown so much and gotten more and more radicalized every day. Everything that I've learned in the last nine months has been through experience and through other people that I've met in this movement who have done the work, and who really know their history and strategy—on unions, on socialism, everything—who've taught me so much, as part of our found family of like-minded marginalized people.

And the impact of generational radicalism was not limited to how it sustained organizers. Even when management fired or pushed out worker leaders, the employees hired as replacements were frequently just as pro-union as their predecessors.

(WELL-RESOURCED) WORKER-TO-WORKER UNIONISM AND ITS TENSIONS

As important as all these dynamics were for SBWU's ability to persevere, two factors were particularly decisive: partners maintained ownership over the campaign and the campaign got a major influx of resources.

Had worker organizers not seen and felt that the union fundamentally remained in their hands, it's unlikely they would have continued risking their livelihoods and dedicating the bulk of their free time for the cause. "I really doubt most of us would have stuck it out this long had this been a staff-driven thing," notes Sarah in Seattle. On the other hand, they were able to keep organizing after the initial upsurge because Workers United (WU) provided major staffing and financial support, as did SEIU later on. In other words, persistence required well-resourced worker-to-worker unionism.

Up through about May 2022, there were only five or six full-time staff working on the campaign, a reflection of WU's small size, the regional unevenness of joint boards' commitment to new organizing, and the fact that the Starbucks battle—far from being a well-prepared-for national decision—had been unexpectedly thrust onto it from below. Fortunately, WU's national leadership embraced the effort and eventually began putting major resources into it.

The preceding months of worker-to-worker effervescence made it next to impossible to superimpose a staff-driven model onto the campaign. But at the same time, partners almost everywhere were actively requesting *increased* staff support. "The demand for more staffers was really coming from below—we do a ton, but especially as time dragged on, capacity issues became real," Sarah recalled.

Threading this needle was not an easy task. Fortunately, one of the staffers who jumped in to support early on was Daisy Pitkin, an experienced WU organizer in Pennsylvania with a radical commitment to developing rank-and-file power. From the summer of 2022 onwards, Daisy headed and helped build up SBWU's national staff-organizing infrastructure. Here's how she describes the campaign's shift in this period:

> Worker-to-worker organizing was the fuel of the campaign, and it never went away—what we ended up having is a union that trusted the workers enough to fund a campaign without trying to control it. Basically, the [WU] union leadership was like, "All right, we trust you guys, here's a big chunk of resources and a strike fund, go beat 'em." So from my vantage point, worker leadership did not die; as time went on, it was supported much more actively and with more intensive resources. And that's important, because I don't know if we can beat a company like Starbucks without a lot of resources.

While virtually all the funding for organizers came from Workers United, it would not have been able to sustain this infrastructure had it not been for the early 2023 agreement by its national parent body, SEIU, to fully fund the campaign's hefty legal fees and to drive forward a robust "corporate campaign" of non-workplace pressure tactics.

SEIU deserves credit for digging so deep for an effort that it neither initiated nor controlled, and whose fight-like-hell strategy went up against some of its leaders' longstanding insistence that organizing at scale requires preliminary policy changes. Not every union would have taken this risk. And Starbucks Workers United could not have soldiered on without this financial support.

But SEIU's wait-and-see approach, which lasted over a year, is also significant. It only got on board after a sustained nationwide grassroots upsurge; after the campaign survived sustained scorched-earth union-busting; and after sharp internal wrangling at SEIU summits. This suggests that while SEIU is less monolithic than left critics assume, pulling it (and other big unions) in a more worker-to-worker direction *does* require lots of bottom-up initiative and struggle.

By January 2023, Workers United had hired about twenty-five staff organizers. A year later, it had thirty-six full-time staff and about twenty worker interns supporting the organizing, not to mention SEIU's slew of lawyers, comms support, researchers, and corporate campaigners. Compared to SBWU's scrappy origins, this was a major transformation, and it brought new tensions and dilemmas (more on this below). But for a national campaign that unionized over ten thousand workers and targeted tens of thousands more, this was still a relatively light organizer-to-worker ratio—far from the 1:100 standard. As with drives like the one at Colectivo, this later iteration of the SBWU campaign often had the best of both worlds: widespread worker-to-worker ownership, combined with substantial union resources.

Partners in unionized stores still ran everything as they saw fit. Parallel to this—and in contrast with "rep"-heavy bargaining traditions—

hundreds of workers over many months deliberated in the National Bargaining Committee to formulate their key proposals to management.

In some (though not all) regions, worker organizers were still primarily responsible for guiding new drives. My survey data for the entirety of 2022—including both the early-year upsurge and the post-May downturn—gives a sense of the proportions: 63 percent of Starbucks drives that year began organizing before getting any outside guidance and/or they were trained exclusively by another worker. And 69 percent of organizers were asked to support drives at other stores. This generally took the form of giving organizing guidance to a new effort, generating new leads by taking shifts at different stores, or participating in "clean plays," big blitzes in which large groups of unionized partners would enter all stores in a city to talk with non-union workers.

Rank and filers also continued to lead campaign comms. Running local and national social media accounts was not a minor responsibility, given the centrality of online agitation for generating new leads, sustaining momentum, damaging Starbucks's brand, and articulating the campaign's message as well as its action plans.

It turns out that extremely online workers can often do a far better job at comms than slick PR firms, especially in industries with a disproportionately young workforce and customer base.[4] For Casey Moore, "this is one of the key things people can learn from this [campaign]: control your social media for as long as possible." Under worker leadership, SBWU racked up over 142 million views on its TikTok videos up through March 2024, not including cross-posting on other platforms, and all without any form of paid advertisements, which many unions and nonprofits rely on to boost views.

It's very difficult for outside professionals to replicate the scrappy authenticity that comes from workers posting about their own experiences, or to learn the idiosyncratic, ever-shifting idioms of younger people online. "I knew that as soon as I didn't understand the latest trend, it'd be important to hand off comms coordination to another chronically online person from the next generation," Casey told me later.

While workers retained an exceptionally high degree of campaign leadership, it's also true that this began to coexist with a large amount of staff input and coordination. To quote Sarah, "It wasn't the staffless Wild West anymore." Daisy underscored that it was a "delicate dance" to provide sufficient but not excessive staff support: "Because the power of this movement is worker-to-worker organizing, I think of providing staff support like a campfire: you want to blow on the campfire to let it grow, but if you blow too hard it's going to go out."

Local organizing activities now much more frequently coincided with big national days of action meant to put pressure on the company at strategic moments around national themes. And workers now leaned on systematic, staff-supported organizing trainings to re-organize their shops (often a necessity due to turnover and firings) or to support new drives regionally.

One of the biggest shifts of the campaign was that it eventually proved necessary to rely far more on time-tested deep organizing tactics. Daisy recalls:

> After the ground was chilled on us and the momentum died down, we had to get back to the fundamentals of good organizing. You have to identify organic leaders and they have to move their coworkers. There's no magic sauce, it's hard work. So we had to shift and dig deep, to do very intensive multi-week trainings with lots of roleplaying on leader identification, mapping, organizing conversations, all those fundamentals. Without that, we couldn't have kept on inching up the number of [election] wins and we couldn't have helped turn around those union stores that were now only union on paper, not reality. And for capacity and experience reasons, we needed a robust staff and intern structure to scale up these trainings.

Not everyone was happy about the increased role for paid organizers. Disputes over staffers' roles and actions were relatively common—and a minority of partners insisted to me that they'd lost a decisive say over national strategy. But it's hard to know what to make of such criticisms, since many of these organizers also acknowledged key instances where bottom-up initiative prevailed in internal debates, such as launching a national weeklong Strike with Pride (against management efforts to take down LGBTQ decorations) and publicly standing in solidarity with Gaza—an action that ended up playing a crucial role in the union's contract breakthrough, as we'll see below.

Moreover, workers and staff almost never uniformly lined up on opposing sides of the campaign's major internal debates, a partial list of which includes: whether to prioritize national days of action or more locally calibrated initiatives; if and when to call for a national consumer boycott; which workers should get paid for organizing (as interns or as full-time staff); the extent to which comms should focus on union-busting or positive demands; how much time to spend on developing internal structures vs outwards-facing outreach; and how to make sure participation was not only deep, but also wide (since not all workers had the same degree of free time for long meetings and debates).

Overall, most partners I spoke with shared Sarah's positive assessment:

> There's a push and pull, for sure. But my experience has been that the staff in general is on board with this being really, really worker run. I think there's a great and constant push from our worker organizers that would never let staff overrun this union—I've definitely seen people check staff when they feel like this is happening. And at the same time, we all know we couldn't do this without any staff support.

Along similar, if somewhat starker lines, most SBWU national leaders recounted a continual push and pull with SEIU. As one organizer put it to me, "Once SEIU got on board there was a daily fight to prevent them from controlling it. But it's also true that we really needed their help, and we were thankful for it."

THE BREAKTHROUGH

After two and a half years of brutal union-busting, why did Starbucks retreat on February 27, 2024?

One factor was SEIU-backed corporate campaigning. In addition to initiating a lawsuit against Starbucks for deceptively using coffee from farms with human rights abuses, an SEIU-driven coalition pursued shareholder activism to pressure the Starbucks board internally. Buying $16,000 of stock—.000015% of the company's total market capitalization—gave it the opportunity to present a rigorously researched case to shareholders that the anti-union offensive was cutting into profits. To promote this message, the coalition decided to run three pro-labor figures for Starbucks's eleven-director board at its upcoming annual general meeting (AGM) in 2024.

This pressure was an embarrassment to the company, and it helped circulate arguments among shareholders about the cost of union-busting. But the available evidence suggests that this was a secondary, rather than primary, factor in why management eventually settled. Though helpful, the campaign did not bring about a shareholder crisis, let alone a rebellion. Hyper-influential proxy advisor firms ISS and Glass Lewis recommended that shareholders vote only for management's eleven directors, not any of the union-backed candidates. As the financial research firm Gordon Haskett noted, "The union won more from that [February 27] agreement than it was likely to win at the AGM."[5]

And the force of this shareholder campaign was almost entirely derived from the damage done to the company's profits and brand by sustained workplace organizing and consumer disenchantment. As the coalition's presentation to the AGM underlined, these losses went well beyond the estimated $240 million the company had spent on fighting SBWU. After the union's first NLRB win on December 9, 2021, "Starbucks shares performed 16.6% worse than the median of Starbucks' peers."[6]

Indeed, management's annual report to the AGM acknowledged (in the most provisional language possible) the costs of workplace organizing to its business and brand: "Job actions and work stoppages have the potential to negatively impact our operations, third-party providers upon whom we rely to deliver product, our sales, and our costs. Additionally, our position with respect to unions and the unionization of partners could negatively impact how our brand is perceived and have adverse effects on our business, including on our financial results."[7]

To management's chagrin, two-plus years of intense union-busting had not succeeded in stopping SBWU. A record-high twenty-one stores filed for elections one week before the February 27 deal, bringing the total to almost four hundred. Here's how Daisy described the relative importance of the campaign's distinct components in forcing management to the table: "Worker pressure and the continuation of organizing all across the country is definitely the number one thing. We saw that this was what the company was most responsive to—and it was the engine that made all the rest of the pieces of the campaign possible, from the consumer brand damage to the pressure on the board."

When I asked how the campaign assessed its workplace-level impact, she replied:

> We can see it in the hundreds of millions they spend on union-busting, but also there's now a clearly nationwide crisis of lower-level management, because union stores are ungovernable and because even in the non-union shops, managers are terrified that they won't be able to prevent a drive at their store. When we started this campaign, most store managers had been with the company five to ten years. Now, a lot of stores have five or six new store managers in one year. We crumbled the frontline of their troops—and they're sending a loud message to the top.

This case tracks with a leaked internal Starbucks survey of white-collar workers in the fall of 2022, which even by that relatively early moment had already registered "historic lows" in staff morale, with only 52 percent saying they "completely agreed" that the company "behaves in an ethical and responsible manner."[8]

Parallel to this workplace level crisis, by late 2023 Starbucks was clearly facing its worst-ever consumer crisis. To a significant extent this was due to its conflict with the union. "Starbucks was running a genuine risk of losing an entire generation of consumers," notes Sarah. "Young people care about unions in a way that was not true even three years ago." *Bloomberg* similarly concluded that the company's consumer-side troubles demonstrated that boycotts could no longer be dismissed as inconsequential noise at Starbucks (or beyond) because "Gen Z in particular has shown they are willing to do more than just post video rants on TikTok, actually putting their money where their mouth is."[9]

From early 2022 onwards, clips of Starbucks workers striking against bad managers and illegal firings have regularly gone viral, exposing the hypocrisy of a nominally progressive corporation. To cite just one example, an August 2022 video of Buffalo partners walking out to protest the firing of thirteen-year employee and union leader Sam Amato has drawn over 32 million views on TikTok.

Parallel to this worker-led media agitation, SBWU has sparked targeted boycotts among key constituencies. When the company illegally closed all its stores in Ithaca after they unionized, Cornell students and baristas took the initiative to get the university to end its contract for Starbucks products. By August 2023, after intensive organizing and direct action, they achieved their goal and, in the process, inspired a movement on over forty other colleges to kick Starbucks off campus.

In a surprising turn of events, consumers' biggest impact came through boycotting Starbucks for its position on Israel-Palestine. This boycott—which ended up costing the company over $11 billion—may very well have been the straw that broke management's back. And it could not have occurred had SBWU been a staff-driven campaign.

Here's what happened: on October 9, 2023, a fired partner decided to tweet from Starbucks Workers United's account "Solidarity with Palestine!" over an image of a Palestinian bulldozer tearing down an Israeli occupation fence. The union deleted it forty minutes later because that person hadn't consulted anybody about the post; in fact, they hadn't been involved in national comms for a long time.

Nevertheless, to try to discredit the union, Howard Schultz egged on Starbucks management to lean into this briefly posted tweet. On October 17, Starbucks execs issued a statement condemning the union's so-called "support for violence perpetrated by Hamas," and the following day Starbucks sued the union for copyright infringement, claiming that the initial tweet as well as Iowa City SBWU's pro-Palestine retweets had led customers to believe the company, rather than the union, supported Hamas.

Faced with this lawsuit, most unions would have retreated, especially at this early moment when the horrors of October 7 were very recent and when the powers that be were viciously smearing virtually anybody with pro-Palestinian views. But SBWU's worker organizers were so outraged by the cruelty of Israel's indiscriminate offensive, and so politically committed to solidarity with Gaza, that they insisted on doubling down. As one organizer explained to me, the ensuing conflict over their push to issue a solidarity statement with Palestine proved to be a crucial test of whether the campaign remained decisively in workers' hands:

> We all just felt really strongly about the issue on principle, and so did our coworkers, so we began a huge internal process to draft a solidarity statement. But some staffers were really against it—they were worried SEIU would cut off funding, since they're not used to not being able to stop things like this from happening. So it was a really scary moment for the campaign, honestly. But you have to give credit to the workers, because

the amount of energy we had on this wasn't stoppable; staff couldn't have prevented us from putting out that statement even if they tried. So we told them that and went ahead with it.

SBWU published its solidarity statement on October 20. Soon after, its legal-political conflict with Starbucks over Gaza got picked up by non-union, pro-Palestinian TikTok accounts, who then on their own initiative called for a Starbucks boycott. By early November, #boycottstarbucks had gone viral online, with its seven thousand–plus videos racking up over 51 million views on TikTok alone. As new Starbucks CEO Laxman Narasimhan lamented to *The New York Times*, the boycott did serious damage to sales in the Middle East, Malaysia, and the US. By December 7, the *Economic Times* was reporting that Starbucks had suffered its worst ever market downfall, "a staggering $11 billion loss in value, marking a 9.4% decline that has set off alarm bells within the company's corridors."[10]

Compounding the company's woes, its big effort to expand in China—long seen as the company's geographic future—had recently been cut off by the growth of state-backed Chinese chain Luckin Coffee, thereby making the US market suddenly all the more important. Daisy summarizes the dynamic: "After the Palestine boycott, all these crises compounded together—and we [the union] became the easiest problem to solve, which is a very good place to be."

VICTORY

Though everybody understands that nothing is final until Starbucks signs the dotted line of a first contract, partners across the country were elated about the February 2024 breakthrough. Cold stores suddenly became hot, organizing momentum accelerated overnight, and over 1,200 of the 10,000 unionized workers nominated themselves or others for bargaining. With wind in its sails, Starbucks Workers United is now well positioned to take on its biggest task yet: unionizing the rest of the company's 200,000 non-union workers.

Big victories always seem inevitable in hindsight. But it's worth remembering that very few people beyond those working on the campaign believed that Starbucks partners could actually win a single store election, let alone a first contract. The doubters and fence-sitters were (and remain) legion. But worker organizers believed in themselves and in their power to make history. And this belief eventually became a self-fulfilling prophecy.

Though it's still possible that Starbucks may try to renege on its deal (especially if Republicans win back the White House), worker-to-worker unionism has proven its mettle in *the* emblematic struggle of the post-pandemic uptick, against one of the largest companies in the world, in the face of the most heinous union-busting campaign in modern labor history. This breakthrough would not have been possible without the spark of inside organizers in Buffalo or without the risky turn to worker-to-worker training during the subsequent unionization explosion. And had workers not maintained their decisive strategic say over the campaign once it received a much needed influx of resources, SBWU would not have taken its bold (and unexpectedly decisive) solidarity action with Palestine. Nor would so many partners have thrown themselves so deeply into the organizing and stuck it out in the face of relentless management harassment and stonewalling.

It seems fitting to close with a quote from one of the thousands who embodied Starbucks Workers United's bottom-up, history-making tenacity. After five years working for and believing in the company, twenty-four-year-old Alydia Claypool and four coworkers in Kansas City were illegally fired in April 2022 for unionizing their stores. "The funny thing is I didn't really step up as a leader until they fired me," she recalls. "But in that moment I realized what the company *actually* was—and ever since I've felt that if I stayed strong and kept fighting for everybody, then maybe it'd show management that firing us was not going to stop this movement."

By late February 2024, Alydia had won back her job with NLRB support. And despite constant turnover and anti-union harassment, she had re-organized her store multiple times. To celebrate her union's leap forward in bargaining, she posted the following on Twitter:

> As the last original worker from our team that started organizing two years ago this has truly been the hardest yet most rewarding two years of my life. It feels so surreal that we finally won.
>
> Being able to tell all our old team that we won and them being so proud makes everything that happened worth it. I'm so honored to be a member of Starbucks Workers United. I never thought I'd be here today. Finally being able to say we won. Being able to prepare to bargain soon.
>
> Thank you to every single person who has supported this movement, and our store. I've been so surrounded by so much love that I feel truly invincible. If you have ever wanted to unionize your workplace the time is now. The fight is always worth it. 🖤 ✊ Solidarity

PART THREE

HOW TO WIN BIG

6

WHICH MODEL CAN WIN WIDELY?

> I think unions are going to have to start figuring out new ways to support worker-led organizing—you know, to create something that's scalable.
>
> CLAIRE CHANG, REI worker organizer

RECENT VICTORIES AT STARBUCKS, Colectivo, Burgerville, and across journalism all show the viability of worker-to-worker organizing. But staff-intensive unionism and thin-but-scalable campaigns also have their fair share of wins. So to assess the merits of these distinct approaches, it's necessary to zoom back out and ask: which unionization models have the potential to successfully build working-class power at scale? A deep dive into the available data on organizing costs will make the answer to this question clear.

CAN STAFF-INTENSIVE ORGANIZING SCALE?

Among those wings of the labor movement still interested in unionizing new workers, the basic case for how to scale up today remains the same as it's been since the 1990s: fund good organizing. Many union organizing directors and staff organizers made this case to me, while complaining of labor's insufficient focus on growth. As one regional organizing director in the Midwest put it, "We don't need to reinvent the wheel, we know how to win—but we need real resources to make that happen."

In many ways I fundamentally agree with this case: unions *do* need to make a dramatic investment in rank-and-file intensive organizing. And the impasse of the AFL-CIO New Voices project doesn't necessarily mean its strategy—better funding, better tactics—couldn't work in more favorable circumstances.

It would be great news for workers if staff-intensive unionism had a plausible path to scaling up. All other things being equal, more staff support and more resources is a very good thing for workplace organizing. US labor would almost certainly be in a better position today if all unions from the 1990s onwards had adopted ambitious funding goals and time-tested organizing techniques. The fact that most unions didn't do so is, on the face of it, puzzling. Why wouldn't unions lean into an organizing approach that had proven its effectiveness? Indeed, in his incisive 2010 book on union revitalization, Julius Getman wrote that "it is a mystery why so few unions" adopted organizing methods that had a clear track record of winning.[1]

Labor scholars have detailed numerous factors that help explain this puzzle, including institutional routinism, risk aversion, organizational atomization, leadership bureaucratization, an over-reliance on establishment Democrats, members' lack of interest in external organizing, and officials' fears of getting voted out if new organizing investments don't pan out or if an influx of new, empowered members vote in different leaders. But one central factor has yet to receive sufficient attention: high organizing costs create a hard ceiling on growth and disincentivize best practices. Though the costliness of unionization isn't necessarily the main hindrance for stick-in-the-mud unions, it *does* go a long way towards explaining the difficulties of organizing-focused unions to pose a viable alternative by spreading widely.

Failing to fully address issues of cost and scale, too many analysts tend to conflate the question of how to win specific drives with the question of how to win widely. For example, one piece recently argues that labor's leap forward "will come from lots of small-scale organizing of the kind this site seeks to highlight and enrich, until that organizing reaches a larger scale."[2]

Most influentially, since the early 1990s labor scholar Kate Bronfenbrenner has argued, on the basis of extensive quantitative research, that by creatively deploying rank-and-file intensive tactics and by providing one staffer for every hundred targeted workers, unions *could* still win despite employer opposition. "The recommitment of the labor movement to organizing is not a futile effort," she and co-author Tom Juravich concluded. "If unions use the right tactics, they can still win, despite the odds."[3] They could do so at scale, Bronfenbrenner argued, by taking on more and more drives and larger and larger campaigns. She acknowledged that this proposed organizing approach was "extremely staff and resource intensive," but insisted that a "lack of resources cannot explain the failure of the majority of unions to organize more aggressively and effectively," since the "costs of not organizing"—that is, continued labor decline—are far greater.[4]

The basic problem with this type of reasoning was noted by organizer Benjamin Day: "By focusing on the means by which certain union election campaigns win and others fail, the organizing literature tends to get mired in a microeconomic perspective that is occasionally, but illegitimately, generalized to the macroeconomic level (i.e., that proliferating winning campaign tactics can reverse [unions' overall] decline)."[5] As union strategist Richard Yeselson observed in his 2013 article "Fortress Unionism," the past two decades of experience had shown that although labor *did* know how to win through well-funded comprehensive campaigns, it turned out to be "economically and logistically impossible" for unions to initiate enough of them to turn things around. He pointed to a simple reason why: in today's decentralized economic conditions it "takes too much time, and it costs too much in money and staff resources."[6]

NOT ENOUGH FUNDS

While improving the tactical *quality* of union campaigns is crucial, it isn't enough on its own to organize sufficiently large numbers of workers for systemic change. To win the unionization war, the harder question is how to exponentially increase the *quantity* of unionization battles. So it's worth asking: could this ambitious goal be reached via staff-intensive means by fully tapping organized labor's coffers?

Let's look at the data. Researcher Chris Bohner found that unions today have roughly $13.4 billion dollars in liquid assets. This, as the author notes, is only "a reasoned approximation," which perhaps somewhat overstates labor's treasuries.[7] Nevertheless, it's clear from Bohner's research that union assets *have* grown considerably over the past decade, and that much of this could go towards generating a robust turn to new organizing.

How far could these assets take labor organizing using staff-intensive means? Though organizing costs vary widely—by company, industry, and degree of employer opposition—the available data suggests that it costs unions between $2,020 and $4,012 on average to organize one worker.[8] Based on the $3,016 midpoint of this cost range, if unions were to use 30 percent of their liquid assets on staffed-up new organizing this would translate into unionizing roughly 1.33 million workers. That would only return labor to about 2015 density levels: 11 percent of the US workforce would be in a union. And using the entirety of labor's liquid assets on organizing would only return labor to 2002 union density, roughly 13.2 percent of the workforce. These would be very significant steps forward, but far below the type of growth needed to decisively beat back corporations and equalize America.

Moreover, these funds aren't readily on hand, awaiting only the decision of national labor leaders to start prioritizing new organizing. As Bohner shows, the vast majority of labor's assets are controlled by thousands of autonomous locals, many of which are deeply entrenched in their risk-averse, service-oriented ways. About 72 percent of labor spending is by locals, 28 percent by national unions, and only .7 percent by the AFL-CIO.[9] This means that today, and for the foreseeable future, even the most ambitious union leaders will have to make hard choices about how to allocate scarce resources.

One of the reasons so few unions adopt best practices is that it's expensive to do so. Case in point is the history of the perpetually cash-strapped hotel organizing powerhouse HERE, whose money troubles led it to merge with UNITE in 2004. Yet in part because HERE's organizing model—which uses lots of staff to train up and support lots of strong worker leaders—remained so costly, much of the UNITE wing of the merger jumped ship only five years later. Among the many reasons for this messy divorce, leaders from UNITE publicly objected to what they viewed as excessive organizing costs; in turn, HERE leaders, not unjustifiably, accused their rivals of chasing shortcuts and of cutting unacceptable deals with employers in the hopes of easing unionization.[10]

Ineffective organizing often has a material base, not just a strategic one. Because it takes so much time, money, and effort to train up large numbers of good staff organizers to identify and guide workers, there's always a strong incentive to cut corners by running hollow campaigns lacking a focus on rank-and-file leadership development. One health care union staffer explained the dynamic as follows:

> In my experience, the problem in [our local] isn't that some of our leaders support a McAlevey [deep organizing] strategy and others in leadership have a different theory, it was more like everyone in leadership knows the right things to say about building a committee and worker leadership and structure tests [public actions to assess a drive's level of support], but

because we're all extremely busy and because we don't know how to train organizers well, we just don't do it, or at least not consistently.

The few existing quantitative financial analyses of union campaigns point to a similar story. Consider Dave Kamper and Alyssa Picard's LM-2 analysis of the rightfully celebrated Las Vegas health care Local 1107 organizing led by Jane McAlevey. As the authors note, "However valuable McAlevey's book is, it does not suggest a solution to the problem of how to pay for organizing—and if we want to rebuild the labor movement, we need to find an answer soon."[11] McAlevey herself acknowledges this in the epilogue of her first book's first edition: "We know how to do the work—it's where the money will come from that's the immediate challenge. That's what keeps me up in the middle of the night these days—it's that I can't yet sort out how we'll pay for what I am confident we actually can do."[12] My book is, among other things, an attempt to find a solution to this challenge.

TARGETING ISN'T ENOUGH TODAY

Recent worker-to-worker campaigns have demonstrated the viability of a new strategy of *seeding* unionization efforts, rather than passively waiting for workers to reach out ("hot-shopping") or exclusively organizing pre-chosen workplaces ("strategic targeting"). Many organizing seeds will fail to sprout, but the total number of drives and strategic campaigns can significantly increase through this approach.

From the 1990s onwards, ambitious organizers and unions have fought hard against labor's prevailing reliance on small-scale hot-shopping. Their arguments against chasing pockets of discontent were sound: isolated workers lacked the punch to bring industries to the table, and unions' limited resources should be concentrated on the most strategic targets. Smart organizing was summed up by Stephen Lerner, lead organizer in the Justice for Janitors campaign: "When a union picks a target instead of letting the target pick the union, workers are more likely to win."[13] This remains the prevailing wisdom today among unions with strong organizing traditions. "Our message to the working class is 'don't call us, we'll call you,'" a researcher from one such union only half-jokingly told me.

The cost-intensiveness of heavily staffed organizing has also made its most effective advocates pick unionization targets (or only follow up with a narrow sliver of organizing requests), rather than consistently responding to or widely seeding worker initiatives. That's a big reason why organizing-focused unions frequently say no to workers who reach out for help.[14] Unions choose their battles judiciously, as one clothing workers' staffer explained to scholar Linda Markowitz:

> Geofelt is a campaign we would not typically conduct. It only has seventy workers. In a perfect world, size wouldn't matter. We could organize anyone who wanted to be in a union. In reality, it takes tremendous resources and time to organize and in many cases the larger size allows you the resources that you need to win and secure a first contract. Unions are not rich organizations. We operate on our members' dues so we have to look practically.[15]

As an alternative to hot-shopping, in their 1990s heyday strategic unions picked out relatively large workplaces and ran big targeted campaigns like Justice for Janitors. Due to their riskiness and exorbitant costs, such ambitious initiatives have fallen out of favor. But organizing unions still generally search for largish-but-winnable targets such as hotels or hospitals.

I'm not arguing for a return to hot-shopping, in which unions passively wait for workers to reach out and do nothing to transform initial wins into company-wide or industry-wide campaigns. Nor am I suggesting that unions stop targeting strategic sites. This *is* still a crucial tactic. Unions should put serious funds into efforts like the Inside Organizer School—a project led by SBWU's founders—to widely train

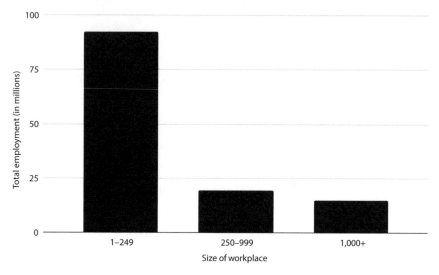

Figure 16. Total US employment by workplace size, 2022. Source: Quarterly Census of Employment and Wages.

a new generation of salts capable of initiating campaigns at pivotal workplaces and companies.

But relying *only* on targeting is a poor fit for our decentralized economy, in which a vast majority of workers work in smallish establishments (see figure 16). In today's sprawled-out conditions—without a relative handful of massive, economically central targets—concentrated targeting has to be supplemented with proactive efforts to seed worker-initiated drives across the entire economy, in workplaces of all sizes—and to turn promising worker responses into ambitious campaigns armed with a rigorous plan to win. As the continued growth of Starbucks Workers United has demonstrated, seeding can be as proactive and ambitious as targeting, its reach is just more scattershot. While most of the four hundred–plus unionized cafes were not specifically targeted by SBWU, a majority of these would also not have begun organizing without the campaign's seeding efforts over multiple years.

Along similar lines, rather than only targeting pre-determined factories, the new UAW has actively encouraged all non-union auto workers to start organizing. As UAW strategist Chris Brooks explained to me, "We didn't know—and didn't want to try to predetermine—where the most heat would be, so we've tried our best to fan the flames everywhere."

From Starbucks to Southern auto, some of the most productive seeding techniques include using high-publicity moments like big union elections and strikes to call on (and provide tools to) other workers to start organizing; holding open online trainings; producing viral social media content to generate new leads; posting digital ads or distributing fliers encouraging people to sign up for organizing support; and developing in-depth, easily accessible training materials for workers to start self-organizing.

And there's no need to counterpose targeting to seeding, even within the parameters of a single campaign. Buffalo showed that winning one election by salting a small workplace can set the stage for a broader grassroots organizing spurt—provided that the union is momentum-savvy enough to seize an opening via national social media agitation, mass onboarding, and worker-to-worker training. Whereas chain reactions tended to spread more organically in the 1930s, in today's conditions they need more proactive and sustained fostering.

NOT ENOUGH STAFF FOR WHIRLWIND MOMENTS

To be sure, increasing funding for new organizing would be a step forward, no matter which model is used. But the burden of proof is on advocates and practitioners of staff-intensive unionism to explain why most budget money should go to a model that is more expensive, that has no potential for exponential takeoff, and (as we will see later) that is generally correlated with *less* effective organizing tactics.

And even if labor's financial assets were greater, this still wouldn't resolve the scale issue because costliness isn't just a question of dollars, but also of time. In the US, like the rest of the world, big advances in unionization tend to come through rapid spurts, not slow-and-steady growth. And time costs make heavily staffed unionism a poor fit for moments of movement effervescence.

There are only a limited number of experienced union staff organizers around at a given time. It takes many months—and often years—to effectively train new ones. Targeted staff-intensive campaigns are generally preceded by months or even years of intensive research about the company, only beginning once enough full-timers are assigned to (or hired for) the effort. And to give helpful guidance in either targeted or hot-shop unionism, it takes organizers many weeks or months to learn the company, to build sufficient trust with organizing committees, and to gather enough information about the particular workplace. That's why in moments when grassroots activity surges up quickly, there are often not enough full-timers on hand. Staff-heavy unionism, in short, can't go viral.

Casey Moore in Buffalo describes the dynamic when their union election sparked a Starbucks unionization wildfire in early 2022: "We believed workers should lead, but also there just literally weren't enough staffers around to reply to all the new stores that were looking to organize." A similar pattern has marked the UAW's campaign to organize the South. Unable to find a sufficient number of staff organizers with the ability and disposition to support the over ten thousand workers who responded to their call to unionize in late 2023, the union has been obliged to plunge forward with relatively few full-timers on board. Sometimes you have to build the plane as you fly it.

SCALABLE BUT SHALLOW CAMPAIGNS

The main alternative to staff-intensive unionism within the labor movement has been thin mobilizations. While much of this has consisted of getting out the vote for Democrats or calling representatives to pass legislation, SEIU has taken the lead in experimenting with new, more scalable approaches that have at least one foot in workplace action.

By the early 2000s, SEIU leaders concluded that the Justice for Janitors staffing model—hiring large numbers of full-timers to support rank-and-file intensive efforts as part of a broader comprehensive campaign—was just too costly to win at scale. In the words of influential SEIU leader and Fight for 15 architect David Rolf: "Efforts to extend the model of traditional unionization are limited" because "it is incredibly time-consuming and expensive to organize a campaign like Justice for Janitors."[16]

Union officials like Rolf weren't wrong to raise concerns about the scalability of the prevailing forms of rank-and-file oriented unionism. On the other hand, Rolf's quote undermines his overarching analysis that trying to build unions workplace by workplace, company by company, is a "dead" approach, made obsolete by the growth of contingent jobs such as subcontracting and gig work. The problem wasn't actually that these workers couldn't be organized, but that top SEIU leaders concluded that it was too expensive to do so in large numbers.

If *cost* is the main stumbling block, then this raises the possibility of finding ways to organize more cheaply via worker-to-worker unionism—an approach that Rolf at no point even considers. Instead, SEIU has experimented with efforts that do not depend as much on intensive workplace organizing, such as transforming large numbers of home health care and childcare workers into potential union members via legislative changes; making questionable *quid pro quos* with employers to enable unionization; initiating campaigns like the Fight for 15 to shame companies and to demand legislators raise the minimum wage; and pushing for sectoral policy changes on a local and statewide level.

These initiatives—especially efforts to "win without workers," as one SEIU proponent of this approach put it—have often been criticized by labor leftists as being top-down and lacking on-the-ground power.[17] What's missing in these critiques is an acknowledgement that SEIU, to its credit, has at least attempted to pose and respond to one of the hardest questions facing labor: in present-day conditions, what will it take to win widely? Rolf is basically right that "the most important single task of today's remaining unions is to seed innovation and discover powerful, scalable, sustainable new models of worker organization.... Any organization fighting for systemic change ... must, by definition, be scalable."[18]

Following SEIU's lead, other unions such as the UFCW have similarly experimented with scalable-but-shallow campaigns. OUR Walmart, for example, leveraged online tools to identify discontented workers willing to participate in press conferences, internal online discussions, and one-day walkouts. As one staff organizer recalled of the later stages of the Walmart campaign, "We're told we're building a base but all we're doing is having people speak to media and 'hope' for change."[19]

Such approaches have helped raise the public salience of workers' demands and they've succeeded in shaming authorities into granting substantial wage increases for millions of workers. Nobody should downplay these victories. But each of these campaigns has been marked by a failing rooted in their avoidance of deep on-the-ground organizing: they've built no self-sustaining worker organizations.[20] SEIU spent well over $100 million on the Fight for 15, which never found an answer to, as Rolf put it, "the question of how fast-food workers would join a union."[21]

Assessing that OUR Walmart wasn't worth the cost, the UFCW eventually dropped its financial support. Most other unions have similarly thrown in the towel on any form of ambitious campaigning beyond the electoral arena. The dominant conclusion among US union leaders—at least those at all interested in dynamics beyond their local fiefdoms—was (and remains) that widespread unionization will only become a reality after labor law reform. Therefore unions in the meantime should double down on electing Democrats and lobbying for legislative changes.

Union leaders are right that this country needs better labor laws—including, as SEIU leaders emphasize, to replace our narrow firm-based collective bargaining system with a broader sectoral bargaining regime, a step that could make it far easier to unionize in today's decentralized context. The problem is that by downplaying deep workplace organizing in the meantime, a "policy first" strategy makes transformative legal reform *less* likely.

If history is any guide, national labor law reform won't get passed without an organizing effervescence that creates intractable crises for economic and political elites. Absent such pressure, labor's half dozen attempts at labor law reform since the late 1970s have failed to overcome Republican intransigence and Democratic insipidity. And even were Congress able to get past the filibuster and pass transformative labor law reform, it's all but guaranteed that our reactionary Supreme Court would shoot it down—unless a powerful insurgent movement compels it to retreat or compels a Democratic administration to pack the Court.

What about sectoral bargaining? It *is* possible that passing sectoral structures like California's SEIU-backed Fast Food Council could pave the way for wide-scale unionization by taking wages out of competition and creating a governmental structure that organized workers could de facto bargain with. But such legislative reforms will remain fragile in the face of corporate backlash unless workers can build real power from below to defend them. And translating such political openings into actual sectoral bargaining—via mass unionization across tens of thousands of scattered establishments—will require a major investment in grassroots unionism in California as well as in regions like the South, where SEIU is backing a promising new Union of Southern Service Workers.

In short, labor law reform and sectoral bargaining are important goals worth pushing for. But to make them a reality will require scaling up power through worker-to-worker organizing.

A WORKER-TO-WORKER ALTERNATIVE

Fortunately, we no longer need to point only to the 1930s for evidence that a cheaper model for building union power is available. Recent experience shows that worker-to-worker campaigns—unlike both staff-intensive unionism and shallow campaigning—are both scalable *and* powerful.

It was precisely because of the need to rapidly scale up that Starbucks Workers United and the NewsGuild were pushed to innovate new organizing structures. "The moment we're in has obliged us to train [workers] quickly, but it's also allowed us to train them effectively," notes Stephanie Basile at the NewsGuild, which unionized 9,741 workers in 212 new units from 2018 to 2023. "It's almost like an intense bootcamp opportunity where you can get years of organizing experience in like a month right now." As she indicates, an ability to swiftly forge good organizers depends not only on effective training techniques, but also on enabling workers to learn in struggle, by taking full ownership of their drives.

What about organizing costs? Financial accounts of specific drives are unfortunately hard to come by. But the available evidence suggests that today's worker-to-worker efforts tend to be significantly cheaper than the roughly $3,016-per-worker average of standard drives. A study of CWA District 4's peer-to-peer organizing model in the 1990s found that costs were significantly lower than in staff-intensive efforts—a drive of 1,800 technical and clerical employees, for example, cost $290 per worker (inflation adjusted for today).[22]

The recent experience of independent unions is also suggestive. It cost the Amazon Labor Union $14 per worker to win their union

TABLE 5
Recent staff-to-worker ratios

Union	Staff-to-worker ratio	Year(s)
Burgerville Workers Union	0 to 1,400	2016–2021
Amazon Labor Union–JFK8	1 to 8,325	2021–2022
Starbucks Workers United	1 to 2,020	2021–2022
UAW–Volkswagen, Chattanooga	1 to 860	2023–2024
UAW–Mercedes, Vance	1 to 2,141	2023–2024
UE–MIT	1 to 1,609	2019–2022
UE–Johns Hopkins	1 to 2,124	2017–2023
UE–University of Chicago	1 to 2,133	2022–2023
UE–Dartmouth	1 to 1,574	2021–2023
UE–University of Minnesota	1 to 4,100	2021–2023
UE–Stanford	1 to 3,410	2022–2023

election at the JFK8 Amazon warehouse in Staten Island.[23] For its part, the Burgerville Workers Union spent $40,000 total to win a first contract that covered about 170 workers, with many of its key provisions covering the entire 1,400-strong workforce. This comes out to $28.57 per impacted worker and $235 per fully covered worker. Even if self-initiated drives that affiliate with established unions and leverage staff support were to cost five or ten times more than their independent counterparts, this would still mean that worker-to-worker unionism is significantly cheaper than the prevailing model.

What about staffing ratios? Here the available data suggests clear differences between union models (see Table 5).[24] In contrast with the 1-to-100 norm of staff-intensive unionism, staffer-less Burgerville workers unionized and won a contract at the first fast food chain in the country. And both SBWU (up through June 2022) and Amazon-JFK8 efforts had staff-to-worker ratios analogous to the low-cost movement unionism of the 1930s.[25] UAW's big recent drives in auto—especially at Mercedes—have also been very lightly staffed.[26]

To get a nationwide sense of differences between these two organizing models, we can look at yearly NLRB data to compare the numbers of new workers organized to the total number of staffers employed by unions. In 2023, the number of workers unionized per staffer was higher than in any other year for which I was able to find data—and almost double the average from 1990 through 2021. It makes sense to infer that 2023's exceptional staffing ratio reflects worker-to-worker unionism's rise.[27]

SCALING UP IN HIGHER ED

I was also able to get detailed data from United Electrical's higher-ed worker leaders and staff organizers, who've led some of the largest and most successful NLRB drives in recent memory. Due to an influx of graduate workers, the national membership of UE more than doubled from 2022 to 2023. These drives had one staffer for as many as 4,100 workers and as few as 1,574. What made it possible to have such consistently low staffing ratios?

One factor was the UE's longstanding organizing philosophy. Here's how this was described by Valentina Luketa, a leader of the unionization effort at Indiana University who went on to become a full-time UE organizer: "Cheaper is part of the model, sure. But the way we talk about it is mostly that to scale up the fights of workers in this country, to have a real movement among the working class for a better society, we're going to have to have a lot more workers organizing other workers. Nobody can hire enough staff to do that."

It's likely that these staffing ratios partly reflect the particularities of universities, which are full of young, progressive people and which generally have less employer repression than the worst private companies. But private universities these days often function almost indistinguishably from corporations and, accordingly, have fought hard and successfully for over two decades to keep grad unions off campus. Until very recently, many union drives in private universities have fizzled or been defeated. Faced with union-busting and ongoing hesitancy among

STEM (Science, Technology, Engineering and Mathematics) graduate workers, for example, the drive at University of Chicago had been underway for fifteen years before it won in 2023. Similarly, drives at Cornell lost by a 2 to 1 margin in 2002 and again in 2017. In contrast, Cornell grad workers won their vote 1,873 to 80 in November 2023.

For a good case study of why higher ed organizing shouldn't be dismissed as anomalously easy, consider the experience at Massachusetts Institute of Technology (MIT), a hard-fought campaign begun in 2019 that played a central role in UE's organizing takeoff. Ki-Jana Carter, a worker leader in the material sciences department, notes that MIT "pulled out the bosses' classic union-busting playbook." The administration blanketed the campus and workers' inboxes with anti-union talking points, including the suggestion that MIT's numerous immigrant students could potentially lose their visas if the union won. Since many STEM grad workers are dependent on professors for their research and employment, management pressured professors to turn lab work meetings into anti-union captive audience meetings. And as so often occurs in contexts of concerted union-busting, a vocal group of anti-union workers emerged, red-baiting the UE and posting fliers claiming that "A Vote for UE is a Vote for Putin."

Further complicating the effort, the vast majority of MIT students are STEM, which has long been the hardest nut to crack in higher ed organizing. Unable to coast as much on pre-existing activist sympathies, MIT's self-initiated drive was thus obliged to spend an extraordinary amount of time and effort winning over skeptics. It built a massive organizing committee of over two hundred workers that reached deep into every corner and layer of the workforce.

Unlike in staff-intensive drives, MIT's worker leaders had already built up a strong training program on their own—and had already begun systematic one-on-one organizing conversations—well before voting to join UE. As Ki-Jana explains, they chose to affiliate because "UE's democratic rank-and-file organizing model was very aligned with both what we wanted to see, what we were already beginning to do, and what kind of support we needed." The approach worked. He recalls the feeling on April 6, 2022, when workers won their NLRB vote 1,785–912: "We just all broke down in tears, nobody could stop cheering or hugging each other. To see four years of work, extremely exhausting work—often emotionally taxing work—to see that pay off was just amazing."

Staffing ratios got even smaller after MIT's victory, in part because workers with UE support founded the Graduate Worker Organizing Committee (GWOC), a national, digitally enabled worker-to-worker structure to strategize and share lessons.[28] MIT's worker leaders were thus able to help train and guide the subsequent drives at Johns Hopkins, Northwestern, and University of Chicago, whose wins in turn provided further worker support and capacity to the drives at Dartmouth, University of Minnesota, and Stanford. Joining this network, while maintaining their autonomy, was a major reason why Chicago's organizers voted to join UE. As one grad leader put it, "We were like, 'Okay, tell us how to fish and then we'll go and fish.'"[29]

Following knockout NLRB wins at each of these universities, GWOC's focus turned to contract campaigns, with MIT organizers teaching their peers nationwide about how they won their first contract in the fall of 2023 through open, mass-participation bargaining and by building a credible strike threat. This focus on worker leadership in first contract campaigns—and democratizing bargaining knowledge—constitutes a dramatic break from the US labor movement's unscalable dependence on full-time "bargaining reps." One New York City staff organizer shared a common complaint with me:

> We do our best to build rank-and-file power and definitely have workers who could support other workers' new organizing efforts—but the first contract question is our big bottleneck. That's where we don't have capacity. Our reps have been on staff for a long time compared to organizers

(and have more power internally), so when we face issues with first contracts, they blame the organizers and say we should slow down on new organizing.

Given the pervasiveness of this bottleneck problem, everything I've written about the urgency of democratizing knowledge is even more true when it comes to negotiating and winning a first contract. To scale up contract campaigns, we'll need many more national worker-to-worker structures, wide-scale online bargaining trainings, open-source contract templates, as well as educational materials like Jane McAlevey's recent study *Rules to Win By*. And if election wins continue to far outpace bargaining capacity, it may also prove necessary to bring back labor's 1930s-era tradition of fighting initially for one-year contracts that do little more than recognize the union, giving workers more time and legitimacy to develop their proposals and their bargaining committees for a subsequent second-round contract battle.

Though the speed and extent to which other unions can move in a GWOC-like direction depends to a significant extent on the workers they're organizing—their degree of confidence, momentum, replaceability, radicalization, fear of employer repression—there's no good reason why all unions shouldn't be trying to move as quickly as possible towards a well-funded worker-to-worker organizing model.

MISSED POTENTIAL FOR SCALING UP

In today's decentralized context, turning a labor uptick into large-scale union growth will likely require far more fostering and resources than a century ago. But despite exceptionally favorable conditions for growth since 2020, funding for new organizing remains abysmally low. The UFCW, for example, spent a paltry 4.6 percent of its 2022 budget on organizing, down from an already low 9 percent in 2013. By way of comparison, from 1953 through 1974 US labor unions on average spent over 20 percent of their budgets on new organizing.[30]

Established unions across the US are mired in a priorities crisis, not a budget crisis. The UFCW—whose net assets increased from $199 million to $522 million between 2014 and 2022—is just one particularly egregious example of the broader trend.[31] Even though the financial assets of the US labor movement nearly doubled from 2010 to 2020, its number of union staffers dropped by 19 percent.[32]

This underfunding of external growth is particularly exasperating because all the available evidence suggests that a well-funded push by unions to support new organizing would find a wide echo. As early as 2017, a national survey found that about 58 million people would vote tomorrow for a union at their workplace if given the opportunity—a major jump since the 1970s and 1990s.[33] There's no good reason why the labor movement today can't aim to reach each of these workers through large-scale salting programs, systematic online organizing trainings, and by tapping its 14.3 million members for worker-to-worker outreach.

My survey of worker organizers suggests that there are a large number of union members who want to help organize new shops but who have never been asked by their unions to do so. Labor scholar Kate Bronfenbrenner's decades-long research on union drives impacting fifty workers or more suggests that about half of such drives have failed to lean on any member volunteers from other shops.[34] And the total percentage among drives of *all* sizes is likely far lower, since smaller drives (fewer than fifty workers) are much less likely to include any external volunteers.

This low level of volunteer involvement is the norm even though member volunteer asks in staff-intensive drives are lighter lifts than in a typical worker-to-worker effort: for example, trying to convince skeptical workers to vote for the union (staff-intensive), rather than being responsible for training and guiding another drive's workplace leaders (worker-to-worker). And this low level of volunteer activity is all the more noteworthy since deploying member volunteers has long been a component of post-Reagan orthodox organizing theory.

Some unions do have a strong record of translating this theory into practice, including the CWA, 1199NE, and UNITE-HERE. For example, Jamai Jackson is a thirty-five-year-old warehouse driver who played a central role in unionizing the Seattle sandwich chain Homegrown in 2022. "I learned so much not only about organizing but even about myself as a person," she recalls. After having provided extensive organizing training in the preceding months, UNITE-HERE Local 8 then asked her if she'd be willing to volunteer to do house visits for a new organizing campaign at Microsoft. Even though she had a fifteen-year-old daughter, and would not get paid for this work, she enthusiastically agreed: "It was a juggle, but I made time for it because it was just really important to me."

Unfortunately, examples like these are the exceptions that prove the rule. Could it be that worker organizers were uninterested in supporting new efforts? My survey research suggests not. Of those respondents who were not asked by their union to help new drives, an overwhelming majority—83 percent—said they *were* willing to volunteer to support other organizing efforts.

It's tragic that so many unions fail to tap these organizers, people who've already shown in practice that they've got the organizing fire in their bellies and who are willing to continue spreading the good word for free.[35] Even if not all these worker leaders subsequently proved able or willing to make good on their volunteering promises, it's clear that unions are leaving a large amount of member power on the table.

A good starting point for large-scale volunteer efforts would be to expand established unions in industries like auto and companies like Kroger where labor already has a beachhead, since worker volunteers have a natural affinity with new potential members and since winning good first contracts is significantly easier when you can leverage areas of pre-existing strength. But since so much of the US economy is non-union, worker volunteers will also have to breach unorganized territory such as Walmart.

Until the labor movement makes an all-in, multi-billion dollar investment to seed and support unionization efforts, there's no way to test the potential for reversing decades of decline. Any massive funding increase would be welcome. But to be maximally impactful, unions should invest as much as possible in worker-to-worker organizing.

7

TACTICS TO WIN BIG

> We have fun [unionizing]—talking to each other, just simply supporting each other, getting people rides to work. We need to get back to the basics, where it's not my family against the world.
> SAMANTHA SEIZ, Rivian EV worker organizer

BUILDING WIDESPREAD WORKING-CLASS STRENGTH is facilitated by, but not reducible to, a lightly staffed organizing model. You also need to find ways to win particular drives and campaigns—no easy task in a country where all the cards are usually stacked against working people.

The reason worker-to-worker unionism is so pivotal for winning big is not just that it's scalable. As I'll show in the following pages, it's also the best vehicle to deploy and develop effective *tactics*. This point, in turn, requires tackling a related question: Which tactical methods are needed to win widely?

To build power from below, it makes sense in most times and places to lean heavily on accumulated experience. Good organizers generally pass on lessons from past struggles and disabuse people of the commonly held notion that it's possible to skip past the hard work of deep organizing because a particular company or industry is somehow unique.

Jamie Edwards from the independent union Trader Joe's United underscored the importance of tried-and-true methods:

> When I'm talking to new stores, I usually have to spend a lot of time convincing folks not to look for shortcuts. We're not the people to be reinventing the wheel, right? We have to focus on doing what works, and then maybe down the road we can make changes that are actually informed by experience—but outside of that, we're not making improvements, we're just doing random shit. So it's really important that people do things by the book, there's a reason why people do it that way.

The example of Trader Joe's United shows that it's possible to operate through a novel form of worker-to-worker infrastructure, while at the same time sticking to time-tested tactics. This is an important point to underscore, since recent debates have often confusingly conflated unionization *models* (who leads the organizing) with unionization *methods* (what tactics they use).[1] But new models don't necessarily require new tactics—or vice versa.

Experience since 2021 has confirmed the relevancy of tried-and-true unionization methods. In fact, the available evidence suggests these are more consistently implemented in worker-to-worker drives than in staff-intensive efforts. At the same time, however, lessons from recent surges in retail, auto, higher ed, K-12, and beyond indicate that organizing orthodoxy should be creatively supplemented—or maybe even sometimes tweaked—during high-momentum whirlwinds.

Jamie's reference to tactical "changes that are actually informed by experience" touches on a real dilemma: How should organizers and unions balance best practices with an understanding that exceptional conditions may require novel organizing approaches? This tension is particularly acute since union growth generally comes in big spurts of excitement, not slow advance under normal conditions. This chapter's final section thus examines how organizers should respond to, and help bring about, high-momentum openings when large numbers of workers surge into motion. In such moments of popular effervescence—when tactical creativity and risk-taking are decisive—a worker-to-worker model becomes especially pivotal.

SOME HISTORICAL BACKGROUND

Today's organizing orthodoxy is not quite as timeless as is often assumed. To understand how we got here and where we may be going, it makes sense to start in 1981. By firing over ten thousand striking air traffic controllers that year, Reagan unleashed a relentless employer's offensive against organized labor and threw union density into a free fall from which it has yet to recover. On a new terrain marked by the one-two punch of increased employer opposition and deepened global economic decentralization, it became clear that unions could no longer rely on the postwar traveling salesman approach of sending in lightly trained and low-motivation union staffers to pitch a union to workers, sign up whoever was willing, and hope for an election win.

Arguing that labor's crisis required dropping the old "service model" in which professional staff substituted themselves for workers, AFL-CIO training manuals and training events from the late 1980s onwards began advocating rank-and-file participation and systematic methods to achieve this goal. Promoting this "organizing model" approach, an AFL-CIO Organizing Institute was founded in 1989 with the mandate to train large numbers of new organizers and to forge a "culture of organizing" across the US labor movement.

Along these same lines, labor scholar Kate Bronfenbrenner's extensive quantitative research since the early 1990s has consistently shown that unions are most likely to win when they run "aggressive and creative campaigns utilizing a grassroots, rank-and-file-intensive strategy, building a union and acting like a union from the very beginning of the campaign. . . . More than any other single variable, having a large, active, rank-and-file committee representative of all the different interest groups in the bargaining unit was found to be critical to union organizing success."[2] To cohere and embolden the workforce, these organizing committees should engage in an escalating series of activities such as mapping a workplace, systematic one-on-one conversations, inoculation against union-busting, and community outreach.

There's a good reason all this might sound similar to the "deep organizing" methodology recently popularized by Jane McAlevey: the Organizing Institute's approach was largely an attempt to promote the best practices refined over the 1980s by aggressive organizing-focused unions, including Local 1199, the union in which McAlevey was trained.[3]

Proponents of these orthodox methods often have suggested that they constitute a revival of 1930s-era unionism. But such claims should be tempered. While both approaches share the goal of high rank-and-file engagement, union organizing back then was far less focused on deploying a series of preparatory steps towards majoritarian strikes and unionization drives, such as bringing workers together via representative organizing committees, identifying and recruiting "organic leaders" (workers with many followers at work), and pursuing systematic escalating actions to build and test supermajority support.

Less sustained fostering was needed in the era of centralized industry because workers tended to be more socially cohesive, and because smaller groups of workers had higher disruptive capacity. Back then, more time than today was spent on agitating workers through leaflets, plant gate speeches, radio broadcasts, and mass meetings. There was also more of a focus on launching disruptive (often minoritarian) workplace actions as triggers for inspiring unionization, which was very often of a pre-majority variety up through the late 1930s.[4] Not until NLRB elections became the norm in the 1940s did unions have a routinized institutional process around which their methods could cohere.

ORTHODOXY PREACHED MORE THAN PRACTICED

By the 1980s, full-time organizers were far less likely to get their heads beaten in, but they also now needed to deploy more systematic, supermajority-oriented methods to win. This is hardly a knock against post-Reagan organizing orthodoxy—effective tactics often have to change in different conditions.

Labor as a whole would be in a significantly better place today had more unions consistently put this orthodoxy into practice. Unfortunately, a rigorous, rank-and-file oriented approach has only been consistently implemented by a minority of militant unions. Despite the concerted efforts of AFL-CIO leaders in the 1990s, the norm in labor has been to use deep organizing tactics only partially and inconsistently. "Although organizer training programs and materials have been emphasizing the importance of these tactics for more than a decade," noted Bronfenbrenner and Hickey in a 2004 quantitative study, "these data suggest that even today only a small number of unions are actually using them, and those that do so tend to use them in isolation, not as part of a comprehensive multifaceted campaign."[5]

Part of the reason for this disconnect between orthodox theory and contemporary organizing practice is that, as we saw in chapter 6, it takes a lot of resources and a high degree of risk tolerance to use a staff-intensive model to pursue deep organizing. Under-resourced organizing departments normally produce stretched-thin staff organizers and weak training programs, which in turn leads to the pursuit of ineffective shortcuts and cookie-cutter methods.

My research, dovetailing with Bronfenbrenner's findings, suggests that a hollow version of post-Reagan organizing orthodoxy is pervasive among those unions that regularly run union drives. Though it has the outside trappings of orthodoxy—namely, escalating quantitative benchmarks to measure support and a verbal commitment to worker engagement—hollow organizing lacks the beating heart of this methodology: identifying, developing, and leaning on rank-and-file leaders. One REI worker organizer thus complained to me about the approach pushed by some UFCW locals: "They had a copy and paste kind of way of doing things, which usually meant cutting a lot of corners."

Without robust worker involvement, tactical best practices can get reduced to lifeless formulas meant more to prevent losing than to enable winning. For example, a standard axiom of unionization orthodoxy is that drives should only file for an election once they have at least 70 percent of authorization cards signed. This is a very good rule of thumb, since intense union-busting normally peels away support. But I found through my interviews that numerous unions adhere to this rule not as a north star for encouraging robust and creative rank-and-file organizing, but primarily as a metric to automatically drop drives when undertrained workers and staffers can't reach the magic number.

Post-Reagan organizing orthodoxy has generally continued to exist more in words than in deeds. "In my experience, the problem was more on execution than the overall strategy when it came to the organizing, especially after we won our vote," notes a worker leader who initiated an AFT-affiliated union drive at California's Dominican College. This discrepancy between theory and practice is sometimes overlooked by advocates of momentum organizing, who tend to unhelpfully lump together labor's orthodox and hollow organizing approaches, failing to acknowledge their often dramatically divergent practices.[6]

BEST MODEL FOR BEST TACTICS

While the best worker-to-worker campaigns might not normally reach the same levels of organizing rigor, discipline, and capacity as the best staff-intensive campaigns, the latter are quite rare, for all the reasons described above. My survey findings suggest that, on the whole, worker-to-worker drives are implementing deep organizing tactics

TABLE 6
Top tactics used by respondents in worker-to-worker drives

Build an organizing committee	93%
One-on-one organizing conversations with 70%+ of coworkers	87%
Make list of coworkers, assess their support	82%
Union-busting inoculation	81%
Win over "organic leaders" (workers with followers)	66%
Organize social events	61%
Map the workplace	59%
Petition with demands	51%
March on the boss/manager	47%
Protest at (or in front of) work	45%
Research company for pressure points	40%
Speak out at captive audience meetings	37%
Leverage elected officials' support	36%
Coalition with community group(s)	35%
Visit coworkers' homes for union outreach	18%

SOURCE: My survey of 2022 worker leaders

more consistently than most staff-heavy efforts. Table 6 lays out the top tactics used by worker-to-worker drives in 2022, a list that can double as a helpful "How To" cheat sheet if you're looking to unionize your workplace.[7] While recent grassroots efforts have invented a new unionization *model*, their *methods* are in many ways straight out of the post-Reagan organizing playbook.

Stephanie Basile from the NewsGuild describes how they've fused tried-and-tested methods into a decidedly untraditional model: "We've set up all sorts of new [worker-to-worker] structures, but I lean on the more methodical side of things. The spirit of it is: we're building something long term—like we're not here to win an election, we're not even just here to win a contract. We're here to build a movement." Furthermore, Basile explains that orthodoxy's pace can be speeded up in urgent situations:

> We get a lot of hot shops reach out to us in an immediate crisis, and I think what our member organizers generally try to tell them is, "Let's do what we need to do, as fast as we can." So we'll try to help them build a

committee and to do the trainings and all the steps real fast—but we don't advocate skipping over these steps.

The NewsGuild's experience, as well as that of Starbucks Workers United after its initial upsurge, underscores how worker-driven infrastructure can go hand in hand with deep organizing's best practices. In this same spirit, countless young worker leaders across the country explained to me that their education in organizing methods came from reading the works of Jane McAlevey or attending an Organizing for Power online training.

The basic reason why worker-to-worker unionism has been so tactically effective is that it helps bake in from the outset *the* crucial ingredient for any strong union campaign: rank-and-file leadership. In contrast, staff-intensive campaigns—even with the best of intentions—often fail to find, retain, and sufficiently develop worker organizers.

Worker leadership is also necessary for the tactical creativity that makes organizing an art, not just a science. It takes a lot of concrete knowledge about a given industry, workplace, and workforce to flexibly align tactics to these particularities, as well as employers' constantly shifting responses. Sarah Pappin gives a good description of what this looked like in Starbucks Workers United:

> A big reason we've been successful is being nimble, being intuitive, and meeting workers where they're at—with a largely younger workforce, we've done some things in ways that are different, like organizing a bunch over group chats and avoiding house calls. A lot of it has been rapidly evolving trial and error. We're seeing what works, and Starbucks and their union busters are constantly doing the same. We figure out something that works really well, then they figure out how to respond, and the cycle continues.

Though talented staffers can immerse themselves deeply enough in a drive and build enough trust with worker leaders to acquire the inside knowledge necessary for this kind of creativity, it's easier for workers themselves to calibrate deep organizing tactics for their coworkers and workplace. Moreover, imbalances of experience, authority, and time availability between seasoned full-time staffers and worker organizers can often lead to unproductive relations of deference. This, in turn, tends to lead to insufficient creativity and democracy in practice.

Organizing ownership is more easily built from scratch than bestowed. Especially if staffers are swamped (as is often the case in underfunded organizing departments), or if they are not deeply committed to rank-and-file power, there's a natural tendency for them to try to do the work themselves rather than train others. Training workers requires a significant time investment on the front end, even if it multiplies overall capacity in the long term.

For the most part, today's lightly-staffed drives are pursuing long-standing deep organizing practices, rather than breaking new tactical ground. Even in times of high momentum, effective unionizing these days normally comes down to the unglamorous work of building relationships of trust between coworkers via countless one-on-one organizing conversations and escalating activities to test, track, and build supermajority support.[8]

Only one tactic listed in table 6 isn't consistently stressed by orthodox trainers and manuals: proactive efforts to socialize. It's worth noting that the prevalence of this approach—used in 61 percent of respondents' drives—shows how the organizing terrain has been transformed over the past century. In an era when coworkers tended to be neighbors who regularly saw each other at the bar or at church, organizers could lean more on such pre-existing networks and activities. But now, when these organic relationships are less common, you often need to create them from scratch.

Though my interviews indicate that many established unions also proactively encourage socializing, this appears to be particularly crucial for sustaining volunteer organizers in drives with relatively light staff support. When I asked Chris Smalls in April 2022 if he could recommend one tactic ALU used to win their election, I was initially a bit surprised by his reply: "Food is the way to the heart. It's as simple as that. If you want to bring people together, you feed them. . . . We made Thanksgiving several times through the year, and not just on Thanksgiving. We had potlucks, barbecues, bonfires. We rejoiced over food, and it wasn't all rejoicing; it was more about conversations."[9]

On a SBWU Reddit "Ask Me Anything," Mari from Seattle described a similar dynamic: "The camaraderie and solidarity cannot be understated, this is the most supportive community I've ever been a part of. Having fun is a part of that too. . . . I love unwinding by playing games with the people I've been organizing with for almost an entire year now."

TACTICAL LIMITATIONS

None of this is meant to suggest that worker-to-worker drives are somehow flawless. For starters, table 6 shows that only a minority (40 percent) of worker-to-worker organizers were part of drives that researched their companies' vulnerabilities. This is a significant shortcoming.

Experience since the 1980s suggests that rank-and-file intensive tactics should be combined with a well thought-out strategic plan to organize a given company and industry. Generally speaking, this requires researching the company's structure, financial dynamics, potential weak points, upcoming expansion plans, and relations to outside leverage points. As Jane McAlevey explains in her discussion of "power structure analysis," rank and filers can and should play a central role in developing such knowledge. Similarly, labor scholar Tom Juravich has been working with unions like Trader Joe's United to develop practices for workers to do their own strategic research without having to rely on paid full-time researchers. The fact that more worker-to-worker drives are not yet doing this kind of strategic planning *is* a significant limitation, indicating an important area for improvement, both among today's grassroots worker leaders and the organizations supporting them.[10]

Underestimating the importance of strategic research is hardly the only common limitation. If I had space to include a chapter on stalled-out or defeated worker-to-worker efforts, it'd describe in detail other frequent errors, including:

- taking on all the work individually rather than building a team;
- confining an organizing committee to a friend group or to self-selecting activists;
- overlooking the importance of winning over influential coworkers;
- overestimating the solidity of union support beyond core supporters;
- relying on loose verbal affirmations of support instead of public actions like signing a union card, participating in a pro-union group photo, or wearing a pro-union button;
- underestimating how many currently supportive coworkers will flip in the face of intense union-busting;
- and underestimating the importance of pre-election one-on-one conversations, relationship building, and supermajority support for winning a first contract.

One of the reasons drives normally need some form of support from battle-tested organizers is to help avoid these standard mistakes. In most unionization efforts, a significant number of workers normally think it's possible to skip past the hard work of systematic one–on-one conversations and escalating "structure tests" to measure and accumulate supermajority strength. This can lead to costly errors if the organizing committee isn't fully committed to deep organizing or if the organizer providing outside guidance—be they a staffer or rank and filer—doesn't convince worker leaders that a more time-tested approach is more likely to win.

A high degree of worker leadership is the source of worker-to-worker unionism's power and scalability. But workers don't automatically make the right tactical calls.

IS ORGANIZING ORTHODOXY ENOUGH?

Deep organizing practices are likely to remain foundational for effective union drives into the foreseeable future. There's a real danger of throwing the tactical baby out with the bathwater when some workers win in unconventional ways, like at Amazon's JFK8. And especially since enthusiastic workers frequently overestimate their momentum, and the extent to which it can be sustained without solidifying their structures, I'm very sympathetic to the impulse of seasoned organizers to err on the side of organizing orthodoxy.

But there are nevertheless good reasons to expect that additions or alterations will be needed to meet high-momentum conditions. Labor movements don't tend to grow gradually over time. Periods of growth are generally concentrated in rare spurts when working-class resignation seemingly overnight turns into action, stasis to forward motion. "Absent the periods of spurt, U.S. union history is characterized by gradual erosion of union density," notes labor scholar Richard B. Freeman in his useful quantitative study on this topic.[11]

It's possible that a national upsurge of 1930s depth will not be repeated again, since workers are more atomized today and since the existence of a federally-sanctioned unionization process provides an escape valve for pressure that might otherwise only get expressed through a unionization explosion. Perhaps in the coming years we'll see multiple punctuated spurts rather than one big upsurge. But without trying to predict the future, it's safe to say that there are moments when even speeding up the pace of orthodox tactics will probably not be enough to meet the moment.

A strategic orientation to developing rank-and-file capacities can take a range of different forms in different contexts. Rob Baril, president of 1199NE—a prototypical practitioner of deep organizing—helpfully points out that time-tested tactics might have to be adjusted in situations of high worker unrest:

> We need to be aware that there are moments in time where yes, it's okay to throw cards [distribute union authorization cards without prior organizing]. You know, 1199 in the 1960s organized a lot of hospitals because you were coming out of the Black Power and Civil Rights riots in cities, and the white executives of hospitals were terrified. So organizers provided direction and vision, but the Black and Latino working class folks at large healthcare institutions—they were already surrounded by struggle over a broader vision of a multiracial democracy and demanding that be extended to their work lives. But we shouldn't forget that as things cooled, that didn't work anymore.

In short, while there are very good reasons to normally err on the side of systematic deep organizing, such an approach can also have costs. Moments can be missed, enthusiasm allowed to cool, scalable opportunities squandered. For that reason, it makes sense to acknowledge that it's possible to err too far in either the direction of too much or too little preparatory build-up. Effectively walking this tightrope is a tricky task, but there's no way around it.

SUPPLEMENTING ORTHODOXY WITH NEW TACTICS

Many elements of what's known as "momentum organizing"—tactics for creating and seizing whirlwind moments—could serve as additions to, not substitutes for, labor's best practices. The following methods aren't generally taught in standard organizing trainings, but a range of unions have implemented them to varying degrees, and they aren't inherently in contradiction with post-Reagan orthodoxy.

Stagger Actions to Build Momentum

Orthodox organizers generally hold the following theory of momentum: workers fighting back and winning will inspire others to do the same. This captures a central dynamic of labor movement growth, as we've seen throughout this book. But numerous examples over the past few years suggest that additional steps towards generating and sustaining grassroots initiative are also possible.

For example, unions can consciously stagger their activities to create a sense of forward motion and to increase the likelihood of organizing contagion. After Buffalo baristas publicly filed for NLRB elections in August 2021, they were surprised to get requests for unionization assistance from a Starbucks store in Mesa, Arizona, and two from Boston. Organizers decided to have the Boston stores wait to file after Buffalo's December 9 NLRB vote—even though they were ready earlier—to create a sense of a national domino effect. Boston filed on December 13, with the following note blasted over social media: "We are proud to stand in solidarity with our partners in Buffalo and throughout Boston, who have inspired us in the fight for equal bargaining power and a democratic work place!"

While the use of escalating actions *within* a given workplace is a standard best practice to win a union election and contract, it is far less commonly used *between* different workplaces. The experience of UAW's 2023 "Stand Up" strike suggests that this approach should be wielded more frequently. Rather than have all workers from one of the Big 3 companies walk out at once, as had always been done in the past, UAW's new leadership chose to start the strike at only a handful of plants, so as to expand to more and more factories as negotiations progressed. Not only did this help avoid depleting the union's strike fund and enable the UAW to flexibly leverage shutdowns against different companies, but, as historian Nelson Lichtenstein points out, "it kept the conflict in a suspenseful news cycle as each new factory was shuttered."[12]

Use Public Attention to Seed New Drives

A good number of unions, particularly in the service sector, understand that public attention and positive media coverage helps workers win.[13] What is far less understood is that moments of high attention and struggle—what momentum organizers call "trigger events"—can also be proactively leveraged to rapidly spread the movement by seeding new drives.

Here, again, Starbucks provides a useful example. Sensing that the eyes of the country would be watching their December 9 vote, Buffalo's worker organizers decided to make the most of the moment by inviting the press to watch them watch the NLRB's vote tally result announcement. In so doing, they inaugurated a new tradition of election victory celebration videos going viral online. And to make it easy for other partners to reach out, they plastered their email contact all over social media while the spotlight was on them.

Neither hot-shopping nor targeted organizing have much need for seeding tactics meant to leverage the excitement of an election win or a strike to launch broader organizing efforts. Though it's difficult to predict if and when such initiatives might catch on, the only way to find out is by trying. To illustrate this, we can compare the UAW's and the Teamsters' approaches to striking in 2023.

The Teamsters ran a good contract campaign and won a good contract that summer by building a credible strike threat. But their decision not to pull the walkout trigger at UPS squandered an opportunity to leverage publicity and momentum to inspire unionization drives at Amazon and beyond. As one driver put it to sociologist Barry Eidlin before a settlement was reached: "Theoretically, we get a good deal [without striking], not everyone would know about it. But we go on strike, it's gonna be on the news 24/7."[14]

The UAW showed precisely how this could be done. At an October union press conference celebrating the victory of their six-week strike,

Fain called it "a turning point in the class war that's been raging in this country for the past 40 years" and immediately pivoted to the new organizing battles to come at non-union holdouts like Mercedes, Toyota, and Volkswagen: "One of our biggest goals coming out of this historic contract victory is to organize like we've never organized before. When we return to the bargaining table in 2028, it won't just be with the Big Three. It will be the Big Five or Big Six." Especially during periods of uptick, *every* high-publicity union fight should be used as a launching pad for organizing the unorganized.

Seize the Moment

With its emphasis on strategic targeting and patient build-up activities, post-Reagan orthodoxy generally has had little to say about seizing openings when they unexpectedly arise. But there's nothing intrinsic to this tradition that precludes it from incorporating the idea that new—and more ambitious—initiatives become possible in whirlwind moments.

Arizona Educators United provides a good example of what this can look like. Founded as a Facebook group on March 4, 2018, that spring AEU rolled out in accelerated fashion an impressive number of structure tests—getting a supermajority of teachers to sign a petition, to wear red on a given day, to organize outreach actions to parents, and to participate in a strike vote. None of that deep organizing would have been possible, however, had AEU's small crew of rank-and-file founders not seized the brief window (roughly February 28 to March 6) when Arizona's educators were hyper-focused on West Virginia's strike and discussing the possibility of replicating it. "People in Arizona were scared to rock the boat—and then West Virginia happened," recalls Garelli. "All of a sudden, the catalyst was there." By way of comparison, similar rank-and-file teacher Facebook groups founded months later in states like Florida never went viral, in part because the fever pitch of early March had already dissipated.

If Arizona shows how organizing orthodoxy can be calibrated for whirlwind moments, the Amazon Labor Union shows that an unorthodox approach doesn't guarantee openings will be seized. Despite being extremely adept at creating and seizing trigger events in their two years of JFK8 agitation, ALU missed an unprecedented opportunity to launch a national campaign to unionize Amazon. With the eyes of the world on them after beating Bezos in April 2022, requests for organizing help began to pour in overnight. Yet for month upon month after their victory, ALU failed to hold a much-promised national training call. This default had numerous causes. A major one was that by going solo rather than affiliating with an established union, JFK8's small crew of organizers lacked the capacity to help pivot nationally. This undercapacity, in turn, went hand in hand with organizers' physical exhaustion after the April election win, their inexperience in systematically training new worker leaders, their interpersonal drama, and Chris Smalls's difficulties delegating organizational responsibility while he focused on spreading ALU's class-struggle message through the media and beyond.

One of the young radicals hired to be ALU staff sent me this dispiriting description of their first day on the job in the fall of 2022:

> I was asked to catalog the many emails that had flown into the union's main inbox, from the contact form and listed email address on the website. There were thousands of unread emails: requests for solidarity from other unions, questions from the press, messages from workers who had been inspired by ALU, and—most heartbreakingly—*over 800 emails from workers who wanted help organizing their Amazon warehouses.*

ALU's experience underscores why scaling up worker-to-worker organizing nationally will require that established unions make an unprecedented financial investment in new organizing. In our decentralized conditions, it takes big resources to win big—even when workers are in motion.

Bend the Rules

It normally makes sense to rigorously adhere to time-tested organizing rules, which crystallize the lessons of decades of accumulated workplace organizing experience. Nevertheless, my interviews revealed that hollow union drives tended to be the most rigidly committed to quantitative benchmarks, while left-leaning, deep organizing unions—with their laser focus on developing worker leadership—were open to occasionally bending the rules. Rob Baril from 1199NE put it like this:

> I think there's a triad of things we need to assess: how deeply felt are [workers'] issues, how strong is their leadership, and how high are their expectations? If one or two of these elevates a lot, it can sometimes allow you to bend the stick on pure models of quantitative based leadership assessment. . . . You *could* win filing at 60 percent—you may not win, you probably won't win, but you at least have a fighting chance.

Along these same lines, Jon Schleuss from the NewsGuild recounted that "when we went public with our union campaign at the *Dallas Morning News,* we had 63 percent support, which was really low, not something we like doing. But the workers only grew from there in terms of their level of support. Sometimes it's worth taking risks." Flexibility also proved essential during UE's big drive at MIT, which filed at only 60 percent of cards. As Valentina Luketa from GWOC recalls, "We saw that if we didn't file at that moment, after months and months of organizing, we were going to lose our momentum." The drive ended up winning 1,785 to 912.

Launch Boycotts

In our interviews, numerous experienced staff organizers vehemently insisted to me that consumer boycotts don't work. And while this *has* generally been true over the past fifty years of labor movement downturn, we know that such actions have worked in previous moments of popular effervescence—for example, in the United Farm Workers' successful boycotts of agricultural companies in the 1960s and early 1970s. And it's a sign of the times that boycotts have recently helped militant unions force management to the bargaining table at Starbucks, Burgerville, and Spot Coffee.

If all the stars align, it may sometimes be possible to launch effective boycotts organically via social media, as seen with Starbucks over Gaza. But since it's so hard to predict what will go viral online, and since not all companies are dependent on hyper-online young consumers, banking on something as risky as a boycott will normally require deep organizing at work and in the community.

Stephen Lerner, who dropped out of high school in the early 1970s to work on the farmworker boycott full time, recalls that

> one of the things that we did was have our people go into stores and fill their shopping carts with food. And we'd put a picket line up, and then all the folks in line would say, "Oh, there's a picket line, I need to respect it"— and they would just leave their full carts. . . . [And] in California people picketed the ports where longshoremen would honor the picket lines for as long as they legally could, delaying shipments of grapes and lettuce.

It's not hard to imagine similar tactics today, from blockades of key logistics hubs to customer-worker sit-ins, occupations, or hard picket lines to shut down stores and workplaces. (One of the few upsides of economic sprawl is that there are countless local targets for community supporters to engage with.) The active, all-out support of other unions—and their willingness to flout legal bans on secondary boycotts—may prove to be particularly decisive. In pivotal moments of struggles, effective labor solidarity obliges much more than press conferences and statements of support.

Provided there was enough popular participation and support across the country, escalating boycott confrontations could help create financial and legitimacy crises for companies, especially those sensitive to their brand. With waves of workers and supporters creating nonviolent havoc, getting arrested, and making headlines, sales could plummet and liberal politicians—as well as key company shareholders—could be pushed to demand management sign a first contract.

Don't Be So Afraid of Losing

It's obviously better for workers to win than to lose. That said, post-Reagan union practice reflects a fear of losing that frequently bleeds into excessive risk aversion. This trepidation is based on real accumulated experience since the 1980s. Lost campaigns have subjected workers to employer repression, prevented further drives at demoralized workplaces for years to come, discouraged parent unions from maintaining funding for new organizing, and undermined the livelihoods of staffers and elected leaders. As HERE's organizing director, Vinnie Sirabella, complained in the late 1980s: "Our national [organizing] program is in jeopardy because of [our staff organizers'] fucking egos. They were afraid to fail. They were afraid to lose their reputation for greatness."[15]

Faced with high stakes and powerful opponents, caution can be useful—but only up to a certain point. An excessive fear of losing is one reason why unions have been so hesitant to seize the recent organizing opening, since a sizable number of today's union leaders were burned by defeats in the 2000s and don't want to repeat the experience. Fear of losing also helps explain why established unions generally remain so hesitant to lean on strikes, labor's strongest (and riskiest) economic weapon.

By way of comparison, a century ago organized labor not only waged more battles than today, it lost them more frequently. Though there's no data on unionization win rates back then, we can compare the success rates of strikes, as compiled by government statisticians. There wasn't a single year from 1900 to 1937 where a majority of strikes were "successes."[16]

NLRB data shows that unions tend to win a higher percentage of elections when they organize significantly less. This makes sense, because if you only take on drives with a high likelihood of success, your universe of potential drives shrinks considerably. As recently as 1976–80, unions ran about five times as many NLRB drives yearly as they do today, but their win rate was only 48 percent. In contrast, as the total number of drives have plummeted in recent decades, labor's win rate has steadily crept upwards, hovering at around 70 percent in recent years.[17] Were labor today to double or quadruple its amount of drives, the total number of wins would shoot up even if success rates dropped back down to 1970s or 1920s levels.

Too much fear of losing can also reflect narrow strategic viewpoints. Things look differently when you're assessing the health of the workers' movement as a whole, not just your particular union local, and when you assess outcomes not just by what you win from employers, but also by how much solidarity, capacity, and leadership you forge in struggle.

Defeated efforts can sometimes set the stage for future victories. Part of the reason Volkswagen workers in Chattanooga won in 2024 was that they were able to build on the accumulated experience of two previous drives that went down to defeat. And if losses inspire others to fight, they can also sometimes strengthen the overall national movement. For instance, even though a spring 2021 hot-shop drive ended up losing its election at the Amazon warehouse in Bessemer, Alabama, it played an important role in boosting the labor zeitgeist and inspiring other Amazon workers. It was not until Chris Smalls witnessed the amount of publicity showered on Bessemer that he agreed with Connor Spence's suggestion to turn JFK8's up-until-then amorphous organizing effort into a union drive.

First contracts, moreover, are not the only ways to judge success. After over a year of systematic organizing, Trader Joe's workers on Manhattan's Lower East Side lost their April 20, 2023, vote 76–76 (NLRB ties go to the company). As one organizer texted me that day, the loss was "excruciating." But the effort was not in vain, because workers kept on organizing and acting as a union. Two months after their election loss, the store's employees collectively walked out after management refused to close the store when unprecedented wildfire smoke from Canada made it unsafe to work.

Becoming less fearful of defeat—and taking a more expansive view of what constitutes a win—is an important step towards overcoming risk aversion, adopting new worker-to-worker techniques, and massively funding new organizing projects.

A key reason the labor movement a century ago was less scared of losing was that it was far less staff-intensive. Here again we see why a worker-to-worker organizing model is necessary to unionize at scale: full-timers will always face stronger pressures not to jeopardize the finances and health of the union that employs them. Precisely because they don't depend as much on paid professionals, mass movements are messy, they throw the dice, and they learn through experience. Sometimes this means you experience heartbreaking defeats, like at Alabama's Mercedes plant in April 2024. But one thing is certain: the only way to win widely is by betting on heroic, tireless workers like those who led the efforts at Mercedes. As worker organizer Sammie Ellis texted me on the night of their loss, "We won't give up."

In short, a more bottom-up approach is necessary to get labor to start waging more battles and to start taking more risks—including, if necessary, tactics that break the organizing rules.

BREAKS FROM ORTHODOXY

Are there any breaks from post-Reagan best practices that could fuel unionization spurts? When I raised this question with interviewees, a few experienced staffers and union leaders insisted to me that unorthodox tactics could never be anything other than counterproductive. But a greater number responded along the lines of the following organizer from a Midwest blue-collar union: "It's *conceivable* that could work, but since it's so much more likely to backfire, it's not the type of thing we should be training workers to do. I'd put it like this: I don't keep a gun in the house, even though there's a chance I might need one someday, because the danger of an accident in the meantime isn't worth it."

This is a very valid concern—so much so that I've gone back and forth debating whether to include the following section in the book. But ultimately I think that we should trust workers enough to discuss tactics that might at some point be relevant, even if in most cases they'll be counterproductive. So with all these warnings in mind, here are some organizing weapons to be kept in the arsenal for potential use at suitable moments.

Openly Unionize from Early On

One unorthodox tactic worth experimenting with is to openly organize from early on, rather than taking the normal route of going public only after securing a majority through hush-hush one-on-one organizing conversations with coworkers.[18]

Going public early is a significant risk, because it gives more space for union-busting before organizers get a chance to talk to and inoculate their coworkers. Yet especially in whirlwind moments, a more open approach can sometimes enable a drive to spread more quickly and confidently. One common tactic in the Great Depression, for example, was to directly pass out union cards and sign up workers at rousing mass meetings. The UAW's new out-in-the-open organizing approach is very much in this spirit.

It's also conceivable that organizing openly from the get-go could make it harder for employers to engage in illegal union-busting, since the cost of such repression would be raised through negative publicity. This was one of the key reasons why Amazon did not initially do more to smash ALU at JFK8, a drive conducted in the open from day one.

TACTICS TO WIN BIG   **197**

Worker organizer Connor Spence recalls that "after firing Chris [Smalls] had backfired so much by getting so much attention, it was pretty clear they didn't want more bad press saying they were breaking the law." Along these same lines, Amazon's annual report for 2022 acknowledged that "our response to any [union] organizational efforts could be perceived negatively and harm our business and reputation."[19]

Regardless of what tactics unions lean on, history also shows that there are exceptional moments when large numbers of workers cast aside any cost-benefit analysis and openly surge into action "too early." Until unions can develop practices and structures allowing them to connect with such spurts, there's a real danger of letting big opportunities slip through their fingers.

Spread as Quickly as Possible

Though it is possible to speed up orthodox organizing, there might also be whirlwind moments that are so pregnant with possibilities that it makes sense to spread the union as widely and quickly as possible by skipping some deep organizing steps.

A caveat before continuing: While throwing the tactical dice may sometimes be worth the risk, this did *not* prove to be true in the vast majority of drives I studied, especially not in the face of hard boss fights. At Mercedes in Alabama, for example, battle-tested UAW staff organizers ultimately agreed with a push from workers to file for a NLRB election without having already publicly tested supermajority support. This unorthodox move reflected not only the reformed UAW's agreement to let workers lead, but also a wager that the benefits of moving quick—leaning on the enthusiasm generated by the Big 3 strike and the recent Volkswagen win—might be worth the risks. Up against Alabama's entire ruling class and a ruthless union-busting campaign, the Mercedes drive may have never made it to an election, or it may have lost by more, had a slower, more orthodox approach been attempted. That said, its hopes that a significant number of unassessed workers would vote Yes were decisively dashed.

Trying to skip past deep organizing fundamentals will backfire in more cases than not. But there *are* exceptions. For example, a worker leader at the New Seasons supermarket chain in Portland explained to me that "our union filed with about 50 percent signed. We wanted to file before management caught wind of our campaign. We won by a margin of more than 4 to 1." Even more unconventionally, the Amazon Labor Union filed for a JFK8 union election with only one-third of cards signed. And, to the surprise of virtually everybody, they proceeded to win their vote.[20]

Given that the main puzzle piece missing for unionizing today's sprawling corporations is the involvement of large numbers of workers and workplaces, prioritizing speed—and breadth over depth—shouldn't automatically be discarded as a plausible tactic.

Consider the experience at Starbucks. Later on in the campaign, after scorched-earth union-busting cooled their momentum, organizers relied on deep organizing tactics like identifying and flipping organic leaders and having systematic organizing conversations. But a different approach was taken in the early whirlwind upsurge, as Brian Murray explains:

> At that point in the campaign, had we tried to be too methodical, it would have been an impediment, because there were hundreds, thousands of workers self-organizing and every time a new store won, it'd inspire others to do the same. So it made sense to ride and stoke that momentum as far as possible, and I don't see how a more systematic approach would have gotten us any further.

In some moments, preparing workers for a long slog ahead could actually be counterproductive. When enough workers take action in the belief that they're destined for a rapid victory over their foes, this belief can sometimes become a reality. Naïveté can have its upsides.

Minority Actions

For good reasons, post-Reagan organizing is all about trying to win supermajorities. But labor history, especially in upsurge moments, is also full of successful actions only taken by a minority of workers at a given workplace or company. Minority strikes were very common in the pre-NLRB era, in part because the nature of factory production made it possible for handfuls of workers to shut down assembly lines. And though the goal always remained to move toward solid majorities, the CIO's big breakthrough in the late 1930s was powered by relatively small groups of workers sitting down. One reason these sit-down strikes spread so contagiously was that they enabled a minority of workers to shut down factories even when the bulk of their coworkers were still too hesitant to strike or to sign a union card. UAW members, for instance, were only a small fraction of GM's workforce during the historic Flint sit-down strike that ultimately forced management to recognize the union in February 1937.[21]

The pervasiveness of effective pre-majority worker actions in the 1930s doesn't necessarily mean that these can be copied today, since production systems and labor laws have shifted so dramatically. But this history should at least open us up to the possibility that in certain times and places it may be useful for a minority to take action before the rest of their coworkers are on board, be it through strikes, blockades, civil disobedience, or nonviolent sabotage.

Since minoritarian actions have a high likelihood of backfiring—by alienating potential supporters or facilitating employer and state repression—the criteria for considering them can't be the righteousness or urgency of the cause. Rather, the question to ask is whether a given action has a good shot at isolating your opponents, building your strength, and directly inspiring larger numbers to join in.

Risky minority actions are most likely to succeed when public opinion is already strongly favorable, even if a majority is not quite yet willing to jump into the fray. It was precisely that type of initiative that launched West Virginia's K-12 rebellion. By late January 2018, discussions at school sites and over educators' viral rank-and-file Facebook page suggested that large numbers were strongly opposed to the Republicans' push to raise health care fees statewide. But only about 150 people showed up to a January 15 union rally at the state capitol.

In this tense and uncertain context, over 250 educators squeezed into Delbarton's Carewood Center on January 23 in Mingo County, a southern region of the state known for its history of mineworker militancy. After staffers informed the crowd that their union leaderships were against any immediate job actions, high school teacher Katie Endicott took to the floor. She called on Mingo educators to galvanize the rest of the state by walking out:

> We cannot leave this room until we decide on a date [for a local work stoppage]. Whether we realize it or not, the eyes of the state are on Mingo County. . . . We just need a spark. If we can do this, if we can stand, then we know that our brothers and sisters in Wyoming [County] are not going to let us stand alone. We know that our brothers and sisters in Logan County will not let us stand alone. The south will stand. And if the south stands, the rest of the state will follow our lead. It may take a week, two weeks, or three weeks, but they will follow Mingo County.[22]

As Endicott predicted, their local walkout on February 2 sparked a wildfire that eventually culminated in a statewide educators strike a month later, an action that inspired the first strike wave since the 1970s, which in turn inaugurated America's current worker-to-worker effervescence.

Leap into the Unknown

Sometimes you have to jump into battle and then figure it out. Take the case of Indiana University grad workers, who wanted to unionize despite being public sector workers in a Republican-dominated state that does not guarantee them collective bargaining rights. Unlike other unions they had reached out to in 2021, "the UE was very much encouraging us, 'just go for it,'" explained worker leader Anne Kavalerchik.[23] Though the Indiana University drive has yet to win a first contract, its month-long strike in April 2022 managed—despite admin threats to fire and cut funding for a thousand strikers—to win all of its other demands. No less importantly, the drive played a crucial role in building UE's momentum, experience, and militant reputation in higher ed, setting the stage for its takeoff in 2022 and 2023.

My point here is not that strategy is less important in moments of effervescence, but rather that it will sometimes have to be developed during the course of struggle itself, not prior to it. Orthodoxy's emphasis on extensive preparatory research and planning makes sense in many circumstances, but it fits poorly with outbursts of worker self-activity. That's not just because workers in such times surge into action before a plan to win is at hand. It's also likely that there are numerous huge corporations for which such a plan can *only* be developed once large number of workers are in struggle, experimenting with new tactics, and collectively pooling their insider knowledge with each other and with full-timers. It was precisely such an iterative grassroots approach that led to the big tactical breakthrough of the 1930s—sitting down to strike, instead of walking out. As one journalist of the time observed, sit-down strikes were weapons "elementally invented by industrial workers."[24]

It's hard to predict if or where powerful new tactics—our modern-day sit-downs—might emerge today. Will drivers and warehouse workers find unexpected ways to identify and paralyze choke points? Will tech workers at mega-corporations figure out how to disrupt online sales, supply chains, and internal communications? Such questions can only be answered in practice, through struggle.

Over the past half-decade rank-and-file leaders have forged a new organizing model capable of scaling up enough power to beat the billionaires. This same spirit of collective creativity will be essential for developing effective tactics during those rare historical junctures when working people seize the reins of history.

PART FOUR

DRIVING FORCES

8

GOVERNMENT POLICY

> Even if you do have fear, once you learn your rights, once you learn the laws that protect organizers and labor in general, you'll know what you deserve, what you can fight for.
>
> ANGIE MALDONADO, Amazon worker organizer

WHAT HAS PROPELLED THE GROWTH in grassroots labor organizing? Getting this answer right is important not only for accurately understanding recent events, but for assessing whether worker-to-worker organizing is likely to quickly fade away or whether it could remain a central component of effective labor organizing for decades to come.

Most accounts of labor's uptick have focused almost exclusively on the galvanizing impact of short-term, contingent factors, suggesting that this is an ephemeral surge that will likely vanish once these circumstances disappear. To quote the *Wall Street Journal*, "Pandemic-related health concerns, tight labor market have led more workers to organize."[1] Along these same lines, numerous union officials raised doubts to me about the movement's staying power, pointing to the exceptional and temporary nature of its causes.

But there are solid reasons to believe that this new bottom-up organizing model is more than an ephemeral historical blip. Skeptical pundits and unionists miss the fact that the emergence of worker-to-worker unionism *predates* the pandemic—as spectacularly seen in the 2018 red state teachers' revolt. And two of the uptick's driving forces are of a longer-term nature: generational radicalization and the spread of digital tools. These two dynamics—which give a particular boost to worker-to-worker unionism, not only unions in general—are likely to continue shaping the labor movement through all its inevitable ups and downs for the foreseeable future. In other words, while labor's post-pandemic momentum could be killed by a Republican electoral sweep, a Fed-induced recession, or scorched-earth union-busting, the organizing landscape will remain molded by the pervasiveness of new information technologies, as well as Gen Z and Millennial activism.

Over the following chapters, we'll examine each of these five driving forces (except the pandemic, which we've already explored at length). Here we start by discussing the importance of governmental policy for boosting labor's uptick, as seen in the tight labor market and the vigorously pro-union NLRB.

CAN THE STATE BOOST LABOR ORGANIZING?

One of the major ways this book parts ways with previous calls for bottom-up unionism is on the question of the state and politics. Most other advocates of grassroots militancy have asserted—based in part on a misreading of the 1930s upsurge—that labor law reform and other transformative state policies can only be a consequence of mass labor struggle, not one of its causes. Shared widely among labor organizers and radicals, this neo-syndicalist stance has been most powerfully elaborated by political scientist Michael Goldfield, who argues that "it is only labor upheavals that have brought us the eight-hour day, the NLRA [the 1935 Wagner Act], and other benefits to workers." Worker

TABLE 7
Five driving forces of worker-to-worker uptick

Factor	Temporal impact
Covid-19 pandemic	Short-term
Tight labor market	Short-term (but prolongable by state policy)
Vigorous NLRB	Short-term (but prolongable by state policy)
Youth radicalization	Mid-range
Digital tools	Long-term

advances are exclusively won through struggles from below, forcing those in power to make concessions to preserve order.[2]

Such claims contain strong grains of truth, but they draw one-sided strategic conclusions. Though unions shouldn't subordinate themselves to politicians or depend on legal reforms to win, the experience of labor's uptick since 2020 shows that electoral politics and policy reforms *can* help workers win widely.

AN EXCEPTIONALLY TIGHT LABOR MARKET

Journalists and other observers have been right to stress the importance of an exceptionally tight labor market for encouraging workplace assertiveness. Employers, unsurprisingly, are unhappy with such a state of affairs, leading to incessant calls on central banks like the Federal Reserve to cool the economy. Dispensing with publicly palatable calls to tame inflation, Australian multi-millionaire Tim Gurner said the quiet part out loud at a property summit in September 2023:

> Unemployment needs to jump 40–50 percent, in my view. We need to see pain in the economy. We need to remind people that they work for the employer, not the other way around. There's been a systematic change where employees feel the employer is extremely lucky to have them, as opposed to the other way around. So it's a dynamic that has to change. We've got to kill that attitude.[3]

Gurner's heartless comments at least have the benefit of pinpointing that unemployment is to a significant extent a policy choice, not—as is usually assumed—the natural result of blind economic dynamics. Whatever their other faults, Congressional Democrats deserve credit for passing the American Rescue Plan in March 2021 and for designing the early pandemic relief packages, which kept the economy running hot and labor markets tight.

Though "the Great Resignation" largely took the form of individuals quietly quitting their jobs from 2020 onwards, it also produced a fair share of collective action. For instance, mass public resignations have become increasingly common. Such moves don't do much to build worker power, but telling your boss to go to hell can be very cathartic. And these public resignations *have* contributed to America's increasingly anti-corporate climate, as seen in the large number of videos, photos, and stories of such actions that have gone viral online.

Record-low unemployment levels seen since 2021 have also significantly decreased the perceived risks of workplace organizing. When asked if "a sense that you could pretty easily get a similar job in case you were fired for organizing was a factor in encouraging you to participate in the unionization effort," an affirmative answer was given by a surprisingly high number of survey respondents—41 percent.

This was particularly true for workers in poorly paid jobs. Bus drivers, disproportionately African American, have leaned on a driver shortage to assert their demands through walkouts and union drives. In the first week of October 2021, for example, Lisa Beauchamp and Missie Savoy led a two-day walkout of school bus drivers in Annapolis, Maryland after their bosses—a private contractor, Student Transportation of America—offered only a 50-cent raise. During the strike, Lisa told a local TV crew: "I love my children that's on the bus. But I also have to eat, too."[4] Missy recalled to me that "after we walked, I said to Lisa, 'What the hell have we done here—they could fire us all.'" When I asked Lisa about this moment, she replied, "Yeah, we were scared, but we all have CDLs [commercial driver licenses], and that's the golden ticket these days because everybody needs us." Midway through the strike, UFCW Local 1994 reached out to the drivers. By the end of the week, they announced their intention to unionize. A month later, they won their union election. And in 2022 they won a first contract.

Similar dynamics have driven much of the unionization groundswell among service and care workers. Union-busting in this new context does not always carry the same punch as it had only a few years prior. Consider the experience at Urban Pathways charter school in downtown Pittsburgh. One day before they went public, the main worker leader was fired. "Everybody knows it was because of unionizing," she told me. But instead of intimidating other teachers, their AFT-affiliated organizing committee subsequently grew stronger and they ended up winning their April 2022 election.

A big shift in terrain should have big consequences for how unions approach organizing. Because a tight labor market makes more workers willing to take risks, unions should seize the moment by massively funding new organizing. And there are also major tactical repercussions. When the fear factor is relatively low, organizers can experiment with waging their drives more publicly from an earlier stage. This, in turn, should enable the unionization process to move more quickly, cheaply, and widely.

Unfortunately, very few unions have pivoted in the new context. Nor have labor and the Left put up a fight—either practically or ideologically—to maintain full employment. This goal has largely fallen off the progressive agenda since the 1970s, even though tight labor markets were central to union strength in the three decades following World War II and even though leaders like Martin Luther King Jr. centered full employment in his "Poor People's Campaign" to uplift the multiracial working class. Experience since 2020 strongly suggests that unions, anti-racist community groups, and their electoral allies should bring this demand back to its former prominence—while simultaneously taking advantage of openings for workplace organizing before it's too late.

THE NEW NLRB

Some of the most ecstatic moments of labor's recent uptick have incongruously occurred in the NLRB's sterile halls. "If you worshiped the concept of being boring, this is the church you would build," one Kickstarter worker told a journalist about their February 2020 NLRB hearing room where union election vote counts take place.[5] Joyful pandemonium broke out when the final vote was counted—the union had come out on top, 46 to 37. And over two years of organizing and struggle later, Kickstarter's workers got another chance to celebrate when in June 2022 they became the first tech workers in the country to win a first contract.

The importance of the NLRB in recent labor struggles has come as a surprise to almost all wings of organized labor. For many decades now, both mainstream labor leaders and their radical critics have tended to look askance at the Board. Like many other leftists, Joe Burns argues:

> Class struggle unionists are deeply suspicious of the role of the government in protecting workers' rights. Our unionism does not consider government institutions such as the National Labor Relations Board and the federal courts to be neutral institutions. Rather, anti-unionism is built into the role of the government as the protector of the billionaire ownership and control of the income-producing segments of society. This fundamental understanding leads to an entirely different approach to unionism and politics [from other labor traditions].[6]

If radicals like Burns have tended to dismiss the potential for pro-labor governmental intervention, labor leaders have long erred in the opposite direction. But on the specific question of the NLRB, their negative stances often haven't been too far apart. Organizing efforts outside of the Board—widely seen as a decrepit, toothless institution—were all the rage among organizing-focused unions in the 1990s and 2000s. And continued assumptions about the NLRB's powerlessness have more recently fueled labor's exceptionally low funding for new organizing as well as a one-sided focus on lobbying for legal reform. Organized labor's prevailing orientation today, as it has been for decades, is to hunker down defensively until legislative changes enable widespread organizing.

These viewpoints reflect reasonable generalizations from bitter experience. The Board *had* failed for many decades to meaningfully uphold workers' federally recognized right to organize and strike. But Littler Mendelson is also right that the NLRB's actions since 2020 have had a "chilling effect" on employers.[7] Indeed, the extent to which the Board has boosted labor organizing since 2020 has been one of the most surprising political developments under Biden. Under Biden-appointed General Counsel Jennifer Abruzzo—a longtime Board attorney who worked as special counsel for the CWA prior to taking the NLRB's reins—the Board has played a significant role in the recent labor uptick. In so doing, it has brought back the crusading pro-union spirit that animated the agency from its 1935 founding until a reactionary counter-offensive purged NLRB leftists in 1938.

Abruzzo's vehemence is hard to square with neo-syndicalist assumptions that the state under capitalism can only take pro-worker action under pressure from below. Rather, as one union leader acknowledged to journalist Harold Meyerson, "We have a general counsel that's pushing the envelope beyond what unions themselves have been pushing for."[8]

Here we'll have to limit ourselves to giving a few examples of how the Board's actions have boosted worker-to-worker drives since 2020. Especially since corporations like Elon Musk's SpaceX are now vigorously challenging the NLRB's constitutionality, it is important to be clear-eyed about what is at stake in the fight to defend and strengthen it.

It's unlikely there would be a national Starbucks unionization wave had the NLRB not sided with Buffalo workers' fall 2021 request to hold store-by-store elections. With the legal guidance of Littler Mendelson, management had been insisting on a city-wide vote, knowing that this would be far harder for the union to win. Brian Murray, one of the Buffalo salts who helped launch the campaign, recalls the situation: "We were hoping at first to go for the whole city of Buffalo. But it eventually became clear that we just didn't have enough stores on board, so the NLRB's decision on whether to let us hold elections at specific stores was absolutely pivotal—had the Board not sided with us we probably would not have moved forward with elections, period."

As a point of comparison, a 2004 IWW union drive at New York's 36th and Madison Starbucks had their request for a single-store election denied by George W. Bush's NLRB, which obliged them to pull their election petition. Of the multiple reasons why the IWW's ongoing efforts to organize Starbucks on a "solidarity unionism" model never caught on, the absence of any legitimizing election wins was certainly one of the most important.

Buffalo's victory on December 9, 2021, electrified service workers across the country. And by going through the NLRB, it gave others a relatively transparent step-by-step process that they could copy. "I think people under-appreciate how important it was that Starbucks's win all of a sudden made it common sense among a wide layer of workers that they could file with the Board to unionize," notes Jonah Furman, UAW's communications director. "Until then, lots of people didn't have any sense of how you'd even begin the unionization process."

Far from bypassing or ignoring the state, today's insurgent worker leaders are doing their best to lean on it. Multiple self-initiated drives got the entirety of their information on the legal steps needed to unionize directly from the NLRB. Vince Quiles, who launched a unionization effort at his North Philly Home Depot store, directly called the local Board office: "I just told them 'Hey, I'm thinking about organizing my workplace' and they walked me through the process. That same morning I started collecting signatures of my coworkers."

Abruzzo's agency has also had a major impact at Amazon. Though untraditional in many other ways, the Amazon Labor Union at JFK8 leaned on and organized through the decidedly old-school NLRB process. ALU co-founder Connor Spence, with the backing of pro bono attorney Seth Goldstein, filed a consistent barrage of ULPs against Amazon from mid-2021 onwards. "All those ULPs, and the fact that we kept on exposing what Amazon was doing to us inside on social media and in the press, put intense pressure on them," Spence recalls. "And so the union busters, who at first were extremely cocky and in everybody's faces, were pretty mild by the time of the vote."

At JFK8, as in the early Starbucks wave, many workers had what I'd call productive illusions about labor law: learning about their legal protections (without fully realizing how weakly these are enforced) gave workers confidence, which boosted their organizing and made it more costly for employers to retaliate. On the evening of their NLRB election victory, with coworkers popping champagne and dancing in the background, I asked ALU co-chair Angie Maldonado about the lessons she'd pass on to others from their win. Not yet realizing the NLRB's role in the recent uptick, I was caught off guard when she highlighted the importance of legal know-how: "Learn your rights. . . . [Management] didn't try anything too crazy [against us] because by that point they had realized that we knew a lot about the laws protecting us."

Angie and other ALU organizers particularly praised Abruzzo for ordering management to let ALU workers campaign out of the warehouse's breakrooms when they were not on shift. From December 2021 onwards, ALU no longer had to rely on furtively talking with coworkers on their way to and from the bus stop outside. Spence notes that this "was pivotal in securing our win because not everybody takes the bus—by being in the breakrooms essentially 24/7 we built a lot more relationships. And being inside legitimized us, because lots of people outside thought we were a third party, that we didn't even work there, even when we were wearing our work badges."

While it's true that Amazon workers have not yet won a first contract, we saw earlier how the NLRB process was instrumental in aiding Colectivo and Burgerville workers to achieve this goal and in getting Starbucks to the bargaining table. In the case of Burgerville's union, it was precisely by leaning more on state structures that their drive was able to continue advancing. As Mark Medina notes, "The reason we filed for an election after two years in a solidarity union campaign was because we all came to see that we had already done everything possible that we could have done [through that approach]."

These are not isolated examples. When asked whether the fact that "federal labor law protects—at least on paper—the right to unionize [was] a factor in helping convince your hesitant coworkers to back the unionization effort," 86 percent of my survey respondents answered affirmatively.

None of this is meant to paper over the major deficiencies of the NLRB, or the Biden administration generally. Countless interviewees complained of how long the Board takes to issue its decisions. Such delays are hugely impactful, because they allow companies to demoralize workers via seemingly endless legal challenges, and because they incentivize illegal union-busting that can take years to remedy.

The good news is that these delays could be partially remedied— even before labor law reform—by sufficiently funding the NLRB. Because the Board's already-low funding levels were frozen in 2014, its staffing numbers dropped by 30 percent from 2010 to 2022, resulting in swamped staffers and excessive delays. And Board funding in 2010 already constituted a 39 percent drop from what it had been in 1978. Imagine how much more efficient and productive the agency could be if it received even a modestly larger slice of what goes to the US military, whose budget in 2020 was exactly 2634 times larger than the Board's.

The NLRB's biggest limitation, by far, is that it hasn't been able to stop large corporations from flagrantly violating labor law. Though Abruzzo is creatively pushing for new, stronger enforcement mechanisms, they generally remain weak. Its powers to force employers to bargain for a first contract are almost nonexistent.

Though Abruzzo's NLRB can't push unions past the finish line, it *has* helped them get into—and stay in—the contest. Leaning on the Board wherever possible today can build worker power in the here and now, while also widely demonstrating the urgency of overcoming its limitations. Put simply, reports of the NLRB's death have been greatly exaggerated.

What are the tactical implications of this surprising development? First of all, rather than waiting for national legislative reform to start large-scale organizing, labor unions should do far more to seize (and enable) Abruzzo's legal openings by initiating bold organizing drives. Fully funding the NLRB would be an important step forward, as would be passing more pro-organizing laws locally and statewide, such as providing unemployment benefits to striking workers, banning captive audience meetings (as Minnesota adopted in 2023), or passing "just cause" protections to prevent unjust firings (which New York City adopted in 2021 for fast food workers).[9] If and when the Republicans take back the White House, these types of sub-national reforms will become particularly important.

STATE SUPPORT AND LABOR STRATEGY

The tight labor market and Abruzzo's NLRB shows why we shouldn't counterpose bottom-up organizing to governmental intervention and electoral politics. Experience at home and abroad shows that labor militancy is most effective when it receives support from—but does not subordinate itself to—elected officials and state actors. Quantitative research on union growth internationally finds that while unions don't automatically grow when the Left is in office, strike waves lead to much higher union growth under Left governments compared to non-Left governments.[10] Conversely, reactionary state governments remain one of the central obstacles to organizing the US South.

Labor organizing and governmental politics are, at their best, mutually reinforcing. Without massive, disruptive strikes and risky union drives, US labor's great leap forward in the 1930s would not have been possible. But the emergence and fate of these actions was always inseparable from the 1932 Norris-La Guardia Act's ban on federal anti-labor court injunctions; from raised working-class expectations generated by Roosevelt's election that same year; from the new administration's famous 1933 proclamation of union rights in Section 7a; from the 1935 passage of the pro-union Wagner Act; from the reluctance of FDR and most Democratic governors (unlike previous elected officials) to smash strikes through armed repression; from the high-profile congressional investigations of union-busting by the La Follette Committee (1936–41); from the legal interventions of the left-leaning NLRB (1935–38); and from FDR's 1937 threat to pack the Supreme Court, which, in conjunction with the sit-down strike wave, forced the Court to uphold the Wagner Act.[11]

It *does* matter who is in government, especially in an epoch of working-class decentralization that makes it more challenging than in the past to tap workers' structural leverage through strikes. Fortunately, the vote of a spatially dispersed worker matters just as much as that of a worker tightly bound to their coworkers.

There are many industries today in which workers' shop-floor struggles can only go so far without political solutions—for example, K-12 and higher ed (increased education funding), media (public funding of journalism), healthcare (Medicare for All), the gig economy (legal recognition of gig workers as workers), and construction, meatpacking, and agriculture (papers for the undocumented). Moreover, industrial policy like the Green New Deal and even Biden's watered down Inflation Reduction Act can take significant steps towards reversing decades of economic dispersal and suburban sprawl, which is as toxic for the climate as it is for working-class cohesion. Pressure from "blue-green" movements combined with anti-corporate elected officials can keep up pressure inside and outside the state to boost the country's unionized green manufacturing base and to build dense, climate-friendly cities knitted together by mass transit, public amenities, and sustainable public housing. More generally, Left electoralism can play a crucial role in boosting class consciousness and confidence, as we'll see in chapter 10's discussion of how Bernie Sanders's two presidential campaigns politicized so many of today's young worker leaders.

While it's appropriate for unions to praise the real steps forward under Biden's administration, it's also the case that the president and other establishment Democrats have studiously refused to use their bully pulpit and federal contracts to try to stop illegal union-busting. Brian Murray from SBWU describes the dynamic:

> We need politicians to be part of our pressure campaign to target companies like Starbucks, to have them face consequences. Unfortunately, so far the only people that have really taken that fight to the bosses have been in the Berniecrat wing of the party. We don't really need more photo-ops of politicians saying unions are good, we need them to call out union-busting, and to publicly demand that CEOs come to the White House to hammer out a deal with their unions.

Recent experience suggests that, as in the 1930s, getting the federal government to sufficiently intervene on behalf of unions will only take place if unions are willing to create crises for, and risk embarrassing, liberal politicians. Unfortunately, this disposition remains exceptionally rare in the house of labor. Tyler Hofmann, a Starbucks worker leader in Richmond, Virginia, recounted a revealing anecdote:

> We recently attended an AFL-CIO Northern Virginia Federation of Labor dinner, where there were a bunch of top union leaders and politicians.

Every single one of the presenters was completely uncritical of Biden and there was even a resounding standing ovation for how great the Biden administration is—but not one single Starbucks barista was clapping or standing up. Whole tables of us were just like, "I don't get this."[12]

Under Shawn Fain's leadership, the new UAW has demonstrated the viability of a more independent approach. By initially withholding a presidential endorsement, openly criticizing the administration's weaknesses, and demanding Biden actively side with them in their Big 3 strike, the union was able to pressure him into becoming the first sitting president to ever walk a picket line. And even after endorsing Biden, the UAW has maintained its independence by quickly demanding a ceasefire in Israel-Palestine and denouncing the suppression of student protestors. Such political autonomy—harkening back to CIO leader John L. Lewis's hardball tactics with FDR and Democratic governors—will be even more necessary to force Democratic leaders to put serious pressure on corporations to grant first contracts.

State policy is not just important for labor's advance. Right-wing governments and policies since Reagan—often with the backing of corporate Democrats—have devastated organized labor and obliged unions to fight countless defensive battles to prevent a further slide backwards. The unfortunate fate of the teachers' movements in West Virginia and Oklahoma can serve as a cautionary tale about the limits of rank-and-file militancy in the face of sustained governmental persecution. Though the 2018 statewide K-12 strikes showed it was possible to fight and win partial battles under conservative administrations, Republican leaders in these states ever since have waged a relentless offensive against educators' unions. By all accounts, the situation today is worse for school workers and public schools than it was on the eve of their inspiring strikes.[13]

A return of Republicans to the White House risks generalizing such a reactionary offensive nationwide against all unions, progressive struggles, and the NLRB. Again, as in the 1930s, the fate of organized labor today remains bound up with the broader fight to defend and expand political democracy against right-wing minoritarianism.

Combining bottom-up militancy with electoral politics is a difficult tightrope to walk—as is forging a broad coalition to defeat Trumpism while simultaneously building political instruments independent of the Democratic establishment. But for those pursuing transformative change, this is the only path forward.

9

DIGITAL TOOLS

> I've never met any of my coworkers in person, but through this organizing (and it's been pretty intense) we've really bonded on a personal level. You know, we're friends now.
> NADIA RAMLAGAN, Public News Service worker organizer

PROGRESSIVES THESE DAYS are more likely to lament rather than celebrate new technologies. An earlier era of optimism, cresting in 2011's internet-fueled rebellions from Tahrir Square to Zuccotti Park, has given way to the pessimistic view that social media only favors misinformation, echo chambers, and right-wing authoritarianism.

Even those who try to find a middle path between these two poles insist that information and communication technologies (ICTs) are ill-suited for building sustainable mass membership organizations like unions. Sociologist Zeynep Tufekci's *Twitter and Tear Gas* thus suggests that digital tools—with their ability to quickly mobilize people without having to first build strong organizations—can promote only ephemeral protests.[1]

This chapter pushes back against these views by looking at how ICTs have boosted grassroots worker organizing.[2] Unlike contingent factors such as the pandemic, low unemployment, and a fighting NLRB, the rise of digital tools constitutes an epochal shift in the organizing landscape. By dramatically lowering outreach and communication costs, they've made it easier for rank and filers to launch workplace struggles without having to rely as much on paid staff and union resources. And by allowing coordination and discussion to take place remotely rather than in person, these tools have hypercharged the reach and scalability of bottom-up strikes and union drives in our decentralized economy.

But turning these potentialities into realities is far from inevitable. Many unions are still reluctant to seriously leverage digital tools. And labor has also had its fair share of internet-driven flashes in the pan, as the alluring promise of digital scalability has often been severed from concerted efforts to build rank-and-file power at worksites.[3]

Avoiding the very real pitfalls of digital tools takes a conscious and protracted decision to *organize*—to develop leaders, persuade skeptics, and consolidate lasting structures—not just *mobilize* existing supporters. Anybody looking for a quick technical fix to labor's problems is sure to be disappointed.

WORKER-TO-WORKER UNIONISM BEYOND THE LOCAL LEVEL

Given that the US has long since moved away from having actual town squares where people regularly engage and debate, the "digital town squares" of social media *can* serve an important knitting-together function, despite the distortions imposed by their profit-seeking owners.

In a pre-digital era, workers could basically only coordinate with other workers on a local level. Newspapers and radio could diffuse tactics and momentum, but it was impossible for workers to regularly meet with those who lived more than a quick walk, train ride, or drive away.

Between annual conventions, it inevitably fell on full-time staffers and elected officials to act as the go-betweens and coordinators of regional and national organizing. In a period like the 1930s, when industry and residency was hyper-concentrated, this posed far less of a constraint on the scope of bottom-up efforts. But as communities and work sprawled out after World War II, the space for grassroots labor organizing shrunk considerably. In such a decentralized context, the few efforts to build peer-to-peer organizing projects in the 1990s never spread widely, in part because, as one of their academic proponents noted, "local membership-based organizing" is most suitable when "the target is near to a local."[4]

But technologies like Zoom now make it possible for workers to coordinate with and train other workers regardless of the distance between them. This was dramatically seen in the 2018 red state strikes, which were initiated over viral rank-and-file Facebook groups involving hundreds of thousands of educators spread out all over their states. One West Virginia teacher's celebratory post to the group noted how winning took a combination of novel digital tools plus traditional union organization: "The truly innovative thing about this strike . . . [is] the incredible impact of social media as a medium for communication, organizing and propaganda. Mother Jones, AFT founder Albert Shanker and Mark Zuckerberg are the true patron saints of this movement. What has been accomplished would have been impossible without their example and inspiration."

Contrary to Tufekci's thesis, these digitally fueled upsurges *did* strengthen sustainable structures of popular power. In the immediate wake of their strikes, the National Education Association affiliate in West Virginia grew 4 percent, West Virginia's AFT branch grew 5 percent, and the Arizona Education Association grew 10 percent.[5] Recent unionization efforts have similarly leveraged digital tools to build workplace power and organization across large spatial divides. As Littler Mendelson notes, "Because of the success unions have had with virtual organizing it does not appear to be going away."[6]

In NewsGuild organizer Stephanie Basile's view, there's nothing new about good staff organizers trying to skill up rank and filers.

What's new, she observes, is the ability to scale so widely and cheaply through digital tools:

> Our union, and our worker organizers, wouldn't be able to connect and train all these shops across the country if we didn't have the era of Zoom. Workers in the Guild now really see and feel like they're part of a bigger movement, not just their own shop, by jumping on our national trainings, mentoring others, or learning from more experienced workers in their pods. In the before times, we'd have to fly out to Akron to meet with and do a training with the shops trying to organize there.

Unfortunately, my interview data suggests that most unions ignore or dramatically underestimate these new digital affordances, either continuing with business as usual or, at most, holding sporadic "check-in" calls between workers of different regions to supplement staff-intensive efforts.

For a sense of how much new technology has shifted the organizing terrain, consider sociologist Daisy Rooks's 2004 observation that "most unions used [organizing] resources to fund salaries for organizing staff, developing and printing communications materials used in organizing drives, and organizers' travel expenses. This last category is often quite substantial—many organizers travel extensively, often living and working out of hotels for a substantial portion of the year."[7]

Times have changed. Union drives still need to pay for some communications materials (though less so than in the past because digital is cheaper and because worker volunteers can do so much). But—provided unions are willing to rely more on workers—they can now avoid most organizer travel expenses by connecting new worker activists to seasoned worker organizers online. As Littler Mendelson notes, "Social media allows the employees access to the best and most experienced organizers around the country."[8]

The ability to train large numbers of workers online exponentially widens the pool of potential volunteer worker organizers who can support new efforts. One of the core innovations of the NewsGuild and UE's Graduate Workers Organizing Committee is that each has used digital tools to put national worker-to-worker guidance—through both one-on-one mentoring and mass trainings—at the heart of their organizing processes.

Though many of the unions highlighted in the preceding chapters have combined locally targeted outreach with national peer-to-peer organizing, it's no longer always the case, as organizer Stephen Lerner argued in 2003, that "to build excitement and energy among workers, and to mobilize community support, there needs to be geographic concentration [of campaigns in particular locales]."[9]

SCALING UP THROUGH NATIONAL TRAININGS

Digital tech not only allows remote peer-to-peer connection across large spatial expanses. It also allows organizations to frontload much of their training material to large numbers of people all at once via open online workshops and training materials. A good example of this approach is CWA's Campaign to Organize Digital Employees (CODE), which depends on regular mass trainings open to any tech or gaming worker. This enables CODE to train much larger numbers (some of whom, though not all, will immediately launch a union drive) and to avoid wasting scarce resources by providing the same Organizing 101 training separately for each new effort. As CODE's training invitation explains, staff only get involved at later stages of the organizing process:

> Our organizing model is heavily worker led, which requires education, discipline, and practice.... The CODE Organizer Training program is designed to teach worker organizers these fundamental skills so they can take agency at work into their own hands. Worker organizers get further training as they work with CODE staff over the course of their specific union campaign around direct action, strategy & tactics, campaign messaging, political education, and more.

The potential for skilling up workers widely via ICTs has also been demonstrated by Organizing for Power (O4P), a multiweek series founded in September 2019 by Jane McAlevey, with support from the Rosa Luxemburg Foundation. Over thirty thousand people worldwide have participated in these free trainings.[10]

McAlevey explained to me that she launched this project to widely disseminate the "skills I learned from extraordinary mentors in the real tradition from the old 1199. They're skills that were beaten out of the movement and worse. So the more we can teach these skills today, the better."[11] O4P has been able to scale up well beyond US borders, training people from 130 countries, with simultaneous language interpretation into Arabic, Bahasa Indonesia, Bulgarian, English, French, German, Hindi, Lithuanian, Portuguese, Romanian, Russian, Serbo-Croatian, Spanish, and Ukrainian. The project's breadth—inconceivable without digital tools—is all the more remarkable given that these fully remote trainings are highly participatory, with each session combining joint "plenaries" for all trainees with small break-out practice sessions led by hundreds of volunteer facilitators.

It's well past time for organized labor to let a thousand flowers bloom by providing as many workers as possible with tools to start self-organizing. Since it now costs virtually the same to train ten workers online as it takes to train ten thousand, and since so many workers today are spread out in small, dispersed workplaces, it makes more sense to plant seeds widely.

To this end, unions could ask their members to invite friends and family to trainings; they could pay for targeted advertisements over social media; or they could mass text and phone bank voters in targeted companies. Of those contacted by this seeding strategy, most probably wouldn't initially respond. But even a fraction of positive replies to this kind of outreach could dramatically increase union leads. And at least some of the non-replies would now have a sense that unions *wanted* them to organize, as well as a point of contact to reach out to later when the spirit moved them.

While open and well-publicized online trainings are a great starting point, there's also a vacuum waiting to be filled by in-depth digital materials to support worker-driven efforts up through a first contract and beyond. The NewsGuild's MOP—with its extensive trackers and training literature to skill up rank and filers—shows some signs of the direction to be headed. The same goes for UAW's nationwide videos on organizing steps and inoculation. But, for the most part, this remains uncharted territory.

Why shouldn't every national union use digital tools to train any worker who wants to learn organizing skills? Skeptics might say that this approach could only work for younger, digitally savvy workforces. But 92 percent of the US population these days has regular internet access, and both the reformed UAW and Teamsters have demonstrated that national webinars and nightly Facebook Live updates can instantly reach tens of thousands of blue-collar workers of all ages—a proof of concept also demonstrated, for reactionary ends, by Trump's savvy digital outreach team.

A more serious stumbling block for getting unions to embrace an online mass outreach approach is simply the dead weight of routine and risk aversion. And this isn't just a technological question. To get large numbers to a mass training, digital savvy isn't enough—you also need to initiate struggles that generate buzz and credibility. Much of Organizing for Power's popularity, for example, arose from workers' and organizers' desire to learn lessons from high-profile actions like the 2019 Los Angeles teachers' strike. Unions who are unwilling to wage big risky battles, and who are unable to immediately leverage these to spread the movement, are unlikely to inspire many people to show up for a training.

ICT-ENABLED UNION DRIVES

To the extent that digital tools lower organizing costs, workers are no longer as dependent as they once were on union staffers to initiate, coordinate, and extend collective action. For instance, it's easier for rank and filers to start self-organizing if they can use Zoom for meetings rather than rent a hall, or if they can directly talk online with coworkers in another city rather than paying a staff organizer to travel.

This doesn't mean there's a technological quick fix for the hard work of organizing. As Vicki Crosson from the *New York Times* tech workers' drive observes, digital tools were very helpful for facilitating the back end of their effort, but "one of the earliest lessons that we realized was that you can't solve organizing with tech—that's not a thing." Casey Moore in Buffalo makes a similar point: "I hear some people say digital marketing is going to save the labor movement, but actually, no, you still have to do the work of organizing people. You're not going to unionize a store just from somebody following and posting on social media."

That said, recent bottom-up drives *have* relied heavily on ICTs—90 percent of survey respondents used some sort of tech for either organizing their meetings or doing outreach to coworkers. Whereas younger and college-educated workplaces were more likely to use denser coordination tools such as Slack or Discord, blue-collar and older workers were more likely to use Facebook or WhatsApp. For instance, Mateo Sanchez (not his real name) is an undocumented factory worker in North Carolina who began a unionization drive at the Panel Systems steel factory in Woodbridge, Virginia, after management unilaterally cut workers' pay. Mateo explained to me that "we set up a WhatsApp to talk about the union when we weren't at work because, you know, a majority of immigrants use WhatsApp." Next, he and a coworker searched over their phones for a union to connect with, eventually landing with the Laborers' International Union of North America.

This new reliance on online tech constitutes much more than a neutral switch from old to new tools. The growing pervasiveness of ICTs specifically boosts worker-to-worker organizing because the cheaper it is to communicate, the less you need to rely on paid staff and established union infrastructure. It costs less to use Spoke or a WhatsApp chat to text updates than to pay a staffer to call members and community supporters. And the same is true for using easy-to-use tools like Action Builder to track organizing data.

In my survey, 68 percent of respondents said a majority of their organizing meetings were done online. Pandemic conditions sometimes made this obligatory for safety reasons. But even once in-person gatherings were safe again, some drives stuck with digital meetings since these were more convenient for many workers, especially those with family responsibilities and those in workplaces with long commutes. As such, all of the Mercedes workers' organizing committee meetings in Alabama were done over Zoom.

Though numerous organizers griped that endless online meetings were draining, others found them productive and invigorating. "I was surprised to find myself feeling recharged on a Zoom call with colleagues a few months back, talking about work, of all things—at 10 p.m. on a Wednesday. They felt it too," recalls Viviane Eng, who helped unionize the nonprofit PEN America, which advocates for freedom of expression."[12] A good meeting, even remotely, can allow workers the ability to speak freely in a way normally blocked at work. As Viviane later told me, "We used to joke that PEN America supported free speech for everyone except the people that work here."

Digital chats were another crucial mechanism for updates, discussion, and socialization beyond management's eyes and ears. Littler Mendelson accordingly warns employers that "social media allows employees to discuss and campaign away from the workplace."[13] To quote Chipotle worker leader Atulya Dora-Laskey, their chat was "a very important space where we could talk, and vent, and talk shit." Fellow organizer Samantha Smith noted that online spaces can also be used for socializing: "People at work, and especially through the group chat, found out they had all sorts of mutual interests. I don't want to brag, but I think this organizing has created a lot of new friendships between people who wouldn't necessarily have known each other or have hung out before."

That said, chats weren't a substitute for tested organizing techniques such as one-on-one organizing conversations. As Atulya explains:

> You really have to be listening way more than you're talking—the 30/70 rule. To be honest, that was a struggle for me, because I never shut up. But we learned that you have to communicate through questions: it's through asking people about their concerns that you can help them see that their issues at work are only going to get resolved by collectively negotiating through a union.

Many drives, like at SoHo's REI, insisted on doing these conversations in person, but others found that holding them remotely was logistically easier or—when dictated by funding limits or geographic distance—logistically necessary. I spoke about this with Jacklyn Gabel, who unionized her Starbucks store in Santa Cruz and became a volunteer SBWU organizer for all of Northern California: "Since so much of this is volunteer based, it's just easier to do Zoom if there's not the funds to cover our gas to drive somewhere." For her part, Kristina Bui from the NewsGuild explains that she often finds remote conversations to be fruitful: "It's really important to have that one-on-one conversation somehow, and not just rely on texting. But in my experience it doesn't feel as essential to always meet in person or to have to sit at a desk next to someone to make that personal relationship work."

I also interviewed several leaders of worker-to-worker drives that were obliged to organize online because their jobs were entirely remote. "The technology has been a game changer for us—we probably couldn't have unionized otherwise, because we're fully remote and spread out over thirty states," notes Nadia Ramlagan, a worker leader at the Public News Service, a private journalism company. Based on the knowledge accumulated through these types of successful remote drives, a group of tech workers produced a great remote organizing guide, *DMs Open*, to share specific tips as well as an understanding that "the principles guiding IRL [in-person] outreach also apply to remote organizing."[14]

Digital tools also make it easier for workers to get the word out about their struggles. Rather than depending on the mainstream press, unions can now take their case straight to the public via social media. For that reason, Casey Moore always advises new drives to keep their cameras on: "Whenever I hear about a store that's about to go on a walkout or a march on the boss, I'm always like 'Record everything!' because that's going to be great to publicize—and otherwise it might not even get picked up by the media."

There's nothing new per se about labor or other progressive causes using independent media to generate national momentum and to stitch together otherwise isolated supporters. Labor and leftist newspapers played that role for decades—as did radio for a brief moment in the 1930s, especially for geographically dispersed locations like Southern textile towns during the 1934 general strike.[15] But independent working-class voices were increasingly iced out of the media as corporations took over the radio waves, as television became dominant from the 1950s onward, and as unions hunkered down into their narrow and depoliticized niches. As such, 1960s social movements were largely dependent on a few TV channels and mainstream newspapers to reach beyond their bases. In contrast, even low-resource worker organizers today can sometimes directly shape the national discourse.[16]

There are many good reasons why the salt trainings led by Buffalo SBWU founders include a session on "TikTok as Class Struggle." Social media hype keeps up momentum, pressures employers, and can generate new leads—"the community," after all, is primarily made up of as-yet-unorganized workers. Jon Schleuss of the NewsGuild notes that "a big reason why organizing has gone viral among journalists is that we're all addicted to Twitter. So we post a lot about our drives, other journalists get excited about these, they say 'I guess we could do that too,' and then they reach out."

Online tools are also crucial for DIY fundraising. Organizers still need money for all sorts of tasks, especially in bigger campaigns. In the same way that online platforms have made it possible for insurgent candidates like Bernie and Trump to lean on large numbers of small donors to organize autonomously from their parties' well-funded apparatuses, so too has digital fundraising fueled worker-to-worker union efforts, in both independent and affiliated efforts.

GoFundMe drives have become a staple of the grassroots unionizing uptick, used for printing costs, food for picket lines, legal fees, strike funds, and material support for worker organizers. A key reason why journalists at the *Fort Worth Star-Telegram* were able to hold out and win a great first contract through their twenty-four-day strike in late 2022 was that they had raised over $51,000 on GoFundMe. Digital fundraising has also helped meet the survival needs of countless victims of union-busting. It's both touching and heartbreaking that hundreds of such fundraisers have been launched to enable fired worker leaders to pay for rent, groceries, and health care expenses for themselves and their dependents.

Whereas philanthropic funding encourages low-risk activities, online fundraising through small donors incentivizes bold, attention-grabbing initiatives. The Amazon Labor Union—which up through its election win depended entirely on online fundraising—was one of the drives that best understood how to leverage ICTs in our media-saturated "attention economy." Cassio Mendoza, ALU's volunteer social media coordinator and a salt at JFK8, recalls their innovative tactics:

> We saw from pretty early on that the best way to fundraise is to try to get a lot of attention online, through Twitter, or news articles, but especially through TikTok videos—about us getting arrested delivering food or showing how bad conditions were inside, things like that. So that's why we would be excited if a TikTok we posted got like a million views—it

wasn't just, "Wow, that was so popular." It was that it would literally translate to like $20,000 in donations to our GoFundMe, because all these new people would find us out for the first time. And that was really important because we didn't have union backing and there *are* hard costs to run a campaign like fliers, food, and union T-shirts.

The fact that ALU has proved to be better at grabbing attention than building deep organization shows that online hype doesn't automatically translate into sustainable power. But the conclusion to be drawn from this isn't that movements should downplay social media, but that they should do everything possible to leverage it for rank-and-file organizing.

THE EMERGENCY WORKPLACE ORGANIZING COMMITTEE

In addition to enabling worker-to-worker strikes and union drives to coordinate beyond a local level, ICTs have also made it possible to found entirely new forms of digitally based organization. One recent project stands out in particular: the Emergency Workplace Organizing Committee.

EWOC is another invention of necessity rather than pre-conceived design. In March 2020, scores of anxious workers began reaching out to the Bernie campaign to ask for help in pressuring employers to provide PPE or sick pay. In response, a handful of labor organizers—myself included—from Bernie's campaign, Democratic Socialists of America, and United Electrical set up a simple Google form to process the requests. As queries kept increasing, our ad hoc crew started reaching out to an expanding circle of experienced labor leftists willing to volunteer their time to remotely help these workers lead fightbacks. Animated by the Bernie campaign's class struggle spirit and its online distributed organizing model, EWOC was born.

Though the initial impetus was to support workers confronting the Covid emergency, EWOC quickly received institutional backing from

UE and DSA and has grown into a much larger project. It aims to address a problem identified by Association of Flight Attendants president Sara Nelson: "There are millions of unorganized workers right now who don't have access to organizing resources, don't have the support of a traditional union, and don't know how to take that first step towards building working-class power." And while my biases on this score are obvious, I agree with her conclusion that "by offering free trainings and organizing guides, and building an army of thousands of volunteers who can offer one to one support to any worker in any industry, anywhere in the country, EWOC is playing a crucial role in labor's revival."

Over 5,000 workers have reached out to EWOC since its founding. In 2023 alone, EWOC handed off sixty-five workplace campaigns representing over 7,000 workers to unions. Over 2,500 workers have participated in our bimonthly, four-part national organizing trainings. And over 1,000 people have volunteered in EWOC, often getting more involved over time via our escalating ladder of engagement, ranging from easy tasks such as texting people about upcoming trainings, to deeply involved responsibilities such as being an "advanced organizer" tasked with guiding new campaigns.

Aiming to help address the organizing vacuum noted by Nelson, EWOC's basic process is simple. Any worker in the US can fill out a short online form and a volunteer organizer will call them back within seventy-two hours to start providing organizing guidance. In 2020 and the first half of 2021, most of this support went towards direct action campaigns like petitions for PPE, paid sick leave, and wage increases. But with the explosion of unionization interest inspired by Starbucks and Amazon in 2022, EWOC's focus turned to helping workers initiate union drives and to helping them find an established union willing to let them affiliate (a task that's sometimes almost as challenging).

"We like to say that unionizing takes 100 steps, and we help workers take steps 1 through 50," explains EWOC national organizer Megan Svoboda.

We're trying to give workers the tools to actually go out and build a union themselves. Of course, not everyone who reaches out to us or who comes to a training will be able to—some get cold feet or others might stop at a petition—but the more people you give those tools to, the more people will actually make it there. I see it like planting seeds of worker power.

There's no way that EWOC could function as a largely volunteer-run project without the low-cost coordination, communication, and digital co-presence afforded by ICTs. It's not just that workers sign up online and participate in remote national trainings. A sophisticated digital back end enables EWOC's volunteers—normally about 250 to 300 are active at a given time—to get onboarded as organizers, to connect with workers who have reached out for support, to track the status of ongoing campaigns, and to coordinate on the cheap without having to live in the same city or to rent local office space.[17]

Rather than monopolize the significant digital innovations required to manage all this data and coordinate so many campaigns with minimal staff oversight, EWOC has actively adopted an "open source" spirit, actively sharing its accumulated technological and training know-how with any union or social justice organization looking to adopt a more distributed model. As EWOC's guiding principles put it, "To build a scalable movement capable of supporting all worker-led organizing efforts . . . we openly share our tools and organizing infrastructure with unions and other allied organizations."

The project's major limitation is that it is still, in the grand scheme of things, very small. Though EWOC punches above its weight and continues to expand every year, the vast majority of workers in the US don't know about it. This reach problem is exacerbated by the fact that we support the initial steps of organizing, rather than the publicity-garnering final stages coordinated by unions. EWOC's organizers have taken initiatives to expand its visibility and contacts, for instance by coordinating more with different unions and getting Bernie, AOC, and

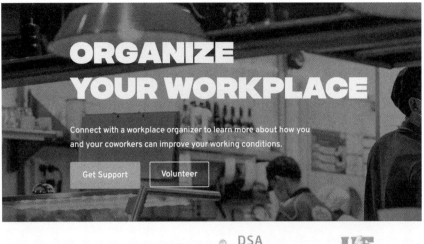

Figure 17. Emergency Workplace Organizing Committee homepage. Source: EWOC.

online streamer Hasan Piker to hype up the project to their millions of online followers. Even with this help, however, most workers who have reached out to EWOC have been in, or adjacent to, the young radicalized milieus around DSA, Labor Notes, and left unionists across the country (including but not limited to UE).

Expanding this model's impact to wider layers of working people will likely require that larger unions start supporting EWOC or start replicating its innovations within their own outreach structures. The replicability of this new approach has already been demonstrated by its diffusion to Britain, where in the summer of 2022 a crew of young labor leftists teamed up with the Bakers Food and Allied Workers Union and the Associated Society of Locomotive Engineers and Firemen to found Organise Now!, a project that has consciously and openly imported the entirety of EWOC's structure and mission.[18]

Though still of relatively limited reach, Organise Now! and EWOC provide a proof of concept for digitally enabled organizing innovations that big national unions and allied organizations can incorporate. Here are the two most important.

Support Any Worker

Unlike EWOC, unions generally only give organizing guidance to workers who have agreed to launch a union drive that will eventually affiliate to their organization; who are in a big enough shop to justify union expenses on winning, bargaining, and servicing their contract; and who are in a locale where the union already has an institutional base.

I've yet to hear a compelling argument against the idea that national unions (or the AFL-CIO) should move in the direction of supporting *any* worker looking for organizing help—even for fights around immediate concessions, even in small shops, even in towns where a given union doesn't already have a base. Doing so would significantly expand the number of overall workplace fightbacks and the number of union drives, especially once word got out that such and such labor union was now an organizing resource for *any* worker in the industry—not unlike how the best worker centers function in immigrant and low-wage communities across the country.

The major obstacle towards making such a radical shift in approach is cost. That's why moving in this direction will require that unions lean on digitally enabled peer-to-peer structures and volunteer help from members, retirees, and young activists. It will require extensive and interactive digital training materials to support workers without staff intensive coaching, as well as gradated approaches for when and how to dedicate major resources to a drive that has caught on—for example, only providing full-time organizer support after workers collect 30 or 50 percent of cards. It might also require building legally firewalled structures, to protect the parent union from having to take legal responsibility for every risky action taken by workers. In other words, it would require that labor start structuring itself more like a movement.

Lean on Volunteers

EWOC has shown that many of the tasks normally done by staff can be effectively done by volunteers. These include guiding new drives, responding to workers who reach out ("intake"), setting up website and online infrastructure, providing trainings, coordinating other volunteers, and researching companies and public policy. EWOC's seeding strategy would be cost-prohibitive without depending on donated labor and without developing robust training as well as apprenticeship processes to onboard people with a wide range of experience levels. With EWOC support, for example, many workers who first contact the project for organizing assistance eventually go on to become volunteers supporting others. To quote Mike Kemmett from the restaurant Barboncino, which in 2023 became New York City's first unionized pizzeria: "EWOC didn't just help us win our [union election] vote. Their support helped to turn bussers and line cooks into labor activists ready and eager to organize other restaurants."

Depending primarily on volunteers rather than staff is pivotal for any project aiming to expand rapidly and widely. "What we straddle is being slightly like an organization, slightly like a movement," Megan explains. "And blending these has meant that EWOC can scale."

Whether unions and allied organizations adopt any of these approaches, fully or in part, remains to be seen. Unfortunately, the internal obstacles are hardly limited to technological deficiencies—some of labor's most digitally savvy initiatives in recent years have been the *least* oriented to putting workers in the driver's seat of their movement. And getting large numbers of people to volunteer is not only an organizational and technical challenge. Above all, it's a question of ambition and political vision. EWOC's experience suggests that people volunteer for big projects that they feel passionately about, that they have ownership of, and that aim to challenge the systemic injustices of neoliberal capitalism. Digital tools can help spread the seeds of worker power, but unions can't tech themselves out of decline.

10

YOUTH RADICALIZATION

> The only thing [my dad] said to me when I told him about [starting a union]—which I was fearful to do because I expected this response—was, "I guess you want to get fired then?" And it was really tough coming from him because I watched him work my entire life and then retire almost on minimum wage.
> BENJAMIN SOUTH, Starbucks worker leader

EVEN THE BEST ORGANIZING MODEL won't get too far if there aren't many people around who are able and eager to put it to use. Fortunately for bottom-up unionism, precisely such a force has begun asserting itself: left-leaning Millennials and Gen Z. Not only are these generations politicized, but they are exceptionally "labor-pilled."

Though many of today's worker organizers are neither young nor lefty, a generational turn to workplace organizing has boosted worker-to-worker organizing, and it will likely continue to do so for the foreseeable future. Unwilling to wait for established unions to step up, young workers have taken the initiative and are pulling the labor movement into more ambitious, more risky, more politically independent directions. To quote Richard Bensinger, "this generation is every organizer's dream—young workers propelled the movement in the '30s, and they're doing it again today."

A LARGE, GROWING, LEFT-LEANING CONSTITUENCY

Before we look at the rise and organizing implications of what Bensinger calls "Generation Union," it's important to underscore that we're talking about a large and growing constituency, not some niche corner of society. By 2025, Millennials and Zoomers will make up over 54 percent of the US workforce, and by 2030 this number will go up to about 66 percent.

Support for unions has surged to 88 percent of those younger than thirty, the highest of any age group.[1] And my survey of worker leaders in 2022 confirms that this isn't just passive support: the median age of respondents was twenty-seven years old—an age similar to most leaders of the 1930s upsurge.[2] By way of comparison, the median age of the current AFL-CIO executive board is sixty-one.[3]

In terms of politics, poll after poll shows that about half of young people in the US now support socialism. And, unlike previous generations, the available evidence suggests that neither Zoomers nor Millennials (who in 2023 were as old as forty-two) are getting more moderate as they get older.[4]

Almost 50 percent of my survey respondents self-identified as radicals (see figure 18). This growth of anti-capitalism within organized labor is a major historical development, not seen since the movement's best organizers were purged by 1950s red-baiting and McCarthyism. Thankfully, decades of divorce between the Left and labor—equally harmful for both—appears to be finally coming to an end.

Some of today's young worker leaders were leftists at the start of their drives; others became so through the course of struggle. As one survey respondent wrote about their political identification: "Radical. Was a Democrat at beginning of campaign." Meanwhile, self-identified progressives ranked second highest among respondents, at just over 30 percent.

A not-untypical snapshot of this spectrum is provided by two young Lansing, Michigan, workers who unionized their Chipotle. When she

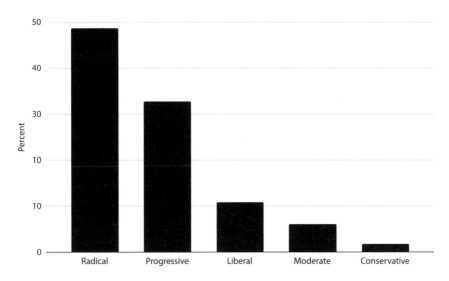

Figure 18. Political identification of survey respondents. Source: My survey of 2022 worker leaders.

decided to start unionizing her coworkers in early 2022, twenty-two-year-old Atulya Dora-Laskey was already an organized democratic socialist, politicized by the 2016 Bernie Sanders campaign. "We're supposed to live in a democracy," Atulya explains. "But in the place where we spend most of our waking lives we have to give up any right to a say. I think unions are a step towards challenging that basic lack of democracy in our society." Samantha Smith, a seventeen-year-old high school student at the time, explains that:

> I had basically zero background in organizing. I had seen TikTok videos of people getting unfairly laid off at work, I had seen Black Lives Matter, and then recently with the push to overturn *Roe v. Wade*, I got really angry. I also had seen what my parents went through during the pandemic—and I knew that me and everybody I grew up with were probably going to get stuck in dead-end jobs for the rest of our lives. So even before getting involved, I knew I wanted to make some kind of difference in the world.

YOUTH RADICALIZATION   243

Though many workers like Samantha moved further to the left through organizing, we also know that the politicization of large numbers of worker leaders predates their unionization drive. When asked whether "a desire to rebuild a militant labor movement in the US" was a major factor spurring them to unionize, 53 percent of respondents answered Yes.

These young activists are not a small fringe of privileged radicals, as the Right likes to portray its ideological foes. Most survey respondents worked in low-wage jobs. Their racial demographics track very closely with that of the young workforce as a whole. And over the course of my research I've been surprised by the extent to which young people seem to be at the center of organizing not only in white-collar professions, higher ed, and retail, but also in many blue-collar jobs. The Amazon Labor Union is one prominent example. Twenty-seven-year-old Angie Maldonado explains:

> One of the main divisions [within the warehouse] was age. Keep in mind that the average age of an ALU organizer is about twenty-six—many older workers tended to be more skeptical of the union. . . . [But] when they found out I was also a mom, and that I was sacrificing all my free time to help build a union, a lot of them really saw how serious this was.

Other blue-collar drives have shared similarly youthful dynamics. One of the reasons Manny A. was able to unionize his FuelCell Energy power plant in 2022 was that his coworkers were mostly young—"mid 20s to low 30s," he estimates. Unlike Manny, they weren't all Bernie supporters who spent an inordinate amount of time watching labor history videos on YouTube. ("I'd start watching one video about how our forefathers fought, and often died, to build unions—and then all of a sudden I realize it's twelve hours later.") But almost everybody agreed that they deserved job security and better pay, and they reacted positively when Manny started sharing news over their employee group chat about the Starbucks and Amazon union drives. After months of

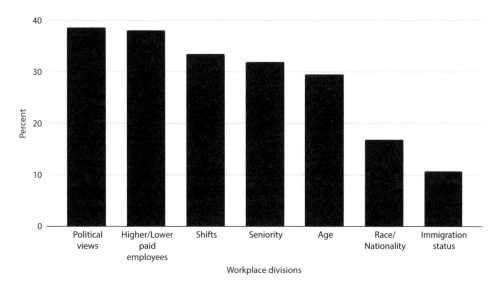

Figure 19. Divides that drives confronted. Source: My survey of 2022 worker leaders. Divisions mentioned by fewer than 10 percent of respondents not included.

bottom-up organizing with IUOE Local 478 support culminated in an election win and a subsequent strike threat, Manny and his coworkers celebrated their own first contract victory in September 2023.

A base among young workers, however, can also pose a problem in age-diverse workplaces, especially when organizers can't flip influential older workers. My survey found that age and especially "political views" were two of the top reported divisions that union drives were obliged to confront (see figure 19).

Vince at Home Depot in North Philly explained to me midway through his drive that "the most fervent supporters I have are a bunch of twenty-year-old kids at my store, who've got the time and the energy to say 'Fuck it, we're gonna play for this [union attempt].'" But a combination of management intimidation and the lack of a representative organizing committee made it difficult to expand support. The drive went down to defeat, 165 to 51.

On a more positive note, youth involvement shifted the organizing dynamics at the Yanfeng auto parts factory outside of Kansas City,

YOUTH RADICALIZATION   **245**

Missouri. UAW drives in 2016 and 2019 had failed, but the union's effort in 2022 succeeded. Why? To quote Sharon Gilliam, an older worker leader involved in each effort: "This time around all the young people were on board."

One particularly crucial young worker was Hafsa Sheik-Hussein, a twenty-four-year-old daughter of Somali immigrants. While attending community college courses online, she had taken a job as an operator on the line at the plant to support her parents and siblings: "I'm kind of the breadwinner in the family, paying all the bills." Though her main motivations for joining the drive were economic, the pro-union zeitgeist also had an impact:

> I had a cousin who worked in Starbucks and he quit because of all the mistreatment and everything that had been going on. And I had been seeing on social media a lot of crews at Starbucks and other establishments walking out and unionizing because they're not being heard by their management. So that was also a push to let me know that I'm not doing anything wrong. This is my *right*.

In Hafsa's experience getting coworkers to sign authorization cards and petitions, it was the younger workers on the line who were the most immediately supportive, while older workers tended to be more hesitant—"I usually had to explain more that the union wasn't just around to take their dues." A large portion of the workforce were Somalis who didn't speak much English and who were initially scared. "At first they thought this was just going to get us all fired and wouldn't lead to anything," Hafsa recalled. "But I had a bunch of conversations with them in our language, to explain that this was going to benefit them, and eventually they got on board." To do the same with older workers from the factory's half dozen other immigrant groups, she convinced young coworkers from those nationalities to similarly flip their hesitant elders. In May 2023, workers voted to join the UAW in a 310 to 26 landslide.

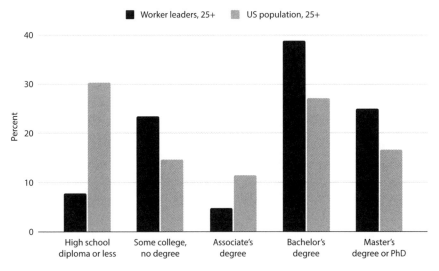

Figure 20. Education levels of worker leaders. Sources: My survey of 2022 worker leaders; National Center for Education Statistics.

Though young worker leaders can be found in all sorts of occupations, it is also true that organizers in 2022's bottom-up drives were disproportionately college educated (see figure 20). The extent to which today's union initiators diverge from the norm shouldn't be overstated: *most* American workers between the ages of twenty-five and forty have some form of college degree.[5] That said, a college-educated pattern clearly exists.

Contrary to what various union full-timers suggested to me, I don't think this means worker-to-worker models are only relevant for degree-holding workers who, the argument goes, are more able to self-organize because they have more time, confidence, and acquired skill sets like public speaking or writing.

While it's true that the types of job people do shapes their ability and willingness to organize, there are numerous reasons to doubt the skeptics' argument. Most lightly-staffed drives in US and world history have been from non-college-educated workers. As recently as the 1990s, the rare peer-to-peer models one could find locally were almost all in blue-collar unions. Assumptions that worker-to-worker unionism only works for the college educated, furthermore, are contradicted by my survey findings that almost 40 percent of respondents aged twenty-five or older did *not* have degrees.

When I asked UE organizer Valentina Luketa to reply to critics who say a worker-to-worker model can't succeed beyond grad students, here's how she responded:

> When people tell me that, what they're really showing is that they don't have much confidence in the capacities of the working class. Do they really think other workers are less capable in some way than grad workers? Obviously, the way we organize at a university isn't going to be identical to when we organize a factory. But workers everywhere are generally capable and smart enough to organize themselves, they can learn all the skills they need to take power.

When I pushed her on the point that some workers have less free time than others, she responded as follows:

> Fair enough—that's why you need a lot of workers organizing a lot of workers and it's also why workers need to find ways to talk to each other at work. But I think the main thing is that when people say they don't have time, that's often because they don't feel like it's *worth* their time, or that they don't have something to contribute. And those are obstacles that can be overcome without needing a ton of staffers.

It's also worth questioning the outdated concept that only blue-collar workers have high levels of disruptive capacity. Working at an auto factory or at a port obviously gives you and your colleagues lots of economic leverage. But we've seen in the slew of teacher strikes since 2018 that K-12 educators can create deep social crises just by refusing to come to work.

And because companies today depend so much on their digital back end, tech workers in all corners of the economy also have a very high degree of structural power. Leveraging this power is an increasingly urgent necessity, since tech workers face an existential occupational threat with the advent of AI, not unlike skilled factory hands a century ago who radicalized to defend their autonomy against deskilling. Perhaps the biggest divergence with the manufacturing workers who led labor's last leap forward, however, is that tech workers tend to be much more decentralized, often working remotely from far-flung locales. And they generally have little interaction with other types of employees at their companies; the average coder who keeps Amazon up and running has probably never stepped into a warehouse. Unsurprisingly, the recent uptick in tech worker unionization has taken place almost exclusively through a worker-to-worker model, allowing tech workers to connect to each other, and to their companies' broader workforce, across large spatial divides.

All that said, the fact that survey respondents tend to have more formal education than other workers *is* a real limitation—especially because so much of US politics today is polarized between those with or without college degrees. And were it the case that the new model depended entirely on self-initiated drives, this would be an even bigger issue, since there would be no proactive way to branch out beyond self-selecting worker activists from similar demographics. But it is possible to actively expand the scope of worker-to-worker unionism by piggybacking off of big battles, by salting strategic workplaces, and by transforming established unions to take risks and organize the unorganized. We saw earlier how the UAW's 2023 strike—itself made possible by a union reform effort supported, among many others, by radicalized grad students—inspired significant numbers of blue-collar employees to organize across the US South.[6]

Except in rare moments of mass effervescence when fear is temporarily swept aside, there will almost always be some layers of workers who tend to be less willing to initiate union drives on their own, even if their desire for one is just as high as others.[7] If the boss can relatively easily replace you, you're generally going to be less willing to stick your neck out. The same holds true if you and your family have less of a financial safety net to fall back on. This pattern didn't correlate in the past with education background for the simple reason that there were so few college-educated workers. As such, in the 1930s it was workers with specialized skills and relatively high pay, like tool and die makers, who tended to initiate unionization drives and strikes.[8]

Given that some people find themselves in structurally disadvantageous positions for labor action, it's reasonable to expect that, like in the past, helping them organize themselves at scale will take extra momentum via trigger events such as UAW's 2023 strike or the draconian 2006 anti-immigrant Sensenbrenner bill, which helped spark millions of undocumented workers to march and strike.

ECONOMIC FRUSTRATION AND CRISIS

What has brought about this labor-focused youth radicalization? The age pattern of today's union revival is in some ways unsurprising, since it's a well-known phenomenon that young people tend to be disproportionately involved in high-risk social movements. Leaving aside the murkier issue of whether idealism tends to erode with age, it's clear that having fewer familial responsibilities increases people's free time as well as their willingness to participate in movements that place their material or physical wellbeing on the line. Young people, accordingly, were at the forefront of America's 1960s rebellions as well as the 1930s labor upsurge.

But since youth initiative is a very novel phenomenon in our modern-day labor movement, timeless sociological factors cannot explain why young workers today are leading new workplace organizing. Until very recently in the US, most unions have complained about the disengagement of young workers. And this remains the norm in other countries.

One central factor driving young Americans to organize is economic frustration. Today's labor insurgencies are in large part responses to (and rejections of) neoliberalism's core pillars: precarity, wage stagnation, indebtedness, and unchecked corporate power. To quote Vince Quiles in North Philly: "I'm 27, I graduated [high school] in 2013, off of the heels of the last major recession, the rise of the gig economy, and the exploitation of the education system by private colleges and student debt collectors. Statistically our generation—you know, Millennials, Gen Z—we walked up into an economy where we were shafted, right?" Thinking the job was initially just a way to pay for his phone bill and car insurance while attending college, Vince found himself stuck working at Home Depot after he had a child: "When stuff like that comes up, you've got to grow up, to be able to take care of your family."

Workers recounted to me countless stories of low pay leading them or their coworkers to live out of their cars, take on multiple jobs, or move back in with their parents; of unfair two-tier wage systems; of the stress of not being able to pay for medical bills for themselves or their families; of physical pains caused by exhausting, repetitive, or dangerous work; of ever-present job uncertainty; of understaffing making it impossible to do the job adequately; of arbitrary, vindictive managers; of broken company promises; of unpredictable scheduling; of unsanitary and dangerous workplace conditions; of thwarted job promotions; and of failed attempts to find jobs in their hoped-for occupation, leading to one low-pay gig after another. Unsurprisingly, better pay, staffing, and job security were the top three demands in the drives of my surveyed worker leaders.

Intertwined with these economic grievances was often a feeling that employers were disrespecting workers' basic human dignity. As Angie from JFK8 put it, "We're treated like robots." The relentless authoritarianism of non-union workplaces was another consistent complaint. Mercedes worker Sammie Ellis explained to me that "it's not just about the money. It's about the control—they [the bosses] have all of it. You say you have an open door policy, but when the door was open, you wasn't listening."

Such feelings were often exacerbated by their age differences with management. "I don't think my manager sees us as adults. During all the union-busting they talked to us like we were little children," explains Laura Rosario, an eighteen-year-old Starbucks barista in Montclair, New Jersey.

Frustration at workplace power imbalances have been exacerbated by a perception that society as a whole is dominated by the ultra-rich, who are hoarding wealth, controlling politics, and bringing society to the verge of climate catastrophe. Consider Atulya's response when I asked her why she thought young people were leading today's union surge: "I think a lot of us feel like we're in the backseat of a car about to head off a cliff and the driver is completely asleep at the wheel—or they're just checking their phone and don't care."

The resulting revival of redistributive demands—*make the rich pay*—constitutes a significant break from the norm in a US progressive movement that has downplayed such concerns for over half a century. As one liberal leader recently wrote in *The Atlantic*, "By focusing on civil liberties but ignoring economic issues, liberals like me got defeated on both."[9]

It can be tempting to explain this resurgent interest in economic demands and unionization as simply a response to rampant inequality and stagnating working conditions. But this fails to sufficiently account for the mediating role of subjective expectations. For example, Thanya Cruz Borrazás at the Nottingham, Maryland, Starbucks explained that her parents' jobs in construction and cleaning services are significantly worse than her own: "They desperately need a union." But because "they believe in the American Dream, [they think] 'just be grateful for everything' even though [their bosses are] treating them like garbage."

There's not much evidence that bad conditions are ever sufficient to get people to organize. Usually, such circumstances lead to low expectations, resignation, scapegoating marginalized populations, or personal desperation. One of Quichelle Liggins's coworkers at Montgomery, Alabama's Hyundai plant took their life in 2023. Another did the same in April 2024. Relentless management pressure was the reason given in one of their suicide notes.

The fact that trust in big business among the US population has recently fallen to 14 percent—an all-time low—underscores that while discontent with corporate America is rampant these days, it isn't on its own enough to spur workers to unionize.[10] Otherwise we'd already be seeing tens of millions of workers of all ages attempting to do so.

For workplace action to emerge, discontent isn't enough. Workers also need to believe they collectively deserve more. That's one of the reasons why college education has been so consequential: though education is no longer a decent proxy for class location, nor an automatic ticket to the middle class, getting a degree does tend to raise one's expectations and, as such, makes many young workers less willing to resign themselves to precarious low-wage jobs.[11]

The same is true for the 2008 economic crisis. By blowing up the prevailing neoliberal economic model's aura of inevitability, the Great Recession ultimately may have been just as important ideologically as materially. My interview data suggests that this was especially true for those generations who hadn't already absorbed decades of unquestioned capitalist common sense. Unlike in the 1960s, polls show that today's youth are significantly more opposed to income inequality than the rest of the population.[12] Realizing that your economic challenges aren't necessarily your own fault can be a powerful stimulant for banding together with others to demand more.

IMPACT OF OTHER STRUGGLES

Heightened expectations are a crucial spur to action. And my survey of worker organizers shows that one major reason they turned to

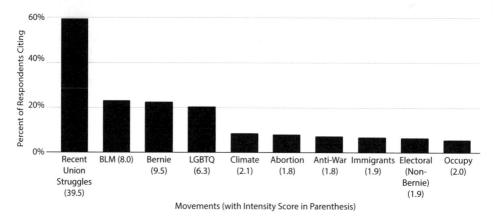

Figure 21. Movement influences on worker leaders. Source: My survey of 2022 worker leaders.

collective workplace action—not just individual acts like quitting—was that they had witnessed and been inspired by outside movements. Over 80 percent of respondents cited at least one popular struggle as a "major factor" in prompting them to unionize.

Figure 21 illustrates that by far the most frequently cited external movement stimulants were labor struggles beyond their own company. These were spurs for close to 60 percent of respondents. And labor's *intensity* of impact was even higher than its *breadth*—that is, many workplace organizers cited labor as the only (or close to the only) movement that spurred them to action. Other movements tended to be listed more frequently as just one of many influences.[13]

These findings confirm a major theme of this book: attention-grabbing worker struggles, momentum, and copycat organizing are crucial for rebuilding a mass labor movement. Over and over, workers said, "If they did it, we can do it too."

While no other movement comes close to labor for inspiring today's young worker leaders, it is significant that over half of respondents cited at least one non-labor struggle as a major spur to their decision to unionize. Of these, Black Lives Matter and Bernie Sanders came out on top—with BLM having the widest breadth, and Bernie having the most intense impact. Wells Fargo's internal company memo was thus accurate enough in warning that "a new generation of employees with activist experience successfully unionized parts of major companies with no prior history of unionization."[14]

BLACK LIVES MATTER

Given that the 2020 Black Lives Matter protests were perhaps the largest in US history, it's not surprising that this insurgent energy fed into a wide range of workplace actions and organizing efforts.

These bottom-up initiatives have exposed the contradiction between corporate anti-racism and working-class anti-racism.[15] Many business leaders, nonprofit execs, and neoliberal Democrats have—under pressure from protests and public opinion—painted themselves in social justice colors, while studiously avoiding any meaningful distribution of resources or power downwards. Among these milieus, we've seen a flurry of milquetoast press releases, trainings on interpersonal etiquette, charity donations, and initiatives to diversify management positions.

Such commitments to social justice, however, do not extend to structural solutions like funding a robust welfare state rather than mass incarceration—or allowing employees to collectively bargain. On the contrary, accusations that unions are racist have recently become a staple of union-busting propaganda. Firms like Littler Mendelson now fluently speak the language of anti-racism and tout the strategic importance of their attorneys' diversity for keeping workplaces union free. In this same spirit, REI responded to its workers' organizing efforts by putting out a union-busting podcast that began with an acknowledgement from Chief Diversity and Social Impact Officer Wilma Wallace that she was "speaking to you today from the traditional lands of the Ohlone people" and in which CEO Eric Artz framed his anti-union case as consonant with REI's continued focus on "inclusion" and "racial equity."

In contrast, recent labor struggles have tied fights against police brutality and systemic racism to pushes for multiracial working-class unity and economic redistribution. Indeed, demands for better pay were slightly higher among the drives of survey respondents of color compared to white respondents.[16]

Organizers at overwhelmingly non-white, low-wage workplaces like Staten Island's JFK8 warehouse saw their struggle for better wages and working conditions as, among other things, a direct way to challenge racial injustice. Amazon further cemented this perception by relying on racist stereotypes to try to discredit Chris Smalls after they fired him. "I'll tell you now, Amazon is definitely the new-day slavery," responded Smalls on his short-lived YouTube show *Issa Smalls World*. "Just think of the job title, it's *picker*."[17]

Along these same lines, Burgerville workers—who had struck in 2018 for the right to wear Black Lives Matter and Abolish ICE buttons at work—posted the following to their Facebook page in late June 2020:

> Earlier this week, Burgerville workers at the Montavilla Burgerville delivered a petition stating that BLACK LIVES MATTER IS A WORKPLACE ISSUE and demanding hazard pay, fair scheduling, and our right to wear antiracist buttons at work. . . . We are not fooled by Burgerville corporate's marketing campaign. . . . [W]e want real, meaningful change. Black Lives Matter in our fight for a living wage, safe conditions, and access to health care during a pandemic that disproportionately impacts Black people.

Across the US, skirmishes with management over meaningful support for BLM were an important starting point for numerous unionization efforts. At disproportionately white workplaces—for example, in journalism and nonprofits—collective demands for better pay were seen as a way to attract and retain more people of color. And the immediate organizational roots of more than a few union drives, such as Forge cafe in Somerville, Massachusetts, began from ad hoc coworker digital chats and carpools set up to support BLM protests. Casey from SBWU describes a similar dynamic nationwide: "When you're going to huge protests and acting in solidarity in the streets, it's not a big leap to ask 'Why can't we do that at our workplaces too?'"

Numerous worker leaders I spoke with saw workplace organizing as a particularly fruitful arena to fight for anti-racist change. Felix Allen, a worker at Lowe's in New Orleans, explains his decision to unionize as follows: "There'd been so many huge protests against police murdering Black people, and I felt like unionizing my store, even if it wasn't directly related to police brutality, was a way to make a real difference in people's lives at a place where we could exert some degree of control." A similar dynamic shaped the political evolution of Leena Yumeen, a Columbia undergrad student and YDSA leader who helped initiate a successful drive to unionize Resident Advisors in the dorms:

> Personally, I was politicized mostly through the Black Lives Matter movement and the experiences that I've dealt with as a woman of color. That's what radicalized me—and it's what radicalized a lot of young people. So I got into politics through issue based things and through further organizing I eventually realized that labor is at an epicenter of everything, that workplace organizing is a very useful axis from which to organize for all our issues.

BERNIE SANDERS

Very few people in early 2015 could have predicted that over thirteen million Americans in the coming election would vote to put a democratic socialist into the White House. But after decades of bipartisan kowtowing to corporate elites, Bernie's cantankerous class-struggle message unexpectedly hit a nerve, especially with young people. Socialism was normalized almost overnight, tens of thousands joined DSA, anti-corporate candidates ran and won across the US, and a new Left media ecosystem of publications, podcasters, and streamers attracted unprecedentedly large audiences. Despite decades of union decline and socioeconomic dispersal, working-class politics was now a force to reckon with in America.

Bernie's impact on labor organizing has not just been a fortunate side effect of his electoral agitation, with its incessant calls for working people to unite against the billionaires. He and congressional co-thinkers in the Squad have proactively used their platforms and resources to actively boost union struggles. Throughout the 2020 campaign, for example, the Bernie campaign texted hundreds of thousands of supporters with requests to show up at local picket lines. Rashida Tlaib has organized workplace organizing trainings for her constituents in Detroit. And Alexandria Ocasio-Cortez and other Squad members have consistently boosted organizing drives, denounced union busters, and helped raise funds for new organizing projects like EWOC.

From an international perspective, it's not unusual that Left electoral politics has done so much to assist workplace organizing. Elections are the arena in which the largest numbers of people engage politically, and global research shows that unions tend to be strongest when backed by workers' parties.[18] But this is a rare phenomenon in a country infamously missing a labor party. As such, the breadth of Bernie's anti-billionaire insurgency has come as a surprise and a challenge to union leaders' longstanding deference to establishment Democrats, as well as US radicals' tendency to downplay the electoral arena.

All this political agitation, amplified by the Left media and groups like DSA and Justice Democrats, has helped create a new class-conscious common sense among millions. "Bernie showed me and a lot of people my age that it's not a bad thing to fight corporations or demand more from your government," explains Vince from Philly. "We're workers, you know, we produce everything, and we deserve more."

The growth of such beliefs among young people has amplified the numbers willing to unionize. It has also eased their efforts. During the successful worker-initiated push to unionize the Public Interest Network's hundreds of canvassers nationwide, one tip passed around between organizers was to have their first one-on-ones with coworkers who had Bernie stickers on their laptops. Similarly, Trader Joe's worker Keenan Dailey in Boulder, Colorado, began assembling an organizing committee by texting "anti-billionaire memes" to his coworkers to see who responded positively.

When I highlighted in my last book that top leaders of West Virginia and Arizona's 2018 teacher strikes were Berniecrats, some critics insisted I was making a mountain out of a molehill.[19] But subsequent events have confirmed the importance of Bernie's impact nationwide. As our survey results demonstrate, no other external stimulus (beyond labor) has played such an intense role in spurring today's grassroots unionization drives.

Most of the Amazon salts who played an integral role in winning the JFK8 election had been politicized by Bernie's campaigns. Similarly, Caden Stearns in Ontario, California, was a Bernie supporter who decided to take a job at his local CVS to unionize it at the height of the pandemic. "Looking back, I was definitely worried like everybody else about getting sick," Caden recalls. "But to be honest I didn't really do a cost benefit analysis—it was more like 'I know the working class is strategically central, I know things are rough right now for these particular workers, so fuck it, let's do it.'" After months of building relationships with coworkers, followed by months of organizing (with the support of UFCW Local 1428), Caden and his coworkers won their election, bringing them under the UFCW-CVS master contract.

As important as salts can be, Bernie's main impact was inspiring people to organize their own workplaces. Maggie Carter in Knoxville was one such worker:

> I didn't know how to define what progressive meant until I found Bernie Sanders, who is one of my heroes in this life, together with Martin Luther King Jr. Ever since Bernie got arrested way back in the day as a student in the Civil Rights protests, he's always stood up for the people who are in

the bottom half of society. And I looked at my parents, who are clearly in that bottom percentage of society, and I realized that Bernie was speaking to people like my parents, people like me.

Unlike her parents, Maggie has actively sought to expose her seven-year-old son to the labor movement: "He loves the union, and likes saying 'Union Yes.' And I've got this cute video of him saying 'Take *that* Howard Schultz.' I don't want to manufacture the way he thinks, but I'd like him to at least see all those things that my parents didn't really point me to, that I had to find on my own."

Whereas organizers in the 1930s could lean more on pre-existing working-class cultures and communities, Maggie's family provides a microcosm of the ways that new cultures of working-class belonging are being built up by young worker leaders who believe that billionaires should not exist.

IMPLICATIONS FOR ORGANIZING

The emergence of Generation Union should be a major boon for the movement. Labor's much depleted bench of dedicated full-time organizers is already starting to get replenished by young cadre who've learned to fight on the job and beyond. New vistas for unionizing high-turnover industries like fast food and coffee have opened up because young activists are more likely to stay at jobs for the sake of the cause, because new hires are often just as likely to be pro-union, and because some management intimidation tactics don't work as well on disaffected Millennials and Zoomers. Countless captive audience meetings in recent years, for example, have backfired because young workers got angry at being "gaslit like crazy," to quote Laura Rosario in New Jersey.

This generational shift also specifically boosts worker-to-worker organizing in a number of crucial ways. Most importantly, increased worker leadership and capacity lowers the need for intense staff engagement. Many young workers are now willing on their own initiative to sacrifice countless hours for the sake of being "part of something big," as Starbucks Workers United puts it. It took an extraordinary amount of dedication and time for the Amazon Labor Union's JFK8 organizing committee of roughly fifteen people to win over a warehouse with more than eight thousand workers. As Angie Maldonado explained to me on the evening of their election victory, "I work twelve-and-a-half-hour shifts for three consecutive days, and on my off days, I'm here [organizing] every day." With their lives entirely consumed by the drive, ALU organizers estimate that they each spent on average twenty-five to thirty hours a week volunteering while off the clock, talking to coworkers in the breakrooms and at the bus stop out front.

When asked what it took to win the union election at JFK8, ALU's elder statesman Gerald Bryson answered: "Some fearless motherfuckers." This bravado gets at something real. But my interviews suggest that young worker leaders on Staten Island and beyond *were* generally scared of what management might do. These fears, however, were outweighed by visions of anti-capitalist change, an eagerness to make history, and intense feelings of camaraderie with co-organizers.

As in the 1930s, worries about retaliation—and anxieties about juggling time-consuming organizing with life's other duties—can be eclipsed by a deeply felt commitment to social transformation. Take the case of Jamie Edwards, who initiated the successful independent unionization drive of Trader Joe's workers in Hadley. Jamie explains that they knew "people get fired doing this. But if I were to not do it for that reason, it wouldn't sit right with me. To be honest, I wouldn't feel like I was actually a legitimate socialist if I were to back down because of that."

POLITICAL IMPLICATIONS

Many new young organizers have come into labor via radical politics and, as such, they've also begun pushing labor in a new political direction. Deep generational fault lines within organized labor have erupted on a range of major political questions, from endorsing leftist candidates like Bernie and the Squad, to Palestine solidarity, to fighting for Medicare for All and the Green New Deal.

With a few notable exceptions such as the Chicago Teachers Union (CTU) and United Teachers Los Angeles (UTLA), even progressive unions capable of pursuing militant tactics at work or in the community remain generally hesitant to break from labor's longstanding electoral strategy—lobbying and getting out the vote for "Blue No Matter Who." Endorsing insurgent anti-corporate candidates remains rare, as does publicly criticizing influential Democrats.

Organized labor's narrow and supplicatory electoral approach may, at best, succeed in temporarily defending the last bastions of union strength, but it does so at the cost of abstaining from the confrontational, class-wide fights necessary to win big for all working people and, in so doing, to definitively isolate the far right.

In today's sprawled-out conditions it's more important than ever for unions to help anchor broader policy struggles of and for the whole multiracial working-class—a strategy that has come to be known as "bargaining for the common good." Taking this approach to its logical conclusion means going beyond pressure campaigns on establishment politicians; it requires developing independent political organizations capable of directly articulating labor's platform within the state and the political arena.

Though still in its incipient stages, a turn to more independent politics inside and outside the Democratic Party could ultimately be one of the biggest changes young people bring into the labor movement via worker-to-worker unionism. And since the fate of workplace organizing is tied by a thousand threads to broader political struggles, this could be a game-changing contribution.

CONCLUSION

It ain't just Mercedes for me. I think all workers have been kicked around for a long time, we *all* need to take a stand.

JEREMY KIMBRELL, Mercedes worker organizer

OVER THE COURSE of this book I've tried to show why only worker-to-worker unionism can build labor's power at scale. If you're not yet in a union, I hope these organizing stories have inspired you to unionize your coworkers *now*, without waiting for an established body to come knocking on your door or inbox. Since you've made it this far, you've got more than enough tips for what to do to get started. There's no good reason why you can't become a working-class hero just like the leaders of the drives at Starbucks, Colectivo, Burgerville, Volkswagen, MIT, the *LA Times*, and beyond.

Workplace organizing *is* a big risk. But nothing less than the fate of economic equality, multiracial democracy, and environmental sustainability hangs in the balance.

And though there's no guarantee that your unionization effort will come out on top, there is a very high chance that you'll build a greater sense of community through the fight. Atulya explained to me how important this was at

Figure 22. Salwa Mogaddedi and coworkers celebrate their union election. Source: Salwa Mogaddedi.

Chipotle: "When we all came together collectively, we got to see different sides of people that we never would have seen otherwise. We saw just how smart people were, how loyal, how creative, how artistic. And we wouldn't have had a chance to see any of that from our coworkers if we hadn't been unionizing."

Workplace organizing is also a sure bet to develop your self-confidence and moral purpose. Here's how a Starbucks barista described this on a Reddit "Ask Me Anything" thread:

> Personally, unionizing has taught me how to advocate and speak up for myself in all areas of my life. I've found my motherfucking calling, dude. There's nothing else I'd rather be doing during late-stage capitalism!!! Is it stressful? Of course. Is it difficult? Nothing worth fighting for is easy. Is the company gonna gaslight and manipulate you? You bet! But don't quit! This is everything!

If you're a labor leader or full-time organizer reading this, I hope to have convinced you to invest in a new organizing model that provides working people with the tools they need to take on key responsibilities normally reserved for staff. Resources, capacity, and experience *are* essential for helping workers and social movements win. But these need to be leveraged in far more scalable ways.

Established unions should start systematically providing tools and funds so that millions of workers can self-organize and train others. Unions can start seeding a far higher number of drives—and they can start saying yes to all to those who reach out for help—by leaning much more on rank-and-file leaders, by holding well-publicized mass trainings, by funding widespread salting at strategic targets, and by seizing high-momentum openings to spread unionization as widely as possible. In other words, the labor movement needs to finally start acting like a movement again.

History will not look kindly on union officials who sleepwalked through the best opening for labor organizing in generations. Those unions who *have* gone all-in on new organizing are showing that another path is possible. When I asked UAW strategist Chris Brooks about how they used momentum and digital tools to plant the seeds of union drives across the country, here's how he replied:

> I like your seeding metaphor, but the term I've been using is that our goal is to be *arsonists*—we should be fanning the flames of workplace organizing. Because the tinderbox is out there, right? Inequality is out of control, workers are coming out of Covid, they're very upset about their lives and the conditions they operate under. We know that anger is there. The question is how do we boost and channel it in the right way, how do we use our staff and resources to dump gasoline everywhere to help workers spread and deepen as many organizing fires as possible? That's why after our strike, we told everybody, "Let's fucking go—let's organize, let's do this, there's a movement happening and it depends on you."

A beautiful thing about these kinds of bottom-up labor struggles is that they put the lie to our society's contempt for the intelligence of working people. Though it's true that popular resignation is the norm in most times and places, history can move faster in weeks or months of mass struggle than over decades of normalcy. When millions of workers transform themselves from spectators to participants, the impossible suddenly becomes possible.

Salwa Mogaddedi in Vernon put it well: "I think it's pivotal to really capitalize on the moments that make everybody realize 'Okay, this is our chance to change everything.'" During such openings—as capitalism's indignities become intolerable, as fear turns to hope—the lyrics of "The Internationale" take on a particularly concrete tactical meaning:

> To make the thief disgorge his booty,
> To free the spirit from the cell,
> We must ourselves decide our duty,
> We must decide and do it well!

Nobody should underestimate what our side is up against. Facing off against the world's most powerful corporations on a decentralized economic terrain is an incredibly daunting challenge, especially when reactionaries run the government. But despite the power of their opponents, rank-and-file organizers are continuing to take big risks to win democracy at work and beyond. Unions should follow their lead.

Acknowledgments

Thanks first of all to everybody who did an interview with me and who filled out the survey. Labor's uptick—and this book—wouldn't exist without your organizing. I wish there had been space to quote each of you and to tell each of your stories.

My manuscript would have been significantly weaker had the following people not read all or sections of it: Ruth Milkman, Joseph McCartin, Barry Eidlin, Gabriel Winant, Micah Uetricht, Michael Kinnucan, Virgilio Urbina Lazardi, Lillian Osborne, Chris Maisano, Elliot Lewis, Honda Wang, Sara Trongone, Ellen David Friedman, Megan Svoboda, Daphna Thier, Jeff Hermanson, Puya Gerami, Kaarthika Thakker, Casey Moore, Sam Lewis, Matt Vidal, Eric Dirnbach, Daisy Pitkin, Chris Bohner, Bill Fletcher Jr., Jamie McCallum, Steve Early, Stephanie Basile, Chris Brooks, Adam Reich, Suresh Naidu, Alex Hertel-Fernandez, Rebecca Givan, Dave Kamper, Shaun Richman, Jacob Blanc, Alita Blanc, and Galit Gun. The manuscript also benefited from numerous discussions with Jane McAlevey before cancer took her from us in July 2024. She would have loved to see the day when workers won on the scale she knew they were capable of.

Naomi Schneider, Aline Dolinh, Julie Van Pelt, and the whole UC Press team did a great job of shepherding this project to fruition. Thank you to Catherine Osborne for the copy edits. I would also like to thank my research assistants, Benjamin Donnelly-Fine and Jacob Robinson.

Much appreciation to my colleagues at Rutgers SMLR for welcoming me into the school—and to my Rutgers AAUP-AFT siblings for welcoming me into our union. For all their dedication, solidarity, and creativity, a big shout-out to everybody involved in the Emergency Workplace Organizing Committee. It's been a pleasure working with you all.

Lastly, I can't thank enough my mom Lita and dad Alan for being fantastic union role models as well as fantastic parents and now grandparents. Biggest thanks of all go to my wife Galit and my son Eli for the laughs, patience, and love.

APPENDIX

Survey and Interview Methodology

To get as good a grasp as possible on the dynamics and demographics of recent rank-and-file oriented drives, my research assistant Jacob Robinson and I made a systematic effort to contact every union drive that went public in 2022. Outreach was done to all 2,072 drives that filed representative election (RC) petitions with the NLRB, a publicly available list. (Note that 457 NLRB RC petitions were withdrawn in 2022 before getting to an election; we reached out to all drives that filed in 2022, though the ones that ended up withdrawing had a very low response rate.)

We also reached out to the 94 known drives that only demanded voluntary recognition (a list provided by the @UnionElections online project, based on daily media and social media searches). Though there is no comprehensive government-compiled list of voluntary recognition attempts, such efforts these days do usually seem to leave an online trace. In any case, all the available evidence strongly suggests that purely "voluntary rec" drives these days are only a tiny minority of total drives, so even were this list partially incomplete, the overall findings would not be greatly impacted.

The contact info for the local or national unions involved in these drives—email, phone, office address, or social media account—were publicly available for all but 18 of the 2,166 total drives. Between January and December 2023, we reached out first by email, if available, and then, if no response was given, through the other available means of contact. The ask made of these unions was to put us in touch with a worker leader (or multiple leaders if there were multiple leaders willing to connect) centrally involved in the given drive, who would participate in our anonymous ten-minute online survey (and potentially an interview) about the drive and today's worker leaders. Every worker we connected with was first asked to fill out the survey. We then did a follow-up interview with as many workers as were willing. (The survey was available in Spanish for Spanish-language speakers and I conducted interviews in Spanish with these workers.)

The union often first connected us with a staff organizer involved in the drive (normally to vet us to make sure we were legitimate labor scholars, not a ruse from employers or right-wingers). We asked these staffers if they would be willing to do a short anonymous interview about their experience; 114 agreed. Most such interviews lasted fifteen to twenty minutes.

We received some form of response to our queries for 1211 drives. Ultimately, 513 workers filled out the survey. For reasons of anonymity we couldn't ask them to include their specific workplace location (only their company, state, and workplace size), which made it impossible to measure the precise number of drives covered in our survey, since some drives connected us to multiple workers. But by triangulating the survey responses with the responses we received to our queries, I estimate that the survey covers roughly 460 drives. In addition, we conducted 214 worker interviews over Zoom, which varied in length from ten minutes to an hour.

The resulting dataset is broad enough to relatively accurately capture the dynamics and demographics of 2022's rank-and-file intensive union drives, of a worker-to-worker, staff-heavy, and edge-case variety. Of my respondents, 69 percent were part of drives that were either worker-initiated or guided by another worker; 23 percent were in drives that began and continued with staffer guidance; and 8 percent were in non-self-initiated drives that received coaching from *both* staffers and workers.

The fact that this dataset doesn't represent a majority of drives that went public in 2022 is not an issue, since I was only trying to get information on drives with a relatively high level of worker leadership. It stands to reason that drives lacking strong worker leaders either did not respond or failed to follow up after responding to the initial inquiry.

Notes

PROLOGUE

1. Unless otherwise noted, all quotations come from interviews I conducted with worker organizers and union full-timers in 2022, 2023, and early 2024.

INTRODUCTION

1. See, for example, Hamilton Nolan, *The Hammer: Power, Inequality, and the Struggle for the Soul of Labor* (New York: Hachette Books, 2024); Jane McAlevey, *A Collective Bargain: Unions, Organizing, and the Fight for Democracy* (New York: Ecco, 2020); Matt Huber, *Climate Change as Class War* (London: Verso, 2022); and Kim Kelly, *Fight Like Hell: The Untold History of American Labor* (New York: Simon & Schuster, 2022).

2. As one West Coast union leader told me in the spring of 2023: "Hate to say it, but I think folks need to keep their heads on straight and not overblow what's going on. I mean I get it, it's exciting that they won elections at Starbucks and Amazon, but I don't see these

kind of drives winning first contracts.... We shouldn't romanticize DIY organizing. So, no, I don't think we should throw out the old playbook just yet." For skepticism in print, see Sam Gindin, "The First Principle of Union Organizing: Spontaneity Isn't Enough," *Jacobin*, July 10, 2022; and Harold Meyerson, "Everyone Who Can Go Union Is Doing Just That," *American Prospect*, May 1, 2023.

3. Clarissa Redwine, "Kickstarter Union Oral History Podcast," *Engelberg Center Live*, 2020.

4. Michael J. Lotito et al., *WPI Labor Day Report* (Littler Workplace Policy Institute, 2022), 27.

5. Lotito et al., *WPI Labor Day Report*, 34.

6. Ralph L. Woods, *America Reborn: A Plan for Decentralization of Industry* (New York: Longmans, Green, 1939), 50.

7. John David Lages, "The CIO-SWOC Attempt to Organize the Steel Industry, 1936–1942: A Restatement and Economic Analysis" (PhD diss., Iowa State University, 1967), 108–9 and Chapter 6.

8. Ruth Milkman and Kim Voss, *Rebuilding Labor: Organizing and Organizers in the New Union Movement* (Ithaca: Cornell University Press, 2004), 4.

9. Kate Bronfenbrenner, *No Holds Barred—The Intensification of Employer Opposition to Organizing Report* (Economic Policy Institute, 2009), 2.

10. For security reasons, I'm using a pseudonym here.

11. Nathaniel Rosenberg and Doug Thompson, "'Nothing Felt Like This': One Baker's Reflections on the Three-Year Colectivo Union Drive," *Milwaukee Journal Sentinel*, July 6, 2023.

12. This decline can't be attributed primarily to a decline in union membership, since the number of union staffers dropped 28 percent from 2002 to 2021, while union membership only dropped 14 percent. Moreover, a rational strategy in the face of continued decline would be to spend far more of labor's increased financial reserves on growth. That said, staffing numbers are only a rough proxy for financial commitment to organizing, since unions also use staffers on other tasks (like member representation and electoral campaigning), and since it's possible to organize more workers with fewer staff when you depend more on volunteers. But since we're not comparing different unions, and since there's no national level data available on union organizing

funding over time, staffing is the best proxy available. Moreover, there's no qualitative evidence suggesting that since the 2000s unions have begun funding organizers more than other staff jobs; if anything, this proxy likely significantly underestimates the decline in financial support for new organizing. For one thing, we know that the AFL-CIO and many national unions have gotten significantly *more* focused on electoral campaigning since the early 2000s; see Timothy Minchin, *Labor Under Fire: A History of the AFL-CIO since 1979* (Chapel Hill: University of North Carolina Press, 2017). Organizers also tend to be the first people laid off in most unions because organizing is normally seen as an "extra" task beyond the organization's core responsibilities (personal correspondence from Shaun Richman).

13. Chris Bohner, *Labor's Fortress of Finance: A Financial Analysis of Organized Labor and Sketches for an Alternative Future: 2010–2021* (Radish Research, 2022).

14. Leah Hunt-Hendrix and Astra Taylor, *Solidarity: The Past, Present, and Future of a World-Changing Idea* (New York: Pantheon, 2024).

15. See, for example, Theda Skocpol, *Diminished Democracy: From Membership to Management in American Civic Life* (Oklahoma City: University of Oklahoma Press, 2003); and Robert Putnam and Shaylyn Romney Garrett, *The Upswing: How America Came Together a Century Ago and How We Can Do It Again* (New York: Simon & Schuster, 2020).

16. INCITE!, *The Revolution Will Not Be Funded* (Durham: Duke University Press, 2017). On the strengths and limitations of foundation-funded worker centers, see Janice Fine, *Worker Centers: Organizing Communities at the Edge of the Dream* (Ithaca: ILR Press, 2006). For a recent analysis of how foundation-funded "alt-labor" groups have sought to expand their reach by leveraging the state, see Daniel Galvin, *Alt-Labor and the New Politics of Workers' Rights* (New York: Russell Sage Foundation, 2024).

17. Dyanna Jaye and William Lawrence, "Understanding Sunrise, Part 2: Organizing Methods," *Convergence*, March 24, 2022.

18. Eric Blanc, "It's Not Enough to Fight—Labor and the Left Have to Be Serious about How to Win: An Interview with Jane McAlevey," *Jacobin*, October 19, 2020.

19. Rosenberg and Thompson, "'Nothing Felt Like This.'"

CHAPTER 1

1. The AFL could afford to be relatively understaffed partly because its narrow organizing approach leaned so heavily on the market leverage of hard-to-replace craft workers. On AFL staffers, see Robin J. Cartwright, "A Business Basis for Unionism," *Organizing.Work*, September 2021.

2. Richard B. Freeman, "Spurts in Union Growth: Defining Moments and Social Processes," in *The Defining Moment: The Great Depression and the American Economy in the Twentieth Century*, edited by Michael D. Bordo, Claudia Goldin, and Eugene N. White (Chicago: University of Chicago Press, 1998), 283–85. On the CIO, see Bob Zieger, *The CIO, 1935–55* (Chapel Hill: University of North Carolina Press, 1997).

3. Kate Bronfenbrenner and Robert Hickey, "Changing to Organize: A National Assessment of Union Organizing Strategies," in *Rebuilding Labor: Organizing and Organizers in the New Union Movement*, edited by Ruth Milkman and Kim Voss (Ithaca: ILR Press, 2004).

4. The precise numbers of SWOC staffers shifted over the course of its multiyear campaign; 275 is an estimate based on the distinct staffing numbers mentioned in John David Lages, "The CIO-SWOC Attempt to Organize the Steel Industry, 1936–1942: A Restatement and Economic Analysis" (PhD diss., Iowa State University, 1967), 32, 107. UE numbers are from M.J. Bonislawski, "Field Organizers and the United Electrical Workers: A Labor of Love, Struggle, and Commitment, 1935–1960" (PhD diss., Boston College, 2002), 83, 89, 262. My tabulation of staff totals incorporates the stated three-year attrition rate of UE staffers.

5. Readers should keep in mind that these ratios are rough estimates since we don't have precise data on exactly how many workers these unions were targeting in their 1930s drives. For example, UE may have targeted more workers than it brought in.

6. Cited in Arne Swabeck, "Why Beck Is Not Their Real Target," *International Socialist Review* 18, no. 3 (1957): 81.

7. Seymour M. Lipset, "Trade Unions and Social Structure: II," *Industrial Relations: A Journal of Economy and Society* 1, no. 2 (1962): 93. From 1961 through 1985, all US national unions for which we have data became even *more* staff heavy; see P. F. Clark, "Professional Staff in American Unions: Changes, Trends, Implications," *Journal of Labor Research* 13 (1992): 383.

8. See James A. Craft and Marian M. Extejt, "New Strategies in Union Organizing," *Journal of Labor Research* 4, no. 1 (1983): 20–21.

9. On "the organizing model," see Richard Hurd, "The Rise and Fall of the Organizing Model in the U.S.," in *Trade Unions and Democracy: Strategies and Perspectives*, edited by Mark Harcourt and Geoffrey Wood (Manchester: Manchester University Press, 2004).

10. Julius Getman, *Restoring the Power of Unions: It Takes a Movement* (New Haven: Yale University Press, 2010), 309.

11. Colette Perold and Eric Dirnbach, *Report: Pre-Majority Unionism* (Emergency Workplace Organizing Committee, 2022).

12. Steve Early, *The Civil Wars in U.S. Labor* (Chicago: Haymarket Books, 2011).

13. Getman, *Restoring the Power*, 73.

14. That said, a higher degree of worker responsibility doesn't automatically ensure that practices of democratic deliberation, collective decision-making, and mass participation are the norm. Rank and filers, for example, can excessively defer to charismatic worker leaders in self-initiated drives. Conversely, some staff-intensive campaigns can do a great job at giving worker leaders a decisive democratic say within the effort. But my research suggests a clear overall trend.

15. Rick Fantasia and Kim Voss, *Hard Work: Remaking the American Labor Movement* (Berkeley: University of California Press, 2004), 127–31.

16. Ruth Milkman, *L.A. Story: Immigrant Workers and the Future of the U.S. Labor Movement* (New York: Russell Sage Foundation, 2006).

17. Lowell Turner and Richard Hurd, "Building Social Movement Unionism," in *Rekindling the Movement: Labor's Quest for Relevance in the 21st Century*, edited by Harry C. Katz, Lowell Turner, and Richard Hurd (Ithaca: Cornell University Press, 2001), 10.

18. Historians of the old Local 1199, for example, identify a "disparity between formally democratic procedures and an effectively centralized chain of command." See Leon Fink and Brian Greenberg, *Upheaval in the Quiet Zone: A History of Hospital Workers' Union, Local 1199* (Urbana: University of Illinois Press, 1989), 199.

19. See Jane McAlevey, *No Shortcuts: Organizing for Power in the New Gilded Age* (Oxford: Oxford University Press, 2016); and Bronfenbrenner and Hickey, "Changing to Organize."

20. See, for example, Staughton Lynd, *Solidarity Unionism: Rebuilding the Labor Movement from Below*, 2nd ed. (Oakland: PM Press, 2015).

21. Joe Burns, *Class Struggle Unionism* (Chicago: Haymarket, 2022), 110.

22. Teresa Sharpe, "Union Democracy and Successful Campaigns: The Dynamics of Staff Authority and Worker Participation in an Organizing Union," in *Rebuilding Labor: Organizing and Organizers in the New Union Movement*, edited by Ruth Milkman and Kim Voss (Ithaca: Cornell University Press, 2004), 65.

23. Sam Gindin, "The First Principle of Union Organizing: Spontaneity Isn't Enough," *Jacobin*, July 10, 2022.

CHAPTER 2

1. William Z. Foster, *Organizing Methods in the Steel Industry* (New York: Workers Library Publishers, 1936), 12.

2. See, among many other works, Walter Galenson, *The CIO Challenge to the AFL: A History of the American Labor Movement, 1935–1941* (Cambridge, MA: Harvard University Press, 1960); and Roger Keeran, *The Communist Party and the Auto Workers Unions* (New York: International Publishers, 1986). Though Communists focused on the biggest workplaces in the biggest industries, a recent study shows that they also organized white-collar service workers in the 1930s because their conception of class was broader, and less patriarchal, than the prevailing CIO norms. See Daniel J. Opler, *For All White-Collar Workers: The Possibilities of Radicalism in New York City's Department Store Unions, 1934–1953* (Columbus: The Ohio State University Press, 2007).

3. Robert H. Zieger and Gilbert J. Gall, *American Workers, American Unions: The Twentieth Century*, 4th ed. (Baltimore: Johns Hopkins University Press, 2014), 91.

4. Ralph L. Woods, *America Reborn: A Plan for Decentralization of Industry* (New York: Longmans, Green, 1939), 65.

5. David Harvey, *The Urban Experience* (Baltimore: Johns Hopkins University Press, 1989), 135. More generally, see Richard Walker, "A Theory of Suburbanization: Capitalism and the Construction of Urban Space in the United States," in *Urbanization and Urban Planning in Capitalist Society*, edited by Michael Dear and Allen Scott (New York: Methuen, 1981), 383–429.

6. For 1939, the "service sector" category refers to "Wholesale and Retail Trade"; "Finance, Insurance, Real Estate"; and "Services." For 2022, with the government's more detailed service classification system, the "service sector" categories refers to "Wholesale and Retail Trade"; "Financial Activities"; "Professional and Business Services"; "Education and Health Services"; "Leisure and Hospitality"; and "Other Services."

7. Jed Kolko, *Urbanization, Agglomeration, and Co-agglomeration of Service Industries* (Public Policy Institute of California, 2008).

8. Charles Brown, James T. Hamilton, and James Medoff, *Employers Large and Small* (Cambridge, MA: Harvard University Press, 1990), 59–64.

9. Kim Moody, *On New Terrain* (Chicago: Haymarket, 2017), 56, 57.

10. Samuel Henly and Juan M. Sanchez, "The U.S. Establishment-Size Distribution: Secular Changes and Sectoral Decomposition," *Economic Quarterly* 95, no. 4 (2009): 427. This countrywide decline in large establishments during a period of deindustrialization is not surprising, since service sector workplaces have always tended to have fewer large worksites. In 1939, only 30 percent of manufacturing establishments employed fewer than a hundred workers—in retail this was 85 percent; in wholesale, 83 percent; and in services, 83.5 percent. See Mark Granovetter, "Small Is Bountiful: Labor Markets and Establishment Size," *American Sociological Review* 49, no. 3 (1984): 326.

11. *Sixteenth Census of the United States: 1940. Manufactures: 1939, Vol. 1*, edited by Thomas J. Fitzgerald (Washington, DC: Bureau of the Census, 1942), 121. Today, only 11 percent of workplaces are of that size. And even warehousing and storage, which due to Amazon's takeoff has doubled its percentage of thousand-plus-worker workplaces in the past few years, has peaked at about 43 percent. Though we don't have aggregate establishment size datasets for the US economy as a whole going back to the 1930s, I've found no evidence that a modest increase in service sector workplace size since then has made up for deindustrialization and plant size decline.

12. *Thirty-Sixth Annual Report of the United States Steel Corporation for the Fiscal Year ended December 31, 1937* (Hoboken: Office of United States Steel Corporation, 1937), 27; Tim Trainor, "The 1936 GM Sit-Down Strike Changed Labor History," *Assembly*, October 7, 2020. We also know that the largest companies were dominated by manufacturing up through the 1970s. The hundred companies with the largest workforces in the world by sector, in 1930, were manufacturing (60

percent), services (6 percent). In 1972 they were manufacturing (71 percent), services (8 percent). In 2002 they were manufacturing (39 percent), services (40 percent). See Howard Gospel and Martin Fiedler, "The Long-Run Dynamics of Big Firms: The 100 Largest Employers, from the US, UK, Germany, France, and Japan, 1907–2002," conference paper delivered at "Studying Path Dependencies of Businesses, Institutions, and Technologies," February 28–29, 2008, Freie Universität Berlin, 26. Similarly, six out of ten of the largest US companies in 1957 were in hard industry; none were in services. (Data compiled by Howard Gospel and provided to author.) Because we know the relative importance of small versus large establishments in manufacturing versus services, we can infer the overall nationwide establishment shift over time driven by these sectoral shifts.

13. Stephen McFarland, "Spatialities of Class Formation: Urban Sprawl and Union Density in U.S. Metropolitan Areas," *Geoforum* 102 (2019): 89.

14. On pre–World War II class consciousness and communities, see Richard Oestreicher, "Urban Working-Class Political Behavior and Theories of American Electoral Politics, 1870–1940," *Journal of American History* 74, no. 4 (1988): 1257–86. On pre-1960s associational life among different classes and ethnicities, see Robert Putnam and Shaylyn Romney Garrett, *The Upswing: How America Came Together a Century Ago and How We Can Do It Again* (New York: Simon & Schuster, 2020), 91–163.

15. Joshua Murray and Michael Schwartz, "Moral Economy, Structural Leverage, and Organizational Efficacy: Class Formation and the Great Flint Sit-Down Strike, 1936–1937," *Critical Historical Studies* 2, no. 2 (2015): 235.

16. Kim Moody, *Workers in a Lean World: Unions in the International Economy* (London: Verso, 1997), 170–72. He was much closer to the mark in 1990 when he noted "the dramatic changes in the relationship of working-class communities to the workplace" due to suburbanization and economic dispersal; see "Building a Labor Movement for the 1990s: Cooperation and Concessions or Confrontation and Coalition," in *Building Bridges: The Emerging Grassroots Coalition of Labor and Community*, edited by Jeremy Brecher and Tim Costello (New York: Monthly Review Press, 1990), 220.

17. Wendell Cox Consultancy, "US Cities with Substantially Same Borders: 1950–2000: Change in Population Density," *Demographia*, 2004. On US suburbanization, see Kenneth T. Jackson, *Crabgrass Frontier: The Suburbanization of the United States* (Oxford: Oxford University Press, 1985).

18. Edward L. Glaeser et al., *Decentralized Employment and the Transformation of the American City* (Brookings-Wharton Papers on Urban Affairs, 2001), 2. On Los Angeles workers and suburbanization, see Becky M. Nicolaides, *My Blue Heaven: Life and Politics in the Working-Class Suburbs of Los Angeles, 1920–65* (Chicago: University of Chicago Press, 2002).

19. Eric Hobsbawm, *The Age of Extremes* (New York: Vintage Books, 1996), 334.

20. Elizabeth Kneebone and Emily Garr, *The Suburbanization of Poverty: Trends in Metropolitan America, 2000 to 2008* (Brookings Institution, 2010).

21. Jackson, *Crabgrass Frontier*, 182, 247; Stephen McFarland, "'The Union Hall was the Center of the Worker's Life': Spaces of Class Formation in the United Auto Workers, 1937–1970," *Journal of Historical Geography* 55 (2017): 20.

22. "1980 Census of Population, General Social and Economic Characteristics, United States Summary," United States Census Bureau; "2019 American Community Survey," United States Census Bureau.

23. Robert D. Putnam, *Bowling Alone: The Collapse and Revival of American Community* (New York: Simon & Schuster, 2020), 213.

24. Matthew E. Brashears, "Small Networks and High Isolation? A Reexamination of American Discussion Networks," *Social Networks* 33, no. 4 (2011): 331–341.

25. Moody, *On New Terrain*, 64, 67.

26. Kim Moody, "Turnover Time: Changing Contours in the Movement of Capital," *Spectre Journal*, May 4, 2023.

27. John Womack, "Labor Power and Strategy," *Democracy Now!*, July 18, 2023.

28. "Color, Nativity, and Citizenship of Employed Persons," *Sixteenth Census of the United States: 1940: Population. The Labor Force* (Washington, DC: US Government Printing Office, 1943), 9; "Employment by Major Industry Sector—Current Employment Statistics Survey" (Bureau of Labor Statistics, 2022).

29. Nantina Vgontzas, "A New Industrial Working Class? Challenges in Disrupting Amazon's Fulfillment Process in Germany," in *The Cost of Free Shipping: Amazon in the Global Economy,* edited by Jake Alimahomed-Wilson and Ellen Reese (London: Pluto Press, 2020), 120.

30. Nantina Vgontzas, "Amazon after Bessemer," *Boston Review*, April 21, 2021.

31. Vgontzas, "A New Industrial Working Class?," 126.

32. Gerald Friedman, *Reigniting the Labor Movement: Restoring Means to Ends in a Democratic Labor Movement* (New York: Routledge, 2008), 92–93.

33. My account of economic and residential decentralization isn't just another way to talk about deindustrialization, as important as this dynamic has certainly been for labor's decline and generalized economic dispersal. Deindustrialization, on its own, can't explain why the numerous non-union factories operating in the US have not remained anything like the hotbeds of organizing they were a century ago. And the strategic conclusions from these distinct accounts diverge considerably: decentralization is a structural obstacle that could be potentially overcome through savvy organizing across spatial divides. In contrast, if the problem is simply that far fewer workers are employed in hard industry, it's difficult to see any potential path towards labor revitalization, since far fewer workers are needed to run factories than a century ago due to automation-driven increases in productivity.

34. Gabriel Winant, "Who Works for the Workers?" *n+1* 26 (Fall 2016).

CHAPTER 3

1. "Mark Medina (Burgerville Workers Union)," *The Docker Podcast*, Episode 37, June 12, 2018.

2. Cited in Arun Gupta, "Beyond the Fight for 15: The Worker-Led Fast Food Union Campaign Building Power on the Shop Floor," *In These Times*, October 25, 2016.

3. Cited in "Audio Report: Burgerville Workers Union Finish Three Day Strike," *It's Going Down*, February 6, 2018.

4. Cited in Arun Gupta, "Fight for 15 Confidential: How Did the Biggest-Ever Mobilization of Fast-Food Workers Come About, and What Is Its Endgame?," *In These Times*, November 11, 2013.

5. Cited in Adam Reich and Peter Bearman, *Working for Respect: Community and Conflict at Walmart* (New York: Columbia University Press, 2018), 151.

6. Teresa Sharpe, "Union Democracy and Successful Campaigns: The Dynamics of Staff Authority and Worker Participation in an Organizing Union," in *Rebuilding Labor: Organizing and Organizers in the New Union Movement*, ed. Ruth Milkman and Kim Voss (Ithaca: Cornell University Press, 2004), 84.

7. Cited in Ashley Rodriguez, "Zoe Muellner and Robert Penner of the Colectivo Collective Take Action," *Boss Barista*, January 13, 2021.

8. Nathaniel Rosenberg and Doug Thompson, "'Nothing Felt Like This': One Baker's Reflections on the Three-Year Colectivo Union Drive," *Milwaukee Journal Sentinel*, July 6, 2023.

9. See Bruce Nissen and Seth Rosen, "The CWA Model of Membership-Based Organizing," *Labor Studies Journal* 24, no. 1 (1999): 73–88. In personal correspondence, Steve Early indicated to me that the CWA's successful 1980–81 campaign to affiliate thirty-five thousand New Jersey state employees trained up workers in all tasks normally assigned to staffers.

CHAPTER 4

1. The breadth of work stoppages is hard to precisely gauge, since US government statisticians only keep tabs on strikes over one thousand workers. My research assistant Benjamin Donnelly-Fine and I manually measured 2020 work stoppages using the methodology developed by the Cornell Labor Action Tracker. The resulting findings on strike occurrences are likely an underestimation, since they miss strikes and sickouts that did not receive any media coverage.

2. Cited in Sarah Hammond, "'This Is Not a Playing Matter': Perdue Plant Employees Walk Out Over Covid-19 Concerns," 13WMAZ, March 23, 2020.

3. Cited in Shelly Bradbury, "More Than 800 Greeley Meat Packing Plant Workers Call Off as Coronavirus Is Confirmed among Employees," *Denver Post*, March 31, 2020.

4. FOX 2 Detroit, "Sterling Heights FCA Workers Say They Held Walkout after Employee Tested Positive," March 17, 2020.

5. Sarah Rahal, "Deaths in Hallways, Unrefrigerated Bodies: Fired Nurses Sue, Cite Covid-19 Conditions at Sinai-Grace," *Detroit News*, June 11, 2020.

6. Cited in Brian Mahoney and Tim Reynolds, "Boycott: NBA Playoff Games Called Off amid Player Protest," Associated Press, August 26, 2020.

7. Michael J. Lotito et al., *WPI Labor Day Report* (Littler Workplace Policy Institute, 2022), 28.

8. Cited in Josh Eidelson, "Whole Foods' Battle against Black Lives Matter Masks Has Much Higher Stakes," *Bloomberg*, August 15, 2022.

9. See Colette Perold and Eric Dirnbach, *Report: Pre-Majority Unionism* (Emergency Workplace Organizing Committee, 2022); and Steve Early and Rand Wilson, "Back to the Future: Union Survival Strategies in Open Shop America," *Talking Union*, April 18, 2012. It's also worth noting that the largest union in the country, the NEA, represents K-12 teachers in many states without bargaining rights.

10. AWU's effort to unionize Google also combines an unorthodox "minority union" approach with time-tested deep organizing tactics to win NLRB votes in sub-units of the company where the union is particularly strong. Winning majority votes in as many units as possible is a crucial piece of the puzzle, because otherwise pre-majority unions can easily ossify into networks of and for left-leaning activists.

11. Josh Eidelson, "Wells Fargo Privately Worries Union 'Resurgence' Could Reach Its Workers Next," *Bloomberg*, April 17, 2023.

12. Sanford M. Jacoby, *Employing Bureaucracy: Managers, Unions, and the Transformation of Work in the 20th Century* (Abingdon: Taylor & Francis, 2004); and Lizabeth Cohen, *Making a New Deal: Industrial Workers in Chicago, 1919–1939* (Cambridge: Cambridge University Press, 1990).

13. The surprising attention bump in 2014 reflects the prevalence of press discussion that year regarding college sports unionization, especially in smaller local newspapers.

14. "How Workers Win: Rebuilding Labor's Power for the 21st Century," Conference, CUNY School of Labor and Urban Studies, May 5, 2023.

15. This conclusion is based on my content analysis of the Newspapers.com data cited above.

16. Cited in Julia Rock, "Fear and Loathing among the Union Busters," *The Lever*, January 31, 2023.

17. In terms of gender, survey respondents were 45 percent women; 35 percent male; 18 percent non-binary; 2 percent other. The racial breakdown was 66 percent White; 14 percent Hispanic/Latino/Latinx; 9 percent Black; 6 percent Asian; 2 percent Middle Eastern; 2 percent Native American; 1 percent other.

18. David Koenig, "Only 9 Percent of Americans Support Car Companies over Striking Auto Workers, AP-NORC Polls Shows," Associated Press, October 12, 2023. Similar support was given to the 2021 John Deere strike; see Tyler

Jett, "Iowa Poll: Majority of Iowans Support Deere Workers over the Company as Strike Enters Second Month," *Des Moines Register*, November 15, 2021.

19. Richard W. Hurd, "The Rise and Fall of the Organizing Model in the U.S.," in *Trade Unions and Democracy: Strategies and Perspectives*, edited by Geoffrey Wood (Manchester: Manchester University Press, 2004), 200–201.

20. Andrew W. Martin, "Organizational Structure, Authority and Protest: The Case of Union Organizing in the United States, 1990–2001," *Social Forces* 85, no. 3 (2007): 1423.

21. José La Luz, "Labor Wars: Time to Set New Priorities?" *New Labor Forum*, October 10, 2016.

22. Bill Fletcher Jr. and Fernando Gapasin, *Solidarity Divided: The Crisis in Organized Labor and a New Path toward Social Justice* (Berkeley: University of California Press, 2009), 61.

23. Ben Smith, "How a New Breed of Union Activists Is Changing the Rules (and Newsrooms)," *New York Times*, May 3, 2020. Prior to the election of reformers to head the Chicago Teachers Union in 2010, the biggest win of the "troublemaking" current associated with Labor Notes came in 1991, when Ron Carey was elected president of the Teamsters with the backing of Teamsters for a Democratic Union, a reform caucus founded in 1976.

24. Harry Kelber, "A New Game Plan for Union Organizing," *Labor Educator*, November 10, 2003.

25. Teddy Ostrow, "Workers Are Transforming America's Most Powerful Unions into Fighting Machines. Yours May Be Next," *Real News Network*, June 26, 2023.

CHAPTER 5

1. "Solidarity Brewing: A Town Hall Discussion with Starbucks Workers," YouTube, December 6, 2021.

2. Strategic Organizing Center, "Brew a Better Starbucks," presentation prepared for Starbucks annual meeting of stockholders, February 2024, 23.

3. Colectivo's drive also demonstrated how managers can side with other employees instead of the bosses. Just after New Year's Day 2021, a shift leader at Ryan Coffel's store, worried about paying his rent, led a collective push to demand the company pay up on time when the company announced that

paychecks would be coming late due to a payroll bug. Higher-ups ordered Ryan to fire the worker. Instead, Ryan resigned from his manager position, asked to be transferred to a different location in Chicago, and ramped up his organizing.

4. This does not mean that full-time comms people are always superfluous. Jeremy Flood's powerful viral videos for UAW's strike and union drives show how professional communications staffers can boost bottom-up organizing, especially in a big national campaign and especially when they deeply understand (and are able to capture) its unique spirit. As one UAW staffer noted to me, "At one plant in the south, there was a 20% increase in the card collection rate after [the] video dropped. And Missouri Toyota workers were so fired up when their video dropped that they made the organizers play it three times." And in SBWU, the degree of staff engagement in national comms eventually increased in the fall of 2023, after Casey Moore stepped down. A comms person from BerlinRosen with an organizing background joined national comms and played, by all accounts, a helpful role.

5. Michael Flaherty and Kimberly Chin, "Starbucks Labor Group Losing Board Battle, Winning Union War," *Axios.com*, March 4, 2024.

6. Strategic Organizing Center, "Brew a Better Starbucks," 27.

7. Starbucks Corporation, *Annual Report Pursuant to Section 13 or 15(D) of the Securities Exchange Act of 1934 for the Fiscal Year Ended October 1, 2023*.

8. Josh Eidelson, "Starbucks Corporate Workers Doubt Company Values in Internal Poll," *Bloomberg*, October 20, 2022.

9. Beth Kowitt and Leticia Miranda, "Starbucks Earnings Are a Warning: Take Boycotts Seriously," *Bloomberg*, February 1, 2024.

10. Liz Alderman, "Starbucks Franchise Lays Off Workers in Mideast amid Gaza-Tied Boycotts," *New York Times*, March 5, 2024.

CHAPTER 6

1. Julius Getman, *Restoring the Power of Unions: It Takes a Movement* (New Haven: Yale University Press, 2010), 310.

2. Nate Holdren, "Strikes Do Not Rise and Fall with the Rate of Profit," *Organizing.Work*, January 27, 2022.

3. Kate Bronfenbrenner and Tom Juravich, "It Takes More Than House Calls: Organizing to Win with a Comprehensive Union-Building Strategy," in *Organizing to Win: New Research on Union Strategies*, edited by Kate Bronfenbrenner et al. (Ithaca: ILR Press, 1998), 33.

4. Kate Bronfenbrenner and Robert Hickey, "Changing to Organize: A National Assessment of Union Organizing Strategies," in *Rebuilding Labor: Organizing and Organizers in the New Union Movement*, ed. Ruth Milkman and Kim Voss (Ithaca: ILR Press, 2004), 54–55.

5. Benjamin Day, "Organizing for (Spare) Change? A Radical Politics for American Labor," *WorkingUSA* 8, no. 1 (2004): 38.

6. Rich Yeselson, "Fortress Unionism," *Democracy: A Journal of Ideas* 29 (2013).

7. Chris Bohner, *Labor's Fortress of Finance: A Financial Analysis of Organized Labor and Sketches for an Alternative Future: 2010–2021* (Radish Research, 2022), 5. In a personal correspondence, Bohner suggests that perhaps a better baseline estimate for labor's coffers is its $17.4 billion classified as "investments," since much of this (for example, stock and bond mutual funds) is relatively liquid. Using such a figure wouldn't significantly alter my argument, but I chose not to make my estimates from "investments" since these also include not-so-liquid assets like real estate.

8. This estimate was reached by triangulating the best available data on organizing costs. Based on an extensive quantitative investigation of union financial records from the mid-1950s through the 1970s, Paula Voos provided two estimates for how much it cost to unionize one worker. One of her models found it cost $580 to unionize one worker in 1980 dollars; the other found it cost $1,568. See Paula Voos, "Does It Pay to Organize? Estimating the Cost to Unions," *Monthly Labor Review* 107, no. 6 (1984): 44. Following the methodology of other scholars (Henry Farber and Bruce Western, "Accounting for the Decline of Unions in the Private Sector, 1973–1998," *Journal of Labor Research* 22 [2001]: 480, 483) I use the midpoint of Voos's two estimates: $1,074 in 1980 dollars, which comes out to $4,012 in 2023 dollars. The AFL-CIO's former Organizing Director Richard Bensinger in the 1990s estimated that unions routinely spent $1,000 per worker; adjusting from 1995 dollars to today, that would be $2,020 dollars. Averaging out Voos and Bensinger's estimates gives us $3,016 in 2023

dollars. SEIU similarly found that it cost "up to $3,000" to unionize one private sector worker; see Yeselson, "Fortress Unionism."

9. Chris Bohner, "Labor's Net Assets Rise by $3.5 Billion in 2021," *Radish Research*, October 18, 2022. My estimates below on projected union growth through expanded funding for organizing are based on 2022 Bureau of Labor Statistics numbers on current union density.

10. Harold Meyerson, "Disunite There," *American Prospect*, February 27, 2009.

11. Dave Kamper and Alyssa Picard, "Mother Jones's Bottom Line: An Analysis of Jane McAlevey's *Raising Expectations (and Raising Hell)*," unpublished paper, 2013.

12. Jane McAlevey, *Raising Expectations (and Raising Hell): My Decade Fighting for the Labor Movement*, 1st ed. (London: Verso, 2012), 315.

13. Stephen Lerner, "An Immodest Proposal: Remodeling the House of Labor," *New Labor Forum* 12, no. 2 (2003).

14. This reluctance to say yes to workers asking for organizing help has long caused friction with worker centers looking to connect their members to unions. See Fine, *Worker Centers*.

15. Linda Markowitz, *Worker Activism after Successful Union Organizing* (Abingdon: Routledge, 2000), 93.

16. David Rolf, *The Fight for Fifteen* (New York: The New Press, 1996), 61.

17. Cited in Teresa Sharpe, "Cultures of Creativity: Politics, Leadership and Organizational Change in the U.S. Labor Movement" (PhD diss., University of California, Berkeley, 2010), 90. For recent critiques, see Jane McAlevey, *No Shortcuts: Organizing for Power in the New Gilded Age* (Oxford: Oxford University Press); and Joe Burns, *Class Struggle Unionism* (Chicago: Haymarket, 2022).

18. David Rolf, *A Roadmap to Rebuilding Worker Power* (The Century Foundation, 2018). My emphasis.

19. "Burnout Culture, Workers as Props: Organizers at United for Respect Speak Out," *Organizing.Work*, May 16, 2020.

20. On the challenges of organizing Walmart—and the tensions of OUR Walmart—see Adam Reich and Peter Bearman, *Working for Respect: Community and Conflict at Walmart* (New York: Columbia University Press, 2018).

21. Rolf, *The Fight for Fifteen*, 93.

22. Bruce Nissen and Seth Rosen, "The CWA Model of Membership-Based Organizing," *Labor Studies Journal* 24, no. 1 (1999): 85.

23. Before its election victory, the union raised $120,000 through GoFundMe. My calculation above was reached by dividing this by 8325—the number of workers in the JFK8 bargaining unit.

24. This table was compiled on the basis of information provided by at least two separate interviewees from each drive. Calculating staffing ratios can be challenging since unions don't always have strictly delineated staff per campaign, nor do they always have consistent levels of staff support over time. Insofar as the provided data made it possible, I account for both: for example, one staffer would count as .5 if they were doing equal work on another campaign at the same time and a drive with one total staffer its first year, and two total staffers its second year, would count here as 1.5 staffers.

25. For ALU, I count Chris Smalls as a de facto staffer, since he worked full time on the organizing and survived in part off money the union raised over GoFundMe.

26. Colectivo's drive may have been slightly more staffed up, though calculating an approximate ratio isn't possible since the union didn't have any full-timers specifically dedicated to the campaign. In part because workers were taking so much of the lead, IBEW staff who were involved in a number of other projects regularly pitched in with strategic and on-the-ground support. The absence of staff dedicated to specific drives makes it similarly difficult to calculate ratios in the NewsGuild. When I asked its president Jon Schleuss if he could estimate a number, he replied, "It's hard to calculate, but my strong impression is because we depend so much on member organizers, our ratios aren't anything close to 1 to 100."

27. From 1990 through 2021, the average number of workers organized through NLRB elections per union staffer was .55; in 2022, it was .68; in 2023 it was .91 (for yearly staffing, see Current Employment Statistics survey, Series ID: CEU8081393001; for NLRB yearly data, see Bloomberg Law's NLRB elections dataset). Readers should keep in mind that this ratio is for *all* union staffers total, not external organizers specifically. It's also worth noting that this does not include workers unionized outside the NLRB. Labor had a few very big non-NLRB wins in the late 1990s through policy-focused mobilizations, such as the unionization of tens of thousands of home health care workers. In these cases, relatively few staff were able to help get large numbers of

workers added to labor's ranks, since the main mechanism to win was legislation (not workplace organizing), since there was no concerted employer opposition, and since the number of workers impacted was so high. Yet as David Rolf notes, similar policy driven wins proved difficult to replicate, since "the legal gray area that allowed Medicaid-paid home care workers to pass state and local bargaining laws is not found in many other sectors" (*Fight for Fifteen*, 61).

28. Along similar lines, grad workers at the Worcester Polytechnic Institute (WPI) that affiliated with the UAW set up regional and national Discord channels to enable direct (if unofficial) nationwide discussion and coordination between the different higher ed drives, including but not limited to the UAW. As Sabine Hahn from WPI explains, "We wanted to be able to talk to other local grad worker organizers directly rather than having to ask a staffer to connect us to another local [worker] organizer if someone had a question or if someone felt like their unit or staff wasn't providing good organizing support."

29. Cited in Derek Seidman, "How a Small Left-Wing Union Is Helping Drive the Unionization Wave in Higher Ed," *Jacobin*, June 7, 2023.

30. Paula Voos, "Trends in Union Organizing Expenditures, 1953–1977," *Industrial and Labor Relations Review* 38, no. 1 (1984): 56.

31. Data on the UFCW's budget was provided to me by organizers involved in efforts to reform the union. For UFCW finances, see Chris Bohner, "UFCW Convention Starts: Assets Up, Membership Down, Reformers in Motion," *Labor Notes*, April 24, 2023.

32. Bohner, *Labor's Fortress of Finance*, 2.

33. Thomas A. Kochan et al., "Worker Voice in America: Is There a Gap Between What Workers Expect and What They Experience?," *ILR Review* 72, no. 1 (2019): 3–38.

34. Personal correspondence.

35. No mention of monetary compensation was mentioned in my survey. In many unions, member "volunteers" receive compensation for their organizing work, often in the form of lost time wages (that is, stipulations in contracts that allow workers to take time off from their normal job for union activities; in such cases, the union covers the missed wages).

CHAPTER 7

1. See, for example, Chris Brooks, "How Amazon and Starbucks Workers Are Upending the Organizing Rules," *In These Times*, May 31, 2022 and Gindin, "The First Principle."

2. Kate Bronfenbrenner, "The American Labour Movement and the Resurgence in Union Organizing," in *Trade Unions in Renewal: A Comparative Study*, edited by Peter Fairbrother and Charlotte Yates (London: Routledge, 2003), 41–42.

3. Richard Hurd, "The Rise and Fall of the Organizing Model in the U.S.," in *Trade Unions and Democracy: Strategies and Perspectives*, ed. Mark Harcourt and Geoffrey Wood (Manchester: Manchester University Press, 2004). For a clear connection between the organizing model and Local 1199, see "Organizing Never Stops," a speech by Bob Muehlenkamp—1199's organizing director—made to the AFL-CIO Organizing Department's national teleconference in 1988 and published in a 1991 issue of *Labor Research Review* dedicated entirely to the "organizing model." 1199's rank-and-file concerted focus has longer roots, going back to the Communist politics of its founders. The one historical monograph on 1199 confirms that rank-and-file intensive tactics and "structure tests" like petitions were deployed during the union's founding hospital drive in 1958; see Leon Fink and Brian Greenberg, *Upheaval in the Quiet Zone: A History of Hospital Workers' Union, Local 1199* (Urbana: University of Illinois Press, 1989), 33, 36, 45, 55, 65, 98. On the other hand, the monograph provides no evidence that the union in its first decades focused on winning over "organic leaders"; to the contrary, it appears that 1199's early rank-and-file leaders were "exceptionally motivated" individuals predisposed to activism, who won leadership and influence through their workplace organizing, not before it (45–48, 97–98). My reading of the historical sources indicates that this was the norm in most left-leaning and industrial unions in the 1930s as well.

4. Indeed, 85 percent of the first contracts won by steel workers in the late 1930s represented only a minority of the workforce, and these types of "members only" contracts were initially as common as majority-exclusivity contracts. See Charles J. Morris, *The Blue Eagle at Work: Reclaiming Democratic Rights in the American Workplace* (Ithaca: ILR Press Book, 2005), 5.

5. Kate Bronfenbrenner and Robert Hickey, "Changing to Organize: A National Assessment of Union Organizing Strategies," in *Rebuilding Labor: Organizing and Organizers in the New Union Movement*, ed. Ruth Milkman and Kim Voss (Ithaca: ILR Press, 2004), 28.

6. Mark Engler and Paul Engler, *This Is an Uprising: How Nonviolent Revolt Is Shaping the Twenty-First Century* (New York: Nation Books, 2017), 51; Brooks, "How Amazon."

7. See also Emergency Workplace Organizing Committee, *Unite and Win: A Workplace Organizer's Handbook* (Chicago: Haymarket, 2024). Unfortunately, because of the incipient nature of most contract campaigns, when I was conducting my survey I didn't include bargaining-specific questions. My impression from interviews was that drives that used rank-and-file intensive methods to win their elections, especially when pursued through a worker-to-worker model, generally carried over this approach to their contract campaigns.

8. It's also worth noting that only a small minority of survey respondents' drives engaged in house calls, a tactic that has long been a staple of post-Reagan organizing orthodoxy for identifying leaders and winning over skeptics. My interviews suggest that this shift away from house calls, in addition to reflecting changed norms about unannounced door-knocking in a cell phone era, also reflects an increased reliance on worker organizers, who are able to speak with their coworkers on the job or after work. Though house visits are still a crucial tool in certain contexts, this tactic's contemporary generalizability is unclear; it seems to be particularly crucial for staff-heavy campaigns, since staffers have few better mechanisms for talking with workers.

9. Christian Smalls, Angelika Maldonado, and Michelle Valentin Nieves, "The Workers behind Amazon's Historic First Union Explain How They Did It," *Jacobin*, April 24, 2022.

10. To the extent that external research support is needed beyond what workers have time and ability to do on their own, there's a need for unions, the AFL-CIO, and support organizations like EWOC to build scalable, volunteer-based research support structures, thereby avoiding the financially unsustainable tendency of unions like UNITE-HERE in the early 2000s to hire "a crazy number of researchers," as one of the union's former staffers described it to me. Fortunately, the radicalization of so many college-educated workers—including those

with a disposition for research, like journalists and grad students—has created a large pool of potential volunteers for precisely such an initiative.

11. Richard B. Freeman, "Spurts in Union Growth: Defining Moments and Social Processes," in *The Defining Moment: The Great Depression and the American Economy in the Twentieth Century*, ed. Michael D. Bordo, Claudia Goldin, and Eugene N. White (Chicago: University of Chicago Press, 1998), 268. For works on labor upsurges, see also Gerald Friedman, *Reigniting the Labor Movement: Restoring Means to Ends in a Democratic Labor Movement* (New York: Routledge, 2008); and Dan Clawson, *The Next Upsurge* (Ithaca: Cornell University Press, 2003).

12. Nelson Lichtenstein, "UAW Strikers Have Scored a Historic, Transformative Victory," *Jacobin*, November 1, 2023.

13. I've been struck in my research by how rarely blue-collar locals do press outreach or public facing work during their drives, presumably on the assumption that few community members would care enough about their drive to support. While public indifference may have been true in the past, this seems far less true today, as can be seen in the outpouring of support for the UAW.

14. Cited in Barry Eidlin, "The Teamsters' UPS Contract: A Win That Leaves Some Unfinished Business," *Jacobin*, August 11, 2023.

15. Cited in Julius Getman, *Restoring the Power of Unions: It Takes a Movement* (New Haven: Yale University Press, 2010), 76.

16. John I. Griffin, *Strikes: A Study in Quantitative Economics* (New York: Columbia University Press, 1939), 91.

17. Henry Farber, "Union Success in Representation Elections: Why Does Unit Size Matter?" *ILR Review* 54, no. 2 (2001): 3–4, 26.

18. Pre-majority unions that are completely or mostly outside the NLRB process, like CWA's Alphabet Workers Union, also illustrate the potential viability of going public early on.

19. Amazon.com Inc., *Annual Report Pursuant to Section 13 or 15(D) of the Securities Exchange Act of 1934 for the Fiscal Year Ended December 31, 2023*.

20. ALU assessed that Amazon's exceptionally high turnover rate, combined with the very large size of its workplaces, obliged the union to file with a minority of cards in order to trigger the NLRB's automatic freezing of the list of potential voters. On the one hand, this is a reasonable and insightful wager,

which may prove useful at further Amazon warehouses. On the other hand, this approach can easily feed into counterproductive shortcuts. Most efforts inspired by JFK8—such as the Home Depot drive in Philly, the Lowe's drive in New Orleans, as well as subsequent ALU drives—that filed with a minority were soundly defeated in their elections. Whether ALU won its election because of, or despite, this type of innovative tactic is difficult to assess, as is the extent to which its subsequent difficulties in moving towards a strong first contract campaign reflected its earlier unorthodox tactics. The fact that ALU has won none of its subsequent elections tells us little about the generalizability of JFK8's particular tactical innovations, since none of the union's subsequent drives (which tended to be driven forward by solo-operating leaders) had *the* pivotal factor enabling success at JFK8: a robust and exceptionally dedicated organizing committee. Absent such a driving force, *any* tactical approach, regardless of its degree of orthodoxy, is almost guaranteed to fail when faced with significant employer opposition. In short, while there has not been enough accumulated experience of success to generalize ALU's tactical innovations, some of these might prove to be effectively replicable elsewhere, especially in other very large workplaces with very high turnover.

21. Joshua Murray and Michael Schwartz, "Moral Economy, Structural Leverage, and Organizational Efficacy: Class Formation and the Great Flint Sit-Down Strike, 1936–1937," *Critical Historical Studies* 2, no. 2 (2015).

22. Cited in *55 Strong: Inside the West Virginia Teachers' Strike*, edited by Jessica Salfia, Emily Hilliard, and Elizabeth Catte (Cleveland: Belt Publishing, 2018), 27.

23. Cited in Derek Seidman, "How a Small Left-Wing Union Is Helping Drive the Unionization Wave in Higher Ed," *Jacobin*, June 7, 2023.

24. Cited in Murray and Schwartz, "Moral Economy," 247.

CHAPTER 8

1. David Harrison and Heather Haddon, "Union Organizing Efforts Rise in First Half of Year," *Wall Street Journal*, July 12, 2022. The quote at the top of the chapter comes from the interview I did with Maldonado on the night of their election victory (Angelika Maldonado, "Here's How We Beat Amazon," *Jacobin*, April 2, 2022), as do her other quotes.

2. Michael Goldfield, *The Southern Key: Class, Race, and Radicalism in the 1930s and 1940s* (New York: Oxford University Press, 2020), 24. My interview data suggests that an attenuated version of this view is also widely shared among unionists who see electoral politics as, at best, harm reduction, but not as a potential tool for working-class *advance*.

3. Cited in Luke Savage, "Real Estate Magnate Tim Gurner Is a Jerk. But He's Saying What All Capitalists Really Think," *Jacobin*, September 14, 2023.

4. Cited in Tim Tooten, "School Bus Drivers' Strike Leaves Students Caught in the Middle," WBAL-TV 11, October 6, 2021.

5. Cited in Simone Stolzoff, "Inside the Fight for Kickstarter's Union," *The Verge*, May 23, 2023.

6. Joe Burns, *Class Struggle Unionism* (Chicago: Haymarket, 2022), 39.

7. Michael J. Lotito et al., *WPI Labor Day Report* (Littler Workplace Policy Institute, 2022), 23.

8. Cited in Harold Meyerson, "The Memo Writer," *American Prospect*, March 30, 2022.

9. On the strategy that culminated in Minnesota's huge array of progressive legislative wins in 2023, see James C. Benton, Patrick Dixon, and Joseph A. McCartin, *Aligning for Power: A Case Study of Bargaining for the Common Good in Minnesota* (Kalmanovitz Initiative for Labor and the Working Poor, 2024).

10. Gerald Friedman, *Reigniting the Labor Movement: Restoring Means to Ends in a Democratic Labor Movement* (New York: Routledge, 2008), 71.

11. On these dynamics, see Eric Blanc, "Can Laws Spur Labor Militancy? A New Look at the New Deal," *Labor Politics*, July 12, 2022; Eric Blanc, "Revisiting the Wagner Act and Its Causes," *Labor Politics*, July 28, 2022; and Lizabeth Cohen, *Making a New Deal: Industrial Workers in Chicago, 1919–1939* (Cambridge: Cambridge University Press, 1990).

12. This critical approach was also made publicly, for example when SBWU declared on Twitter in November 2022 that "Pres. Biden forcing railroad workers to accept a deal they voted down is a betrayal of working class people."

13. In contrast, the increasingly "purple" political context in Arizona, now with a Democratic governor, has allowed more space for Arizona's educators' movement to wrest more partial wins and prevent major lurches backwards.

CHAPTER 9

1. Zeynep Tufekci, *Twitter and Tear Gas: The Power and Fragility of Networked Protest* (New Haven: Yale University Press, 2017).

2. I am certainly not the first to argue for the importance of digital tools in supporting bottom-up workplace organizing. See, for example, Richard B. Freeman and Joel Rogers, "Open Source Unionism: Beyond Exclusive Collective Bargaining," *WorkingUSA* 5 (2002): 8–40.

3. See, for example, "Burnout Culture, Workers as Props: Organizers at United for Respect Speak Out," *Organizing.Work*, May 16, 2020.

4. Bruce Nissen and Seth Rosen, "The CWA Model of Membership-Based Organizing," *Labor Studies Journal* 24, no. 1 (1999): 74.

5. Eric Blanc, "The Red for Ed Movement, Two Years In," *New Labor Forum* 29, no. 3 (2020): 66–73.

6. Zoe Argento et al., *Inaugural Report of Littler's Global Workplace Transformation Initiative* (Littler Mendelson, 2021), 34.

7. Daisy Rooks, "Sticking It Out or Packing It In? Organizer Retention in the New Labor Movement," in *Rebuilding Labor: Organizing and Organizers in the New Union Movement*, edited by Ruth Milkman and Kim Voss (Ithaca: ILR Press, 2004), 196.

8. Argento et al., *Inaugural Report*, 34.

9. Stephen Lerner, "An Immodest Proposal: Remodeling the House of Labor," *New Labor Forum* 12, no. 2 (2003).

10. By way of comparison, the AFL-CIO trains about 900 to 1,500 people a year, through in-person trainings that cost about $250 per person, not including participants' travel and lodging expenses, to be paid by sponsor unions.

11. Eric Blanc, "It's Not Enough to Fight—Labor and the Left Have to Be Serious about How to Win: An Interview with Jane McAlevey," *Jacobin*, October 19, 2020.

12. Viviane Eng, "How Unionizing Sparked a New Sense of Possibility in Me," *Jacobin*, December 1, 2022.

13. Argento et al., *Inaugural Report*, 33.

14. Emily Mazo et al., *DMs Open* (Collective Action in Tech, 2022).

15. Vincent J. Roscigno and William F. Danaher, *The Voice of Southern Labor: Radio, Music, and Textile Strikes, 1929–1934* (Minneapolis: University of Minnesota Press, 2004).

16. On the relationship of media, geography, and social movements, see Craig Calhoun, "Community without Propinquity Revisited: Communications Technology and the Transformation of the Urban Public Sphere," *Sociological Inquiry* 68, no. 3 (1998): 373–97.

17. In contrast with top-heavy nonprofits, EWOC initially functioned with no staff before hiring Megan Svoboda as a full-time organizer in 2021 and adding two additional staffers in 2022–23 to meet workers' growing demand for support.

18. Unions, labor studies departments, and "alt-labor" organizations should also consider building EWOC-like structures to provide two more key types of support for worker-initiated drives: research (of companies, policy, etc.) and legal aid. These tasks, which normally absorb an inordinate amount of resources, could likely be scaled up through volunteer teams of lawyers (with the aid of law students) and volunteer researchers.

CHAPTER 10

1. "The State of Labor Unions Polling," *GBAO Strategies*, August 25, 2023. The quote at the top of the chapter is from "The Highs and Lows of Being a Starbucks Union Organizer," *Death, Sex & Money*, July 20, 2022.

2. See Walter Galenson, *The CIO Challenge to the AFL: A History of the American Labor Movement, 1935–1941* (Cambridge, MA: Harvard University Press, 1960), 132; and William Haskett, "Ideological Radicals, the American Federation of Labor and Federal Labor Policy in the Strikes of 1934" (PhD diss., University of California, Los Angeles, 1957), 59.

3. Independent analysis by author, based on publicly available data.

4. John Burn-Murdoch, "Millennials Are Shattering the Oldest Rule in Politics," *Financial Times*, December 30, 2022.

5. "Educational Attainment in the United States: 2021," United States Census Bureau.

6. One of the benefits of self-initiated drives among workers with higher replacement costs (graduate workers, journalists, etc.) is that they free up labor's staffers to focus on strategic corners of the economy that may require extra organizing support. They also train large numbers of young organizers who can subsequently support such efforts as salts, staffers, or union reformers.

7. We shouldn't assume that getting a college degree itself is the reason why such workers today are more likely to self-initiate a drive. It's just as plausible that this divergence reflects the fact that college-educated workers are disproportionately located in jobs with relatively higher replacement costs and/or in jobs with higher concentrations of young workers, both of which facilitate organizing.

8. On the prevalence of "skilled" and "semi-skilled" workers in prior labor organizing, see, for example, Steve Babson, *Building the Union: Skilled Workers and Anglo-Gaelic Immigrants in the Rise of the UAW* (New Brunswick: Rutgers University Press, 1991); Ronald Schatz, "Union Pioneers: The Founders of Local Unions at General Electric and Westinghouse, 1933–1937," *Journal of American History* 66, no. 3 (1979): 586–602; and Eric Blanc, *Revolutionary Social Democracy: Working-Class Politics across the Russian Empire (1881–1917)* (Leiden: Brill, 2021).

9. Caroline Fredrickson, "What I Most Regret about My Decades of Legal Activism," *The Atlantic*, September 18, 2023.

10. Lydia Saad, "Republican Confidence in Big Business Remains Scarce," *Gallup*, July 26, 2023.

11. Ruth Milkman, "A New Political Generation: Millennials and the Post-2008 Wave of Protest," *American Sociological Review* 82, no. 1 (2017): 1–31.

12. Milkman, "A New Political Generation," 7–8.

13. To measure an intensity score, I weighed answers heavier when respondents listed fewer movement influences. Citing one movement influence suggests that this particular influence had more of an impact on an individual than if a movement was cited as one of many other influences. The intensity score was compiled as follows: each respondent had up to 1 total point for influences: listing 1 movement would garner that movement 1 point, listing 2 movements would garner each movement .5 points, and so on. The score constitutes the total aggregate of points for that movement among all respondents.

14. Cited in Josh Eidelson, "Wells Fargo Privately Worries Union 'Resurgence' Could Reach Its Workers Next," *Bloomberg*, April 17, 2023.

15. For a critique, see Olufemi Taiwo, *Elite Capture: How the Powerful Took Over Identity Politics (and Everything Else)* (Chicago: Haymarket, 2022).

16. My survey found that 90.4 percent of white worker leaders participated in drives where pay was a top demand; this was true for 91.3 percent of nonwhite respondents.

17. Chris Smalls, "Ep. 2: The Autobiography of Malcolm X: Chapters 5–8," *Issa Smalls World*, April 30, 2021.

18. Bruce Western, *Between Class and Market: Postwar Unionization in the Capitalist Democracies* (Princeton: Princeton University Press, 1997).

19. For my response to these criticisms, see Eric Blanc, "Did Bernie's Campaign Lead to the Teachers Strikes?," *Jacobin*, November 7, 2019.

Bibliography

Alderman, Liz. "Starbucks Franchise Lays Off Workers in Mideast Amid Gaza-Tied Boycotts." *New York Times*, March 5, 2024.

Argento, Zoe, et al. *Inaugural Report of Littler's Global Workplace Transformation Initiative*. Littler Mendelson, 2021.

"Audio Report: Burgerville Workers Union Finish Three Day Strike." *It's Going Down*, February 6, 2018.

Babson, Steve. *Building the Union: Skilled Workers and Anglo-Gaelic Immigrants in the Rise of the UAW*. New Brunswick: Rutgers University Press, 1991.

Benton, James C., Patrick Dixon, and Joseph A. McCartin. *Aligning for Power: A Case Study of Bargaining for the Common Good in Minnesota*. Kalmanovitz Initiative for Labor and the Working Poor, 2024.

Blanc, Eric. "Can Laws Spur Labor Militancy? A New Look at the New Deal." *Labor Politics*, July 12, 2022.

———. "Did Bernie's Campaign Lead to the Teachers Strikes?" *Jacobin*, November 7, 2019.

———. "It's Not Enough to Fight—Labor and the Left Have to Be Serious about How to Win: An Interview with Jane McAlevey." *Jacobin*, October 19, 2020.

———. "The Red for Ed Movement, Two Years In." *New Labor Forum* 29, no. 3 (2020).

———. "Revisiting the Wagner Act and its Causes." *Labor Politics*, July 28, 2022.

———. *Revolutionary Social Democracy: Working-Class Politics across the Russian Empire (1881–1917)*. Leiden: Brill, 2021.

Bohner, Chris. *Labor's Fortress of Finance: A Financial Analysis of Organized Labor and Sketches for an Alternative Future: 2010–2021*. Radish Research, 2022.

———. "Labor's Net Assets Rise by $3.5 Billion in 2021." *Radish Research*, October 18, 2022.

———. "UFCW Convention Starts: Assets Up, Membership Down, Reformers in Motion." *Labor Notes*, April 24, 2023.

Bonislawski, M.J. "Field Organizers and the United Electrical Workers: A Labor of Love, Struggle, and Commitment, 1935–1960." PhD diss., Boston College, 2002.

Bradbury, Shelly. "More than 800 Greeley Meat Packing Plant Workers Call Off as Coronavirus Is Confirmed among Employees." *Denver Post*, March 31, 2020.

Brashears, Matthew E. "Small Networks and High Isolation? A Reexamination of American Discussion Networks." *Social Networks* 33, no. 4 (2011).

Bronfenbrenner, Kate. "The American Labour Movement and the Resurgence in Union Organizing." In *Trade Unions in Renewal: A Comparative Study*, edited by Peter Fairbrother and Charlotte Yates. London: Routledge, 2003.

———. *No Holds Barred—The Intensification of Employer Opposition to Organizing Report*. Economic Policy Institute, 2009.

Bronfenbrenner, Kate, and Robert Hickey. "Changing to Organize: A National Assessment of Union Organizing Strategies." In *Rebuilding Labor: Organizing and Organizers in the New Union Movement*, edited by Ruth Milkman and Kim Voss. Ithaca: ILR Press, 2004.

Bronfenbrenner, Kate, and Tom Juravich. "It Takes More Than House Calls: Organizing to Win with a Comprehensive Union-Building Strategy." In *Organizing to Win: New Research on Union Strategies*, edited by Kate Bronfenbrenner et al. Ithaca: ILR Press, 1998.

Brooks, Chris. "How Amazon and Starbucks Workers Are Upending the Organizing Rules." *In These Times*, May 31, 2022.

Brown, Charles, James T. Hamilton, and James Medoff. *Employers Large and Small*. Cambridge, MA: Harvard University Press, 1990.

Burn-Murdoch, John. "Millennials Are Shattering the Oldest Rule in Politics." *Financial Times*, December 30, 2022.

"Burnout Culture, Workers as Props: Organizers at United For Respect Speak Out." *Organizing.Work*, May 16, 2020.

Burns, Joe. *Class Struggle Unionism*. Chicago: Haymarket, 2022.

Calhoun, Craig. "Community without Propinquity Revisited: Communications Technology and the Transformation of the Urban Public Sphere." *Sociological Inquiry* 68, no. 3 (1998).

Cartwright, Robin J. "A Business Basis for Unionism." *Organizing.Work*, September 2021.

Clark, P. F. "Professional Staff in American Unions: Changes, Trends, Implications." *Journal of Labor Research* 13 (1992).

Clawson, Dan. *The Next Upsurge*. Ithaca: Cornell University Press, 2003.

Cohen, Lizabeth. *Making a New Deal: Industrial Workers in Chicago, 1919–1939*. Cambridge: Cambridge University Press, 1990.

Craft, James A., and Marian M. Extejt. "New Strategies in Union Organizing." *Journal of Labor Research* 4, no. 1 (1983).

Day, Benjamin. "Organizing for (Spare) Change? A Radical Politics for American Labor." *WorkingUSA* 8, no. 1 (2004).

Early, Steve. *The Civil Wars in U.S. Labor*. Chicago: Haymarket Books, 2011.

Early, Steve, and Rand Wilson. "Back to the Future: Union Survival Strategies in Open Shop America." *Talking Union*, April 18, 2012.

Eidelson, Josh. "Starbucks Corporate Workers Doubt Company Values in Internal Poll." *Bloomberg*, October 20, 2022.

———. "Wells Fargo Privately Worries Union 'Resurgence' Could Reach Its Workers Next." *Bloomberg*, April 17, 2023.

———. "Whole Foods' Battle Against Black Lives Matter Masks Has Much Higher Stakes." *Bloomberg*, August 15, 2022.

Eidlin, Barry. "The Teamsters' UPS Contract: A Win That Leaves Some Unfinished Business." *Jacobin*, August 11, 2023.

Emergency Workplace Organizing Committee. *Unite and Win: A Workplace Organizer's Handbook*. Chicago: Haymarket, 2024.

Eng, Viviane. "How Unionizing Sparked a New Sense of Possibility in Me." *Jacobin*, December 1, 2022.

Engler, Mark, and Paul Engler. *This Is an Uprising: How Nonviolent Revolt Is Shaping the Twenty-First Century*. New York: Nation Books, 2017.

Fantasia, Rick, and Kim Voss. *Hard Work: Remaking the American Labor Movement*. Berkeley: University of California Press, 2004.

Farber, Henry. "Union Success in Representation Elections: Why Does Unit Size Matter?" *ILR Review* 54, no. 2 (2001).

Farber, Henry, and Bruce Western. "Accounting for the Decline of Unions in the Private Sector, 1973-1998." *Journal of Labor Research* 22 (2001).

Fine, Janice. *Worker Centers: Organizing Communities at the Edge of the Dream*. Ithaca: ILR Press, 2006.

Fink, Leon, and Brian Greenberg. *Upheaval in the Quiet Zone: A History of Hospital Workers' Union, Local 1199*. Urbana: University of Illinois Press, 1989.

Flaherty, Michael, and Kimberly Chin. "Starbucks Labor Group Losing Board Battle, Winning Union War." *Axios.com*, March 4, 2024.

Fletcher, Bill, Jr., and Fernando Gapasin. *Solidarity Divided: The Crisis in Organized Labor and a New Path toward Social Justice*. Berkeley: University of California Press, 2009.

Foster, William Z. *Organizing Methods in the Steel Industry*. New York: Workers Library Publishers, 1936.

FOX 2 Detroit. "Sterling Heights FCA Workers Say They Held Walkout after Employee Tested Positive." March 17, 2020.

Fredrickson, Caroline. "What I Most Regret about My Decades of Legal Activism." *The Atlantic*, September 18, 2023.

Freeman, Richard B. "Spurts in Union Growth: Defining Moments and Social Processes." In *The Defining Moment: The Great Depression and the American Economy in the Twentieth Century*, edited by Michael D. Bordo, Claudia Goldin, and Eugene N. White. Chicago: University of Chicago Press, 1998.

Freeman, Richard B., and Joel Rogers. "Open Source Unionism: Beyond Exclusive Collective Bargaining." *WorkingUSA* 5, no. 4 (2002).

Friedman, Gerald. *Reigniting the Labor Movement: Restoring Means to Ends in a Democratic Labor Movement*. New York: Routledge, 2008.

Galenson, Walter. *The CIO Challenge to the AFL: A History of the American Labor Movement, 1935–1941.* Cambridge, MA: Harvard University Press, 1960.

Galvin, Daniel. *Alt-Labor and the New Politics of Workers' Rights.* New York: Russell Sage Foundation, 2024.

Getman, Julius. *Restoring the Power of Unions: It Takes a Movement.* New Haven: Yale University Press, 2010.

Gindin, Sam. "The First Principle of Union Organizing: Spontaneity Isn't Enough." *Jacobin*, July 10, 2022.

Glaeser, Edward L., et al. *Decentralized Employment and the Transformation of the American City.* Brookings-Wharton Papers on Urban Affairs, 2001.

Goldfield, Michael. *The Southern Key: Class, Race, and Radicalism in the 1930s and 1940s.* New York: Oxford University Press, 2020.

Gospel, Howard, and Martin Fiedler. "The Long-Run Dynamics of Big Firms: the 100 Largest Employers, from the US, UK, Germany, France, and Japan, 1907–2002." Conference paper, "Studying Path Dependencies of Businesses, Institutions, and Technologies," Freie Universität Berlin, February 28–29, 2008.

Granovetter, Mark. "Small Is Bountiful: Labor Markets and Establishment Size." *American Sociological Review* 49, no. 3 (1984).

Griffin, John I. *Strikes: A Study in Quantitative Economics.* New York: Columbia University Press, 1939.

Gupta, Arun. "Beyond the Fight for 15: The Worker-Led Fast Food Union Campaign Building Power on the Shop Floor." *In These Times*, October 25, 2016.

———. "Fight for 15 Confidential: How Did the Biggest-Ever Mobilization of Fast-Food Workers Come About, and What Is Its Endgame?" *In These Times*, November 11, 2013.

Hammond, Sarah. "'This Is Not a Playing Matter': Perdue Plant Employees Walk Out over Covid-19 Concerns." 13WMAZ, March 23, 2020.

Harrison, David, and Heather Haddon. "Union Organizing Efforts Rise in First Half of Year." *Wall Street Journal*, July 12, 2022.

Harvey, David. *The Urban Experience.* Baltimore: Johns Hopkins University Press, 1989.

Haskett, William. "Ideological Radicals, the American Federation of Labor and Federal Labor Policy in the Strikes of 1934." PhD diss., University of California, Los Angeles, 1957.

Henly, Samuel, and Juan M. Sanchez. "The U.S. Establishment-Size Distribution: Secular Changes and Sectoral Decomposition." *Economic Quarterly* 95, no. 4 (2009).

Hobsbawm, Eric. *The Age of Extremes*. New York: Vintage Books, 1996.

Holdren, Nate. "Strikes Do Not Rise and Fall with the Rate of Profit." *Organizing.Work*, January 27, 2022.

Huber, Matt. *Climate Change as Class War*. London: Verso, 2022.

Hunt-Hendrix, Leah, and Astra Taylor. *Solidarity: The Past, Present, and Future of a World-Changing Idea*. New York: Pantheon, 2024.

Hurd, Richard. "The Rise and Fall of the Organizing Model in the U.S." In *Trade Unions and Democracy: Strategies and Perspectives*, edited by Mark Harcourt and Geoffrey Wood. Manchester: Manchester University Press, 2004.

INCITE! *The Revolution Will Not Be Funded*. Durham: Duke University Press, 2017.

Jackson, Kenneth T. *Crabgrass Frontier: The Suburbanization of the United States*. Oxford: Oxford University Press, 1985.

Jacoby, Sanford M. *Employing Bureaucracy: Managers, Unions, and the Transformation of Work in the 20th Century*. Abingdon: Taylor & Francis, 2004.

Jaye, Dyanna, and William Lawrence. "Understanding Sunrise, Part 2: Organizing Methods." *Convergence*, March 24, 2022.

Jett, Tyler. "Iowa Poll: Majority of Iowans Support Deere Workers over the Company as Strike Enters Second Month." *Des Moines Register*, November 15, 2021.

Kamper, Dave, and Alyssa Picard. "Mother Jones's Bottom Line: An Analysis of Jane McAlevey's Raising Expectations and Raising Hell." Unpublished paper, 2013.

Keeran, Roger. *The Communist Party and the Auto Workers Unions*. New York: International Publishers, 1986.

Kelber, Harry. "A New Game Plan for Union Organizing." *Labor Educator*, November 10, 2003.

Kelly, Kim. *Fight Like Hell: The Untold History of American Labor*. New York: Simon & Schuster, 2022.

Kneebone, Elizabeth, and Emily Garr. *The Suburbanization of Poverty: Trends in Metropolitan America, 2000 to 2008*. Brookings Institution, 2010.

Kochan, Thomas, et al. "Worker Voice in America: Is There a Gap Between What Workers Expect and What They Experience?" *ILR Review* 72, no. 1 (2019).

Koenig, David. "Only 9 Percent of Americans Support Car Companies over Striking Auto Workers, AP-NORC Polls Shows." *Associated Press*, October 12, 2023.

Kolko, Jed. *Urbanization, Agglomeration, and Co-agglomeration of Service Industries*. Public Policy Institute of California, 2008.

Kowitt, Beth, and Leticia Miranda. "Starbucks Earnings Are a Warning: Take Boycotts Seriously." *Bloomberg*, February 1, 2024.

Lages, John David. "The CIO-SWOC Attempt to Organize the Steel Industry, 1936–1942: A Restatement and Economic Analysis." PhD diss., Iowa State University, 1967.

La Luz, José. "Labor Wars: Time to Set New Priorities?" *New Labor Forum*, October 10, 2016.

Lerner, Stephen. "An Immodest Proposal: Remodeling the House of Labor." *New Labor Forum* 12, no. 2 (2003).

Lichtenstein, Nelson. "UAW Strikers Have Scored a Historic, Transformative Victory." *Jacobin*, November 1, 2023.

Lipset, Seymour M. "Trade Unions and Social Structure: II." *Industrial Relations: A Journal of Economy and Society* 1, no. 2 (1962).

Lotito, Michael J., et al. *WPI Labor Day Report*. Littler Workplace Policy Institute, 2022.

Lynd, Staughton. *Solidarity Unionism: Rebuilding the Labor Movement from Below*. 2nd ed. Oakland: PM Press, 2015.

Mahoney, Brian, and Tim Reynolds. "Boycott: NBA Playoff Games Called Off amid Player Protest." *Associated Press*, August 26, 2020.

Maldonado, Angelika. "Here's How We Beat Amazon." *Jacobin*, April 2, 2022.

"Mark Medina: Burgerville Workers Union." *The Docker Podcast*, Episode 37, June 12, 2018.

Markowitz, Linda. *Worker Activism after Successful Union Organizing*. Abingdon: Routledge, 2000.

Martin, Andrew W. "Organizational Structure, Authority and Protest: The Case of Union Organizing in the United States, 1990–2001." *Social Forces* 85, no. 3 (2007).

Mazo, Emily, et al. *DMs Open*. Collective Action in Tech, 2022.

McAlevey, Jane. *A Collective Bargain: Unions, Organizing, and the Fight for Democracy*. New York: Ecco, 2020.

———. *No Shortcuts: Organizing for Power in the New Gilded Age*. Oxford: Oxford University Press.

———. *Raising Expectations and Raising Hell: My Decade Fighting for the Labor Movement*. London: Verso, 2012.

McFarland, Stephen. "Spatialities of Class Formation: Urban Sprawl and Union Density in U.S. Metropolitan Areas." *Geoforum* 102 (2019).

———. "'The Union Hall Was the Center of the Worker's Life': Spaces of Class Formation in the United Auto Workers, 1937–1970." *Journal of Historical Geography* 55 (2017).

Meinster, Mark. "How Unions Can Lay the Ground for the Next Upsurge." *Labor Notes*, October 15, 2020.

Meyerson, Harold. "Disunite There." *American Prospect*, February 27, 2009.

———. "Everyone Who Can Go Union Is Doing Just That." *American Prospect*, May 1, 2023.

———. "The Memo Writer." *American Prospect*, March 30, 2022.

Milkman, Ruth. *L.A. Story: Immigrant Workers and the Future of the U.S. Labor Movement*. New York: Russell Sage Foundation, 2006.

———. "A New Political Generation: Millennials and the Post-2008 Wave of Protest." *American Sociological Review*, 82, no. 1 (2017).

Milkman, Ruth, and Kim Voss. *Rebuilding Labor: Organizing and Organizers in the New Union Movement*. Ithaca: Cornell University Press, 2004.

Minchin, Timothy. *Labor Under Fire: A History of the AFL-CIO since 1979*. Chapel Hill: University of North Carolina Press, 2017.

Moody, Kim. "Building a Labor Movement for the 1990s: Cooperation and Concessions or Confrontation and Coalition." In *Building Bridges: The Emerging Grassroots Coalition of Labor and Community*, edited by Jeremy Brecher and Tim Costello. New York: Monthly Review Press, 1990.

———. *On New Terrain*. Chicago: Haymarket, 2017.

———. "Turnover Time: Changing Contours in the Movement of Capital." *Spectre Journal*, May 4, 2023.

———. *Workers in a Lean World: Unions in the International Economy*. London: Verso, 1997.

Murray, Joshua, and Michael Schwartz. "Moral Economy, Structural Leverage, and Organizational Efficacy: Class Formation and the Great Flint Sit-Down Strike, 1936–1937." *Critical Historical Studies* 2, no. 2 (2015).

Nicolaides, Becky M. *My Blue Heaven: Life and Politics in the Working-Class Suburbs of Los Angeles, 1920–65*. Chicago: University of Chicago Press, 2002.

Nissen, Bruce, and Seth Rosen. "The CWA Model of Membership-Based Organizing." *Labor Studies Journal* 24, no. 1 (1999).

Nolan, Hamilton. *The Hammer: Power, Inequality, and the Struggle for the Soul of Labor*. New York: Hachette Books, 2024.

Oestreicher, Richard. "Urban Working-Class Political Behavior and Theories of American Electoral Politics, 1870–1940." *Journal of American History* 74, no. 4 (1988).

Opler, Daniel J. *For All White-Collar Workers: The Possibilities of Radicalism in New York City's Department Store Unions, 1934–1953*. Columbus: The Ohio State University Press, 2007.

Ostrow, Teddy. "Workers Are Transforming America's Most Powerful Unions into Fighting Machines. Yours May Be Next." *Real News Network*, June 26, 2023.

Perold, Colette, and Eric Dirnbach. *Report: Pre-Majority Unionism*. Emergency Workplace Organizing Committee, 2022.

Putnam, Robert D. *Bowling Alone: The Collapse and Revival of American Community*. 20th Anniversary Edition. New York: Simon & Schuster, 2020.

Putnam, Robert, and Shaylyn Romney Garrett. *The Upswing: How America Came Together a Century Ago and How We Can Do It Again*. New York: Simon & Schuster, 2020.

Rahal, Sarah. "Deaths in Hallways, Unrefrigerated Bodies: Fired Nurses Sue, Cite Covid-19 Conditions at Sinai-Grace." *Detroit News*, June 11, 2020.

Redwine, Clarissa. "Kickstarter Union Oral History Podcast." *Engelberg Center Live*, 2020.

Reich, Adam, and Peter Bearman. *Working for Respect: Community and Conflict at Walmart*. New York: Columbia University Press, 2018.

Rock, Julia. "Fear and Loathing among the Union Busters." *The Lever*, January 31, 2023.

Rodriguez, Ashley. "Zoe Muellner and Robert Penner of the Colectivo Collective Take Action." *Boss Barista*, January 13, 2021.

Rolf, David. *The Fight for Fifteen*. New York: The New Press, 1996.

———. *A Roadmap to Rebuilding Worker Power*. The Century Foundation, 2018.

Rooks, Daisy. "Sticking It Out or Packing It In? Organizer Retention in the New Labor Movement." In *Rebuilding Labor: Organizing and Organizers in the New Union Movement*, edited by Ruth Milkman and Kim Voss. Ithaca: ILR Press, 2004.

Roscigno, Vincent J., and William F. Danaher, *The Voice of Southern Labor: Radio, Music, and Textile Strikes, 1929–1934*. Minneapolis: University of Minnesota Press, 2004.

Rosenberg, Nathaniel, and Doug Thompson. "'Nothing Felt Like This': One Baker's Reflections on the Three-Year Colectivo Union Drive." *Milwaukee Journal Sentinel*, July 6, 2023.

Saad, Lydia. "Republican Confidence in Big Business Remains Scarce." *Gallup*, July 26, 2023.

Savage, Luke. "Real Estate Magnate Tim Gurner Is a Jerk. But He's Saying What All Capitalists Really Think." *Jacobin*, September 14, 2023.

Schatz, Ronald. "Union Pioneers: The Founders of Local Unions at General Electric and Westinghouse, 1933–1937." *Journal of American History* 66, no. 3 (1979).

Seidman, Derek. "How a Small Left-Wing Union Is Helping Drive the Unionization Wave in Higher Ed." *Jacobin*, June 7, 2023.

Sharpe, Teresa. "Cultures of Creativity: Politics, Leadership and Organizational Change in the U.S. Labor Movement." PhD diss., University of California, Berkeley, 2010.

———. "Union Democracy and Successful Campaigns: The Dynamics of Staff Authority and Worker Participation in an Organizing Union." In *Rebuilding Labor: Organizing and Organizers in the New Union Movement*, edited by Ruth Milkman and Kim Voss. Ithaca: Cornell University Press, 2004.

Skocpol, Theda. *Diminished Democracy: From Membership to Management in American Civic Life*. Oklahoma City: University of Oklahoma Press, 2003.

Smalls, Chris. "Ep. 2: The Autobiography of Malcolm X: Chapters 5–8." *Issa Smalls World*. April 30, 2021.

Smalls, Christian, Angelika Maldonado, and Michelle Valentin Nieves. "The Workers behind Amazon's Historic First Union Explain How They Did It." *Jacobin*, April 24, 2022.

Smith, Ben. "How a New Breed of Union Activists Is Changing the Rules (and Newsrooms)." *New York Times*, May 3, 2020.

Stolzoff, Simone. "Inside the Fight for Kickstarter's Union." *The Verge*, May 23, 2023.

Strategic Organizing Center. "Brew a Better Starbucks." Presentation prepared for Starbucks annual meeting of stockholders, February 2024.

Swabeck, Arne. "Why Beck Is Not Their Real Target." *International Socialist Review* 18, no. 3 (1957).

Taiwo, Olufemi. *Elite Capture: How the Powerful Took Over Identity Politics (and Everything Else)*. Chicago: Haymarket, 2022.

Tooten, Tim. "School Bus Drivers' Strike Leaves Students Caught in the Middle." WBAL-TV 11, October 6, 2021.

Trainor, Tim. "The 1936 GM Sit-Down Strike Changed Labor History." *Assembly*, October 7, 2020.

Tufekci, Zeynep. *Twitter and Tear Gas: The Power and Fragility of Networked Protest*. New Haven: Yale University Press, 2017.

Turner, Lowell, and Richard Hurd. "Building Social Movement Unionism." In *Rekindling the Movement: Labor's Quest for Relevance in the 21st Century*, edited by Harry C. Katz, Lowell Turner, and Richard Hurd. Ithaca: Cornell University Press, 2001.

Vgontzas, Nantina. "Amazon after Bessemer." *Boston Review*, April 21, 2021.

———. "A New Industrial Working Class? Challenges in Disrupting Amazon's Fulfillment Process in Germany." In *The Cost of Free Shipping: Amazon in the Global Economy*, edited by Jake Alimahomed-Wilson and Ellen Reese. London: Pluto Press, 2020.

Voos, Paula. "Does It Pay to Organize? Estimating the Cost to Unions." *Monthly Labor Review* 107, no. 6 (1984).

———. "Trends in Union Organizing Expenditures, 1953–1977." *Industrial and Labor Relations Review* 38, no. 1 (1984).

Walker, Richard. "A Theory of Suburbanization: Capitalism and the Construction of Urban Space in the United States." In *Urbanization and Urban Planning in Capitalist Society*, edited by Michael Dear and Allen Scott. New York: Methuen, 1981.

Western, Bruce. *Between Class and Market: Postwar Unionization in the Capitalist Democracies*. Princeton: Princeton University Press, 1997.

Wendell Cox Consultancy. "US Cities with Substantially Same Borders: 1950–2000: Change in Population Density." *Demographia*, 2004.

Winant, Gabriel. "Who Works for the Workers?" *n+1* 26 (Fall 2016).

Womack, John. "Labor Power and Strategy." *Democracy Now*, July 18, 2023.

Woods, Ralph L. *America Reborn: A Plan for Decentralization of Industry*. New York: Longmans, Green, 1939.

Yeselson, Rich. "Fortress Unionism." *Democracy: A Journal of Ideas* 29 (2013).

Zieger, Bob. *The CIO, 1935–55*. Chapel Hill: University of North Carolina Press, 1997.

Zieger, Robert H., and Gilbert J. Gall. *American Workers, American Unions: The Twentieth Century*. 4th ed. Baltimore: Johns Hopkins University Press, 2014.

Index

AFL-CIO: age of leaders, 242; lack of focus on union transformation under New Voices, 109; low amount of funds, 157; previous turns to new organizing, 14–15, 38–39, 109–10, 153–54; promoter of deep organizing, 177–78, 291; relationship to Democratic Party, 220, 275; staff intensivity in 1990s, 38–39; Wisconsin support for Colectivo union, 83

Alphabet Workers Union, 98, 293

Amazon, 18, 56, 59–61, 100, 198, 249

Amazon Labor Union (ALU): anti-racism of, 256; average age in, 244; Chris Smalls, 13–14, 107, 184, 191, 195, 256; decision to become a union, 195; dedication of, 261; economic grievances, 251; filing with a minority of cards, 199, 294; going public early, 197–98; inability to pivot to national organizing, 191; staffer at JFK8, 167, 289; support of NLRB, 215–16; union victory celebration, 13; use of social media, 233–34; use of food as tactic, 184

American Federation of Teachers (AFT), 27, 38, 180, 211, 224

anti-war movement, 22, 254

Arizona 2018 educators' strike, 10, 190, 224, 295

Black Lives Matter, 22, 94, 254–57

Burgerville Workers Union (BVWU): anti-racism of, 256; contract campaign, 69–74; faced with union-busting, 71–72; gains won, 73–74; limitations of, 74; NLRB elections, 70, 216; no staff, 167; roots of, 68–69; strategic goals of, 68–69; 2019 strike, 72–73

Chicago Teachers Union (CTU), 110, 262
Chipotle union, 7–8, 230–31, 252–53, 264
climate justice, 1, 22, 218–19, 252, 254
Colectivo union: community support, 17; contract campaign, 81–82; faced with union-busting, 79–80; feeling of victory, 28; NLRB support, 80; organizing tactics, 78; relations with IBEW, 67, 75–78, 81, 83; roots of, 74–75; victory at, 82–83
Communication Workers of America (CWA), 38, 85, 115, 166, 173, 226
Communist Party, 36, 47, 50, 278, 291
Covid-19 pandemic, xi–xii, 11–13, 74–75, 79–80, 92–94, 209

Democratic Socialists of America (DSA), 82, 136, 234, 257–58, 262
digital tools: for brand damage and community support, 81, 193, 215; comparison with prior media, 232; enabling national trainings, 226; enabling remote organizing, 228–32; enabling worker-to-worker organizing beyond local level, 11, 223–26; facilitating worker-initiated drives, 5; for fundraising, 233–34; growth of pro-union sentiment on, 17, 106; limitations of clicktivism, 23; lowering organizing costs, 225–28; optimism and pessimism regarding, 222; in red state teachers' strikes, 11; as spurs to organizing, xii, 96, 120, 224; as union diffusion mechanism, 161, 188–89, 232; worker-run comms, 81, 127, 140–41
distributed organizing, 23–24, 234–36
Duke grad workers union, 1

economic decentralization: differences from 1930s, 51–52, 57, 249; impact on organizing, 5–6; implications for political strategy, 218; implications for tactics, 62–63, 103, 165, 223–24; logistics, 59–61; precluding hyper-targeting, 51; raising organizing costs today, 52, 61, 155–56, 171, 177, 191; relationship to deindustrialization, 53–54, 282; as spur for seeding, 160; suburbanization, 57–58; workplace size decline, 54–56
1199 union, 7, 44, 178, 187, 277, 291
Emergency Workplace Organizing Committee (EWOC): dependence on volunteers, 239–40; filling a gap, 235; founding of, 234; limitations of, 236–37; impact on book research, 27; reliance on digital tools, 236; as a scalable project, 236; seeding strategy, 235–36; shift from issue campaigns to unionization, 235; support from DSA and UE, 235; supporting any worker, 238–39

hollow organizing, 44, 157–58, 179–80
Home Depot union drive, 13–14, 214–15, 245, 251, 258

immigrant rights, 22, 250, 254
Industrial Workers of the World (IWW), 35, 47, 68–70, 214
internal democracy: importance for building power, 23, 26; importance in Burgerville campaign, 70; importance in Colectivo campaign, 77; limitations in recent social movements, 23; limitations in staff-intensive drives,

40, 76–77; in tactical decisions, 183; limitations in New Voices era, 43, 109; worker-to-worker model as important for, 26, 40, 70, 89, 98, 277
International Brotherhood of Electrical Workers (IBEW): and Colectivo union, 67, 75–78, 81, 83

Kickstarter union, 3–4, 212

labor law, 6–9, 15–16, 20, 37, 165, 212–21
Labor Notes: on democracy as power, 253; impact on Colectivo drive, 78; impact on Shawn Fain and new UAW, 112–13; influence on labor uptick, 16; longstanding focus on union transformation, 48; longstanding push for worker leadership, 47; relationship to union reform, 110, 285
LGBTQ struggle, 110, 124–25, 131, 142, 254
logistics, 55, 59–61, 193
Lowe's union, 100, 257, 294

McAlevey, Jane: challenges scaling up her advocated methods, 157–58; deep organizing methods, 45, 157; democratizing knowledge of contract bargaining, 171; impact on young organizers, 182; influence on labor uptick, 15–16, 78, 182; Organizing for Power, 227–28; overlap with organizing model, 178; on persuasion, 25; on power-structure analysis, 184
media attention on labor, 73, 104–6, 120, 127, 189–90
Medieval Times union, 16
Milford Regional Medical Center union, 97

minor league baseball union, 96
momentum organizing, 23, 187–96

National Labor Relations Board (NLRB): attacks against, 213; impact in 1930s, 217; implications for labor strategy, 217–21; importance of for Burgerville union, 70; importance of for Colectivo union, 80, 82; importance of for Starbucks union, 122–23, 129, 149, 214; Jennifer Abruzzo, 105, 213; Kickstarter drive, 212; leftist skepticism of, 212; limitations of, 130, 217; as spur towards labor uptick, 15, 134; support for ALU, 215–16; support for Home Depot union, 214–15; tactics before creation, 178, 200; underfunding of, 216; union skepticism of, 212–13
NewsGuild: commitment to deep organizing tactics, 181–82; development of Member Organizer Program, 10; digital tools enabling national movement, 225; on drawbacks of worker-to-worker model, 90; first contracts, 84, 166; growth via Twitter, 232–33; on importance of deep organizing, 45; pods, 87–88; recent transformation of, 110–12; on remote conversations, 231; roots of Member Organizer Program, 84–85; staff-to-worker ratios, 289; on taking tactical risks, 192; trainings, 87; on training up worker leaders quickly, 166; worker-to-worker mentorship, 89

Occupy, 22, 254
organizing tactics: bending the rules, 192; boycotts, 192–94; at Burgerville,

organizing tactics *(continued)*
69–70; at Chipotle, 16; at Colectivo, 77–78; common limitations of worker-to-worker model, 184–86; deep organizing tactics, 176, 183; deep organizing through new model, 45; differences with 1930s, 178, 200, 291; downplaying of by some radicals, 48; early on at Starbucks, 128; flexibility, 182; going public early, 197–98; limitations of orthodoxy during spurts, 186–87; main tactics used by worker leaders, 181; minority actions, 200–201; orthodox methods compatible with unorthodox model, 182; overcoming fear of losing, 194–96; persuasion, 24–25; possibility to speed up organizing orthodoxy, 181; relation to economic decentralization, 62–63; seizing high-attention moments, 188–91; socializing, 183–84; spreading as quickly as possible, 198–99; staggering actions, 188; used in Vernon, CT, Starbucks drive, xiii; at YogaWorks, 24;

pre-majority unionism: few practitioners of, 98; at Google, 98; paving the way for easier organizing conditions, 102–3; pre-contract material concessions granted by management, 98–100; pre-contract worker transformation, 100–102; relevance of, 97
public opinion on labor, 17, 103–8

REI union, 16, 98, 103, 114, 153, 180
right-wing authoritarianism, 1, 22, 220–22, 233

salting, 42, 68, 118–20, 160, 214, 259
Sanders, Bernie, 113, 129, 136–37, 219, 234, 257–60
seeding, 157–61, 227–28, 235–36
Service Employees International Union (SEIU): Fight for 15, 76, 163–64; as promoter of new organizing, 38; push for sectoral bargaining, 165–66; relations with SBWU, 139, 142–44, 146; search for scalable power, 15, 162–64; split from AFL-CIO, 39
social movements: decline of mass membership organizations, 21–22; impact of mass media on in previous generations, 232; social movement unionism, 43–44; weak-but-wide and strong-but-small impasse, 22–24; youth involvement in, 250
spontaneity, 9, 42, 49, 70, 92–95, 118
staff-to-worker ratios: changes in 2022 and 2023 compared to previous years, 167–68, 289; of 1199NE, 44; growth of staff post–World War II, 37–38; in 1930s, 36–37, 276; of recent worker-to-worker drives, 167–68; since 1980s, 36–38
Starbucks Workers United (SBWU): age gap with union busters, 252; Bernie Sanders's impact on, 259–60; centrality of queer workers, 124–25, 131, 142; contract breakthrough, 143–49; drive in Vernon, CT, xi–xv; early tactics, 128; early worker-to-worker approaches, 126–27; faced with union-busting, 128–31; Gaza boycott, 145–47; grievances at, 122–23; importance of NLRB for early union growth, 214; Jaz Brisack, 107; later

deep organizing tactics, 141; national growth in late 2021–early 2022, 120–22; no blueprint for, 26; opinions of Biden administration, 219–20; pre-contract victories, 134–36; relations with SEIU, 139, 142–43; relations with staff and Workers United, 137–42; risks of involvement, 95; roots of, 118–20; SEIU corporate campaign, 143–44; seizing high-attention moments, 189; solidarity built, 132; staffing ratios, 167; staggering actions, 188; strikes at, 132–34; tactical flexibility, 182; transformation of participants, 136–37; use of social media, 232; worker-led social media, 140–41

Star Garden union, 96–97

Teamsters union, 16, 37, 75, 189–90, 228, 285

tight labor market, 13, 15, 99, 123, 207–12

turnover, 68–70, 81, 102–3, 141, 260, 294

undergraduate student worker unions, 96

union-busting: acceleration in 1980s, 38; at Adoption Star, 8–9; at Amazon, 198, 215–16; anti-racism of, 255; at Burgerville, 71; at Colectivo, 79–80; declining impact in some contexts, 211; GoFundMe as a response to, 233; media attention on, 106–7; at Medieval Times, 16; at Mercedes, 198; at MIT, 169; politicians' reluctance to call out, 219; at Starbucks, 119, 128–31, 181, 252

union diffusion via inspiring struggles, 14, 16, 106–7, 118, 254

union funding for organizing, 18–19, 46, 110, 157–58, 171–72, 213

unionization costs: as block to scalability, 2, 6–7, 15, 154–57; as impediment to effective tactics, 157; increased by decentralization, 52, 61, 155–56, 171, 177, 191; low costs a century ago, 35–37; lowered by digital tools, 225–30; as spur to wide-but-shallow campaigns, 163–65; time costs, 161–62; of worker-to-worker model, 166–71

union routinism and risk aversion, 7–8, 113, 154, 172–74, 194–96, 228

union transformation: via bottom-up union drives, 113–15; limitations under New Voices, 108–9; of NewsGuild, 85, 110–11; of teachers' unions, 110; of Teamsters, 285; of UAW, 111–13, 249; UFCW reform, 114–15; worker-to-worker organizing and, 20–21

United Auto Workers (UAW): digital materials, 228; drive at Hyundai, 25; drive at Mercedes, 198–99, 230, 251–52, 263; drive at Rivian, 175; economic grievances, 253; graduate students in, 112–13; political independence of, 220; recent transformation, 20–21, 111–13; seeding approach, 161; seizing high-attention moments, 189–90; Shawn Fain, 2, 21, 107–8, 112, 220; staffing ratios, 167; stance on Israel-Palestine, 220; staggering actions, 188; strategy of, 2, 265; win at Volkswagen, 3, 21, 113, 167, 190, 198; youth in recent drives, 246

United Electrical (UE) union, 36–37, 98, 167–70, 201–2, 235–37, 248

United Food and Commercial Workers (UFCW) union: bus drivers affiliate, 210–11; CVS workers affiliate, 259; hollow organizing, 180; lack of organizing democracy, 76; local fiefdoms, 114–15; Local 400, 14; OUR Walmart, 15, 76, 164; search for scalable campaigns, 15, 164; underfunding of organizing, 171–72; union reform, 114–15; weak contracts, 109

United Teachers Los Angeles (UTLA), 110, 228, 262

UNITE-HERE, 38–39, 44, 157, 173, 292

Walmart, 5, 53, 56, 60, 174

West Virginia 2018 educators' strike, 10–11, 190, 201, 220, 224, 259

Women's March, 22

worker centers, 22, 275, 288

worker-to-worker unionism: case studies of victory, 67–90, 117–51; common tactical limitations, 184–86; definition of, 40–49; differences with hot-shopping, 42–43; differences with 1930s grassroots unionism, 48; differences with previous forms of grassroots unionism, 40; differences with social movement unionism, 43; differences with staff-intensive left unionism, 44–45; different forms of, 40–41; government policy as booster of, 207–21; importance for contract campaigns, 71, 170–71; importance for effective tactics, 175–205; importance for internal democracy, 26, 40, 70, 89, 98, 277; importance for scalable power, 2, 5–6, 19, 43–46, 153–73; importance for stronger contract campaigns, 170–71; importance of digital tools for, 223–40; importance of staff and resources, 46–47; youth radicalization as booster of, 241–61

youth radicalization: age divisions in drives, 245–46; Bernie Sanders's impact on, xii, 136, 254, 257–60; Black Lives Matter impact on, 255–57; centrality in recent surge, 136, 208–9, 242–47; centrality of economic grievances, 250–53; and college education, 247–50; comparison with AFL-CIO age, 242; desire to build a militant labor movement, 244; implications for union politics, 261–62; implications for union strategy, 260–61; in red state teachers' strikes, 11; large demographic, 242; similar to 1930s, 241; worker leaders' identification as radicals, 243–44

Founded in 1893,
UNIVERSITY OF CALIFORNIA PRESS
publishes bold, progressive books and journals
on topics in the arts, humanities, social sciences,
and natural sciences—with a focus on social
justice issues—that inspire thought and action
among readers worldwide.

The UC PRESS FOUNDATION
raises funds to uphold the press's vital role
as an independent, nonprofit publisher, and
receives philanthropic support from a wide
range of individuals and institutions—and from
committed readers like you. To learn more, visit
ucpress.edu/supportus.